FACES
IN THE
SMOKE

Also by Douchan Gersi

Explorer
Jeremy P. Tarcher, Inc.
Los Angeles

Tawa et Sekapan, Enfants Dayak de Borneo
GP Rouge et Or
Paris

Aventures dans la Jungle de Borneo—Kalimantan
Presses de la Cité
Paris

Borneo
Robert Laffont
Paris

Sahara
Presses de le Cité
Paris

La Dernière Grande Aventure des Touareg
Robert Laffont
Paris

Iken, le Petit Seigneur des Sables
GP Rouge et Or
Paris

La Minute du Moi–poems
C.E.L.F.
Brussels

FACES
IN THE
SMOKE

*An Eyewitness Experience of
Voodoo, Shamanism, Psychic Healing,
and Other Amazing Human Powers*

DOUCHAN GERSI

JEREMY P. TARCHER, INC.
Los Angeles

Library of Congress Cataloging-in-Publication Data

Gersi, Douchan.
    Faces in the smoke : an eyewitness experience of voodoo, shamanism,
psychic healing, and other amazing human powers / by Douchan Gersi.
        p.   cm.
    ISBN 0-87477-595-7
    1. Parapsychology—Miscellanea.   2. Occultism—Miscellanea.
3. Shamanism—Miscellanea.   4. Gersi, Douchan.   I. Title.
BF1999.G3885   91-10699
133—dc20   CIP

Jeremy P. Tarcher, Inc.
5858 Wilshire Blvd., Suite 200
Los Angeles, CA 90036

Distributed by St. Martin's Press, New York

Design by Tanya Maiboroda

Manufactured in the United States of America
10 9 8 7 6 5 4 3 2 1
First Edition

To Love, pure Magic,
the most precious gift
that the Creator has given
to humans.

To those I love.

We are what we think.
All that we are arises
with our thoughts.
With our thoughts
We make the world.

GOTAMA BUDDHA

Contents

Acknowledgments

To Jazi, for accepting the many lonely nights; Maeva and Jason, for not disturbing me too much; Steve Henningson, for providing me with working computers; Kiki Braekman, for helping me with his friendship; Mick Viet, for his "amical" support; Georgina and Marc Otte, and Minou and Steven Ball, for providing me with a roof of love; Ralph Strauch, for providing me with his knowledge, which helped me formulate a better understanding of "Psychic Healing"; Michel Drachoussoff, for leading me to the shamans and sorcerers of the Andes, sharing with me his personal experiences with them, and letting me use the results of his year-long study; Emmanuel Braquet, for being my spiritual guide among Howling Dervishes; Claude Jannel, for sharing with me his knowledge of the Toradjas; Geretta G., Paul and Rosemary Grey, and Elliott Salter, for their never-ending patience.

Many thanks to Jeremy P. Tarcher, Inc., beginning with Jeremy, my friend and publisher, who continues to believe in me; Rick Benzel, for having tried to give me a creative direction; Aidan Kelly, for being a patient and talented editor; and to Paul Murphy, Jennifer Boynton, and all the others who made this book real.

And many thanks for those who loved my previous book *Explorer* and have let me know it.

Introduction

I am an explorer. I have spent most of my life traveling in parts of the world where the understanding of man takes on another dimension. I have lived with headhunters in Asia and with tribesmen of the Amazon. I have shared the way of life of ancient tribes in Africa and of the Tuareg people who dwell in the Sahara Desert. I have followed the silent but persistent call of Bushmen in the Kalahari and of Papuans in New Guinea. I have studied the magic of Voodoo, approached sorcerers in Africa, and investigated the powers of shamans.

Many people believe that we spend our lives following the path drawn for us by fate. I, however, believe that I have held the reins of my own destiny. I became an explorer because I wanted to somehow reexperience the wild feelings of my African childhood. And my quest for magicians, shamans, and sorcerers, my search to understand their real powers, arose from my need to find answers to the questions left by the mysterious events experienced at that time in Africa.

As political refugees, my parents and I left Czechoslovakia—where I was born—and moved deep into the Belgian Congo (now called Zaire), where I spent my childhood and part of my adolescence. Tribesmen were my neighbors; jungles and savannahs became my playground. There, I first got high on doses of adrenalin whenever I flirted with fear of the unknown. I was fed tales of mystery and African mythologies. I lived according to realities different from those of our modern world, and many times I witnessed amazing and inexplicable things that found a home inside my child's wild imagination. Let me share with you three of these stories.

Because we were living in a region infested by deadly snakes, my parents received—from Belgian missionaries living in a nearby Catholic mission—a small, black, flat, shiny stone. They were told that it was able to remove venom, poisons, and infections from wounds.

When asked about the origin of this stone, the missionaries told my father that, long ago, a medicine man from India had, at the time of his death, revealed to two Belgian missionaries the secret process for making the black stone, on the condition it never be commercialized. Since then, the missionaries had continued to make the stones and distribute them to their missions all over the world.

The stone wasn't a magic object; it had been made by hand from different plants and carbon compounds that, when mixed together, create a chemical imbalance. The black stone would try to rebalance itself by sucking out and absorbing chemicals contained in poisons, venom, and pus. After it had been used, one could easily cleanse the stone by putting it first in milk, which can also absorb venom, poison, and pus, and then in water for a day. The chemical imbalance of the stone would be perfectly restored.

Did it work? Not only did the missionaries' black stones save wounded tribesmen, but our stone saved my mother's life when she was bitten by a black mamba, a snake that is very dangerous because of the large dose of venom it injects. She was carried to my father by the natives working for him. He first inserted the point of his knife into the wound to make it bleed. Then he applied the black stone to the wound, in contact with the blood, and it stuck firmly to the wound by itself for hours, absorbing the venom. When no venom was left, it fell off.

I grew up with the family's black stone. Now I have my own, and keep it with me whenever I go on an expedition. Without it I wouldn't be alive today, having been bitten twice by a cobra, three times by a black scorpion, and many times by venomous spiders such as black widows. Thanks to it I also have survived deeply infected wounds. And during my travels in the Sahara and Afghanistan, I met nomads who carried black stones—similar in shape and density to mine, and with the same spectacular properties—that were made by their medicine men.

☾

Because of my Catholic education, I was raised with the idea that a human being consists of a physical body and of a soul. When the body dies, the soul, being immortal, lives on. In my teens, I was confronted with the truth of this belief when a strange occurrence happened to my mother.

We had a servant named Joseph. He had no family, and had been loyal to us for many years. One morning, my parents found him lying in the kitchen unconscious. They brought him to the hospital in the nearest city, Luluabourg (now called Kananga), about sixty miles away—a two-hour drive on a winding dirt road.

The attending doctor diagnosed Joseph as having a large brain tumor. Joseph never regained consciousness, but my mother went to visit him each time she had to go to the city. A few weeks later, she learned from the doctor that Joseph would soon die, although he didn't know if it was a question of hours or days. Because the hospital's policy was to bury the body in a pauper's grave if no one claimed the deceased, my mother made arrangements with the hospital to have Joseph buried in a coffin with a decent funeral.

One night, as she often did, my mother got up in the middle of the night to go to the bathroom, lighting her way with a candle. As was true of all the rooms in the house, from the bathroom you could look into a large dining/living room, into which the front door of the house opened. Suddenly she heard a door creaking. Thinking that one of her three children was coming out of a bedroom, she called our names one by one. Then she heard footsteps approaching the bathroom, and the door slowly opened, revealing Joseph.

Before she could express her surprise at seeing him in the house and her joy at knowing he was alive, Joseph put his finger on his lips and whispered, "I came to thank you for having arranged my funeral. It's really very nice of you." She screamed with terror, and Joseph disappeared abruptly.

Awakened by my mother's cry, my father rushed to the bathroom with his handgun. After reassuring her that there wasn't any danger, he listened to her tell of having seen Joseph alive and well and standing in front of her. Her screams had awakened me also, and I came to the bathroom door, where I heard the whole story.

My father then went to check the front door of our house. It was locked. He calmed my mother and me, assuring her that she probably had had a dream. We all went back to bed. The clock showed 2:30 A.M.

The next morning, my mother went to the city to visit Joseph. He wasn't in the hospital anymore; his body had been sent to the morgue, awaiting delivery of the coffin. He had died during the night—between 2:00 and 3:00 A.M., according to a nurse. Later, my father concluded that it must have been Joseph's soul that had appeared to my mother after his death.

I was about ten years old when I witnessed a ceremony of sorcery in which the night watchman of our estate used a magic doll to kill an enemy. The watchman's name was Moduku, and the ceremony took place in Moduku's small house, which my father had built at one end of our estate, just behind the farm.

Moduku, a small and vigorous man in his late fifties, was my friend. I didn't see him a lot during the daytime, for that was when he slept. But as often as I could, I escaped through my bedroom window after my parents went to bed, and joined Moduku by the campfire burning in front of his small, one-room house, where he filled my imagination with amazing stories about wildlife, about the customs of his tribe, and about each of the scars that covered his body—so many that I couldn't count them all. Many scars were from deep wounds made by deadly machetes during fights with tribal or personal enemies.

"Tell me the story of this one!" I said one day, pointing at the huge scar that crossed his chest.

"Someone tried to kill me while I was asleep, last year. His machete slit my ribs and my lungs."

I asked him why he didn't die from that wound.

"Nothing can kill me, because I am a powerful sorcerer; I'll die only the day I decide so!

"Usually I get even with those who have tried to kill me, except with the man who did this," he continued, putting a finger, whose extremity was missing, along the scar I had pointed to.

"How do you get even? Do you kill them? Do you fight with them?" I asked.

"Oh no, I hate fighting! I use . . . magic!"

I asked him to tell me everything that one could do by using magic, and he did. I even asked him to teach me how to do magic, but he always replied that I would have to wait until I grew up.

Late one morning he joined me while I was hunting snakes, which were a nuisance because they would eat our eggs and feed on our small chickens. "How come you aren't sleeping?" I asked, surprised to see him.

"I came to tell you something very important: the man who wounded my chest has come and settled nearby," he said. "Would you help me get even with him?"

"Oh yes!" I replied. Helping a friend accomplish an act of vengeance seemed to me, at that age, obvious and normal; and I was excited at the idea of witnessing a ceremony of magic.

"I need you to bring me a small, live, black chicken tonight!"

Before all the chickens were locked up for the night in the hen-houses, I stole one and brought it to Moduku and asked him if I could come back later that night and watch his ceremony. He said yes.

I wasn't very hungry that evening, and the time my parents took to go to bed seemed an eternity. At last their bedroom lights went off, and I made the journey to Moduku's house.

Inside his house, which was filled with dark smoke, Moduku, his face covered with sweat that reflected the small campfire beside him, looked wild as he crouched over the scattered feathers and bloody remains of the chicken. As I entered, he ignored me, continuing his barely audible chanting. I was so excited and scared that I remained speechless. I watched him make a small doll out of rags and grass; he then covered it with thin black feathers and blood, which he poured from a calabash. Then, continuing his mysterious incantations, he lit the contents of the calabash, and heavy smoke poured from it. Staring at the calabash, he began an unintelligible and monotonous chant.

Slowly the smoke became very strange. Colors began to form bizarre faces—not human faces, nor those of animals or birds, but faces nonetheless. I watched the faces in the smoke as Moduku, holding the doll in the smoke in one hand, and three long thorns with the other, trembled and repeated over and over more incomprehensible words. The sweat covering his face dripped onto the doll. Suddenly, he drove the thorns simultaneously into the doll—one in the head, one in the heart, one at the navel. He had become so hysterical and frenzied, his body trembling all over, that I got scared and ran away. I almost fell from my window as I climbed back into my room. And after long sleepless hours, I had a series of nightmares, in which the strange faces I had seen in the smoke appeared.

The noises and voices of a gathering crowd awoke me very early in the morning. Reaching the veranda, I saw my father getting into the truck with a group of natives who looked frightened. As he drove away, I asked my mother what was going on. She said to go back to bed, but I waited out of her sight for my father to come back.

When he returned, from my hiding place I heard everything he said. In a voice filled with emotion, he told my mother that he had seen the watchman of the nearby sawmill, dead, stone-cold dead, and yet still standing on his feet, leaning against the wall of his hut. Between his fingers were the ashes of a cigarette that had continued to burn after he died. According to my father, the man had been dead for eight hours at least. He said that, to his knowledge, only lightning could suddenly kill a man like that, leaving him in that standing position. But since there had been no thunder that night, my father said, the man must have been struck by a magic death. But strangely enough, all the natives my father questioned said the man couldn't have had time to make enemies, for he had been brought in by the sawmill company only two days before.

I rushed to Moduku's little house and found it empty and clean. All traces of the ceremony were gone, and there was no message for me. Moduku, with all his personal belongings, was gone.

Thus I grew up, taking for granted everything I heard, learned, and saw, like the amazing properties of the black stone, the ghost of Joseph, and the mysterious powers of Moduku, who knew the secret of killing by magic. But when, at my father's death, we moved to Belgium and I entered college and tried to live according to the modern world's reality, I began struggling with the constrictions of rationalism. I found myself doubting my own memory. Whenever I shared my African stories, everybody around me would begin to laugh. "You're so naive, Douchan!" they would say. So I dedicated my adulthood to finding out if what I had learned, heard, and seen during my African childhood was real, and, if it was real, to what reality it belonged. I wanted to know if I would see faces in the smoke elsewhere—and I did. I found them while studying Voodoo in Haiti for five years. I found them among the Tuareg of the Sahara Desert and the shamans of the Andes. In fact, among almost all people who live according to realities other than ours, I have been able, in one way or another, to see faces in the smoke.

1

Peoples of Tradition and the Modern Perspective

Most of us think of tribesmen as *primitive* people, but I prefer to call them *peoples of tradition.* By this term I refer to all peoples who live following age-old traditions instead of moving with the flow of the twentieth century, whether they are part of the Third World or developing countries, or of Fourth World societies, which remain outside the modern world.

We think of peoples of tradition as being backward, ignorant, naive, acting from instinct, lacking intelligence, and believing in false realities. We see their customs and beliefs as passé, old-fashioned, full of contradictions and superstitions from which we have escaped, thanks to our so-called civilized intelligence. They claim to communicate with the *invisibles* and to use supernatural powers, while we build computers and spaceships.

Yet superstitions are not dead in our modern civilizations. In our societies, there are people who believe in God, in Jesus Christ as the Son of God, and in the Holy Spirit. Some believe that the Virgin Mary became pregnant by the direct action of the Holy Spirit, and that Jesus was raised from the dead. Similarly *impossible* beliefs are held by those of the Jewish faith and other Western religions. Many in the West now follow the ways and beliefs of Eastern religions. Are they naive? Many of our most renowned scientists belong to churches, believe in God, and carry out the precepts of traditional faiths. Are they superstitious?

To me, these considerations suggest that we are all really one humanity. Peoples of tradition may lack the tools and technology we have in the West, but fundamentally they have the same needs we do—to love, to create a family, to believe in a higher force, and to survive. Their ways of feeling, thinking, dealing with life and death, and so on differ from those of Westerners, because they have their own perceptions of reality. It is the diversity of realities that separates us from the peoples of tradition and that creates the cultural and religious differences between the societies of the modern world. Beyond differences in language, a people's worldview of reality governs the way they dress, eat, believe, think, reason, feel, and behave.

There is one area, at least, where I find that peoples of tradition are more advanced than we: the powers of the mind. Indeed, one of the most striking and perplexing aspects of my many years among such people is the number of strange events I have witnessed, mysteries that range from divination to telepathy, from flying men to those who can walk through walls, from miraculous healings to magic deaths, from humans in a trance who are possessed by *entities* to people who can endure the most horrifying self-inflicted pain, from men who claim to converse with divinities to evidence of life after death. What is amazing is that, in many of the various rituals and events I have attended, whatever magic was being performed actually worked—or at least it seemed so to me. Most of us have a hard time accepting amazing feats of strength, endurance, willpower, psychic and supernatural powers, and mind over matter. As Westerners, we have come to accept the tenets of science: that whatever cannot be experimentally proven must be false; that whatever cannot be explained rationally must be fake; that whatever cannot be duplicated in a laboratory must be sheer fraud.

Yet I have experienced a mystical and often frightening world, in which human beings seemingly invoke the powers of spirits. I have met people who have chosen to use their powers not for economic or technological advancement, but for cultural and spiritual survival. I have seen the effects of strange and mysterious forces that a person can use to control his or her destiny and keep his or her identity and dreams alive—dreams we all have, dreams of freedom, of somehow finding a link between ourselves, the universe, and a god. These powers come from the repetition of age-old ceremonies, and their effectiveness has insured the survival of different societies for many centuries.

Over the years, I have given a great deal of thought to these mysteries (some of which were recounted in my previous book, *Explorer*).

I have analyzed them from many perspectives, and I keep coming to the conclusion that *there must be some truth to them*. At the verfact that such rituals evolved so similarly throughout the world must provide a certain validity. Why would a people invent such ceremonies as piercing themselves with needles or hanging themselves on hooks if they did not truly believe that the ritual would result in some spiritual connection to a cosmic truth?

Jung touched upon some of the answers. His analysis of our collective unconscious seems to suggest that we carry within our minds the patterns of magico-religious rituals and skills that have existed since we first evolved from the cosmic chaos. I had read Joseph Campbell's discussions of mythology—the stories that mankind passes on, generation after generation—and I wondered what truth lay behind those stories. Is it possible that our myths indicate actual ancient happenings and powers?

Might it be that the rituals still practiced by peoples of tradition reflect rituals that all of mankind across the planet used to perform? We know that Christmas and Hanukkah are celebrated at the same time of year as older pagan winter festivals dedicated to the sun god, and Easter and Passover likewise occur at the time that pagan spring festivals were held. Could it be that some of the rituals practiced by peoples of tradition represent the most basic beliefs once shared by mankind, even if no corresponding ceremony exists today in our modern societies?

For instance, when we yawn or open our mouth (other than to eat or talk), we tend to put our hand in front of our mouth, thinking we are doing it out of politeness. We also believe that makeup, nail polish, earrings, bracelets, and rings are all simply aspects of our culture's delight in beauty.

Without knowing it, however, we are carrying on many age-old rituals that reflect our ancestors' belief in spirits and invisible forces around us. Our behavior and the logic of our thinking, consciously or unconsciously, are still organized by myths and the truths that form the basis of belief. As Joseph Campbell writes in *The Power of Myth,* "Mythology is the song of the universe, the music of the spheres—music we dance to, even when we cannot name the tune."

I believe that some of our behaviors can be explained by studying the peoples of tradition. For them, wearing earrings is still part of a magical ritual that prevents malicious and sly spirits from penetrating the human body through the natural openings of the ears. Attracted by something shiny, evil spirits prefer entering the rings' holes rather than ears . . . until they get lost. Perhaps by widening their earlobes, some tribes, like the Dayaks of Borneo, create more chances for these evil spirits to get lost. This probably holds true for nose rings as well.

Besides covering the mouth, many tribes ensure full-time protection against evil spirits by coloring or tattooing the lips, gums, or chin. Some use eye makeup to protect, restrict, or focus mind powers. Others color finger and toe nails, palms, and the soles of the feet or wear various hairstyles, hand and foot bracelets, and rings to establish and reinforce a magical border between the extremities of the visible body and the invisible world surrounding them.

Quantum physicists have recently confirmed that liquids have a memory that may hold information. Peoples of tradition, like the Dogons of Africa, have known this since the dawn of their existence. They call this phenomenon *the memory of water*. For them, water that has been part of a ritual continues to hold the magic of the ritual; anyone who uses it will continue to get the benefits of the ritual. Does this differ from the holy water, consecrated by a priest, that Roman Catholics use for baptism and for making the sign of the cross when they enter a church?

Long ago, the Chinese, too, believed in the memory of liquids. Before drinking, they would stare at their drink, impregnating it with the power of their thought or wish. The sound of clinking glasses was supposed to chase away evil spirits, which could interfere with the success of the ritual. Drinking the thought-impregnated liquid was believed to imbue the entire body with that thought, so that the wish would become a reality. It is from that ancient Chinese tradition that we have inherited our ritual of making a toast, which we usually perform without any idea of its potential *magic*.

The mysterious powers that I have witnessed many times in magic healings, trances, levitation, and so on might similarly represent old abilities and knowledge that all mankind used to have, whether to contact forces outside of us or to make use of powers (psychic and otherwise) that are still within us.

One possible scientific explanation of our modern inability to tap the supernatural may be found through understanding the triune-brain theory, which posits that, throughout evolutionary history, the brain developed in phases, so that the human brain is really three different brain systems, one built upon the other. Dr. Paul McLean calls these three major brain systems the reptilian, old mammalian, and new mammalian; whereas for Carl Sagan our triune brain is composed of the reptilian inner core, the limbic middle core, and the neocortex. The brain's bottom, or reptilian, layer maintains some of our primeval instincts and urges and is responsible for our most primitive behaviors; it deals with sex, aggression, and various other drives, such as hunger. Sagan also postulates that in dream states our reptilian brain takes over. The middle, or limbic, layer is responsible for our emotional behaviors. The top layer is responsible for our more intellectual behaviors and thinking; it deals with such things as language.

In relation to our modern world, peoples of tradition may seem backward, ignorant, naive, instinctual, and lacking in intelligence because, for whatever reasons, they don't use the most evolved part of the brain to the extent that peoples of the modern world do. Instead, they rely more on those parts of the brain that allow them access to altered states of consciousness, like dream states. They are more in touch with man's primeval urges and ancient abilities to connect with spirits and other cosmic forces. Also, through meditation and the ecstatic experience induced by trance and gestural magic, they are in tune with a cosmic repository of energies as well as the ancient wisdom and knowledge that, as some scientific research suggests, is carried in our mind-body systems—in our genetic memory. In this way they gain access to powers that we use only rarely and don't truly understand with our civilized conscious minds.

Our ability to do what peoples of tradition can do may have disappeared because we no longer use these early-brain systems. Are we suffering from brain atrophy? Does technology stop us from using these parts of our brain? I think neither is true. Perhaps as we use our brain's top layer—its rational and logical functions—more and more, we have increasingly turned off, at least temporarily, the other brain systems, which provide us with the ability to communicate with others in more emotional, psychic forms, and to do things that at first seem impossible. I suggest that it is our culture that has encouraged this emphasis on the rational, with religion and science playing major roles.

By repressing our sexuality, our civilized religions have forced us to turn off those parts of our brain that deal directly and instinctively with sexuality. Our tenets being only those backed up by science, which, for us, is the guarantor of truth, we keep ourselves in the reasoning frame of our brain's top layer, and we reject our feelings. Technology and rationalism, therefore, are preventing us from expanding toward other realities.

Even in our modern societies, however, there are people who, for whatever reasons, seem to be in tune with aspects of the brain that allow them to perform paranormal phenomena. Such phenomena—often called *psychic* or *psi* phenomena—refer to events that cannot be explained by the current laws of physics or psychology. As Willis

Harman, president of the Institute of Noetic Sciences, and Howard Rheingold note in their book *Higher Creativity*:

> Since the early 1960s, there has been increasing public acceptance that such [paranormal] capacities do exist. Police departments on several continents have made frequent use of psychics in the solution of crimes. Archaeologists have employed psychics to assist in the location of buried sites and artifacts. Mining and oil companies have used clairvoyants to locate underground deposits. There has also been active interest in military applications of psychic phenomena on both sides of the Iron Curtain. In the United States, various military and intelligence agencies have sponsored, supported, or conducted research into the strategic applications of these capacities.

The field of psychic abilities is called *psi*. The scientific study of psi, or psychic, phenomena is called parapsychology or psychical research. There are parapsychology institutes in the United States, as well as psychical-research departments in dozens of universities throughout the world. The Parapsychological Association, created in 1957, was admitted to the American Association for the Advancement of Science in 1969.

Although the methods used in parapsychological experiments are based on proper scientific principles, psi phenomena are very controversial, because their acceptance will require some major revisions in current scientific theories. However, new developments in the physics of relativity and subatomic particles may accommodate explanations of psi within a scientific framework. The strange universe described by these areas of science can easily include the concept of a consciousness that can span time and space. Harman and Rheingold write that if the results of certain studies conducted by the Stanford Research Institute (SRI) are accurate,

> the ability to know what is happening at a place one has never visited is not a rare talent but a trainable skill, latent within all of us. This training primarily involves the removal of negative unconscious beliefs that it can't be done. . . . Research on psychokinesis has been conducted . . . by equally prestigious organizations—with equally startling results. One such experiment was conducted by Robert Jahn, dean of engineering and applied sciences at Princeton University. . . . In both the SRI . . . and the Princeton . . . research, the findings indicated that the perennial wisdom may be right, we may all know unconsciously how to perform these kinds of extraordinary feats. We simply need to remove the negative belief that inhibits us from doing them. In

the end, when the meager evidence available today is closely examined, it appears that John Lilly was right when he said that it is not clear that there are any limits to the abilities of the human mind that are not fundamentally "beliefs" about the limits of that mind.

About PSI

Psi covers a wide range of often-interrelated phenomena. Although it is not easy to categorize them, psychic phenomena are usually divided into three main classes for purposes of investigation: extrasensory perception (ESP); psychokinesis (PK); and survival phenomena—that is, evidence of life after death.

Extrasensory perception involves information coming into the mind of an individual from outside.

Psychokinesis involves the effect of the individual's mind on his or her environment (something coming from the mind that affects the surroundings)—sometimes called mind over matter. It includes teleportation (moving an object from one place to another without direct physical contact), production of thermal or electromagnetic effects at a distance, levitation, astral projection (the ability to leave the physical body and go elsewhere), thought photography (creation of images on unexposed films by thought), psychic healing, and walking on fire.

Survival phenomena involve all events that appear to be caused by souls of the dead or nonmaterial entities. They include channeling, mediumship, and séances, as well as poltergeists, hauntings, and other ghostly apparitions. We will deal with the latter two categories later in the book. Here I would like to consider ESP in particular.

About ESP

Extrasensory perception may be defined as having knowledge of something without use of the five normal senses or logical deduction: a dream that turns out to be true; an occasion when, as you reach for the phone to call someone, it rings because that person unexpectedly decided to call you. The frequency of these and other events can lead to the feeling that there must be some explanation beyond mere coincidence. Perhaps there is some aspect of human beings we don't know about yet, a link between us and our universe that we have not yet identified, that could account for such events. The attempt to clarify how and why such experiences happen is a major part of parapsychological research.

Although it is not easy to differentiate between them, ESP phenomena are usually divided into four types: telepathy, clairvoyance, precognition, and retrocognition. They also include seeing auras, or luminous fields, around a person; and dowsing—that is, locating desired objects, like water.

Telepathy is the faculty to connect with others, at whatever distance. (Such abilities are very common among the Tuareg of the Sahara Desert.)

Clairvoyance is the perception of objects or events currently happening at a distance. Literally, the word means "clear seeing" and applies to those who see psychically. Their impressions often take the form of pictures. (Edgar Cayce, for example, was considered an amazing clairvoyant.) Other psychics receive their impressions in the form of spoken words or messages that only they hear; this is properly called *clairaudience.* Those who get a feeling that comes in neither words nor pictures have *clairsentience.*

Precognition is the perception of future events. Its history stretches back to prebiblical times, when oracles and prophets interpreted their dreams or other omens as describing future events.

Retrocognition is the perception of events in the past of which one has no ordinary knowledge from reports or histories. An example might be sensing something that happened to a person as a child, without having been told that the event had occurred.

Clairvoyance and precognition continue to be the subject of experiments in parapsychology laboratories. Some of these tests have produced positive results, suggesting that these powers may actually exist. But such indications raise major philosophical problems. If one can see the future, does this mean that the future already exists? Can it be changed? What does this do to the concept of free will?

ABOUT DIVINATION

The field of parapsychology also recognizes divination abilities as belonging to the realm of ESP. According to *Webster's New Collegiate Dictionary,* divination is the art or act of foretelling the future or seeking to uncover hidden knowledge by the aid of supernatural powers. When one thinks about divination, images of mysterious Gypsies reading palms or telling fortunes with cards immediately come to mind.

In the Fourth World and the other cultures of tradition, divination is used to foresee whether intended actions will get the invisibles' approval or disapproval—that is, whether such actions will succeed or fail. Three major methods are usually used:

△ rituals for calling upon invisibles for advice about a decision

△ careful observation of nature for signs that can be interpreted as good or bad omens

△ clairvoyance and precognition—that is, using man's powers and abilities without spiritual or divine intervention

Auguries, or Divination Rituals

Auguries, or divination rituals, are specific kinds of ceremonies performed to determine the answers that invisibles—gods or spirits—have for those who consult them. Even in our own culture, such rituals have an important history. For example, for hundreds of years peoples of ancient Greece and Asia Minor would never dream of undertaking any important project without consulting the Oracle of Delphi, who received answers from Apollo (in the classical period).

Almost all peoples of tradition believe that divination rituals are the easiest way to involve the invisibles—spirits, souls of ancestors, or divinities—in their everyday lives. Such rituals answer their questions or confirm their decisions.

Carrying out auguries is the task of the spiritual leader, who will use his mediumistic talents to become the intermediary between the invisibles and the people, and, by using various methods, will read the invisibles' messages.

Among the many techniques of divination by peoples of tradition, one of the most widespread is the examination of the organs—livers, gall bladders, and other organs—of sacrificed animals. On the other hand, throughout the Andes diviners examine the position of fallen coca leaves. Both techniques are also used as ways to diagnose and cure illness.

Omens

Divinities sometimes express their feelings about decisions people are about to make without being called upon through a ritual. (The Latin word *augur* originally referred to the priest who was in charge of observing certain signs—such as lightning and thunder, or the flight pattern and song of birds—considered to be signals of the gods' will. *Augurium* was the art of interpreting omens.) So, before undertaking any action, peoples of tradition carefully observe nature, searching for signs that can be interpreted as good or bad omens, such as the spontaneous movement of stones as one passes by; or encounters with specific birds, snakes, and lizards; or the special cries of certain animals.

Clairvoyance and Precognition

Clairvoyance methods (I will use this term for clairvoyance, retrocognition, and precognition) allow a person to see the past or the present, or predict the future, using human powers only, without divine intervention. Often, some focus of attention or concentration is used, and so the methods are described as *reading* the answers from various things. Among the objects read are: the human hand, coffee grounds, tea leaves, crystal balls, tarot or ordinary playing cards (cartomancy), sand, bones, salt, water, yarrow stalks or coins (the I Ching), and runes.

About Psychic Healing

Every human society has health practitioners. Depending on the culture they belong to, they are called physicians, healers, acupuncturists, shamans, witch doctors, medicine men, sorcerers, or something else. All such healers have theories and models of how the body works, and of what kinds of things go wrong with it and why, providing them with a basis for diagnosis and treatment according to the healing traditions in which they work. (A *healing tradition* is a coherent body of thought and practice concerned with health, illness, and healing; *healing* is the process by which the body moves from illness to a more healthy condition; a *healer* is someone who functions to aid the process of healing; a *diagnosis* is the process through which the healer identifies and classifies an illness according to his particular healing tradition; a *treatment* is what he does to alleviate the illness and aid the healing process.)

One healing tradition might see illness as a blockage of the flow of the life force, or vital force, and treat it by sticking pins into the patient to restore that flow. Another might see it as possession by an evil spirit and treat it by a form of exorcism. A third might see it as a consequence of imbalanced energies in the patient and treat it by restoring internal harmony. A fourth might see the same illness as an invasion of hostile beings and administer poisons to destroy the invaders; this is the common approach of contemporary Western medicine, which calls the invaders *microbes* and the poisons *antibiotics.*

Many books have been written about the effectiveness of some parallel systems of medicine—that is, systems other than the one that is commonly practiced in our Western world, like homeopathy, acupuncture, and so on. And with the coming of the so-called New Age era, many writings acquaint us with psychic healing and other healing traditions that are based on the power of the mind, on mind/body interaction, and on the fact that consciousness may affect matter, and that illness may be due to a psychological state of mind.

But in fact we are not becoming aware of anything new: the so-called New Age is an era of the rediscovery of many healing traditions that were practiced thousands of years ago. Some have been kept alive by the Fourth World and other cultures of tradition.

Since the dawn of mankind, every culture has practiced a healing tradition. In Egypt, South America, and other parts of the world, skulls have been found that show signs of skillful bone surgery performed at least ten thousand years ago. Some skull bones had already begun to heal, proving that the patients survived, perhaps for years. Other skulls show evidence of four or more operations. To perform these operations without modern anesthetics or antibiotics, these ancient surgeons must have possessed incredible techniques and knowledge of healing.

Few of these ancient healing traditions have disappeared: some have been kept alive by peoples of tradition; many have been revived by other cultures and enriched with their own knowledge. Among those healing traditions that survived history, some have reappeared in our Western world. Homeopathy, for instance, traces its roots to the healing traditions of the mages of Babylonia, the sages of China, and the god-priests of Egypt.

Hippocrates, the father of medicine, was among the first to appreciate this heritage. About 400 B.C. he wrote, "Opposites are healed by opposites," and "Illness is produced by likes and, by the likes that he takes, the patient comes from illness back to health; fever is suppressed by what produces it, and is produced by what suppresses it. So, in two opposite manners, health is restored."

In a few sentences, Hippocrates thus established the principles of two main healing traditions: allopathy (from the Greek *allos,* which means "opposite"), which is our classical medicine; and homeopathy (from the Greek *homoios,* which means "similar"). Hippocrates was also the one who discovered the therapeutic effects of diet and exercise—he taught the art of eating and the art of walking, and treated his patients with diet, exercises, and herbs, concentrating on which elements of the human body were out of balance—and who claimed that many illnesses are related to the spinal column. In 1875, the American osteopath Andrew Taylor Still confirmed that there was a relation between the spinal column and some organs, and between articulations and tissues.

He also concluded: "There where blood flows normally, illness is unable to develop, for our blood is able to produce all the useful principles to insure a natural immunity and fight against illnesses."

The Western healing tradition reflects the fundamental separation of man and nature so basic to the Western worldview. "Today, illness doesn't mean what happens to man in his whole, but what happens to his organs," wrote Stefan Zweig in *La guérison par l'esprit.* With progress in surgery (that is, knowledge of the body), bacteriology (that is, knowledge of illnesses), and pharmacology (that is, knowledge of chemicals that fight illness), our medicine became analytic. Western healing practitioners like to think of medicine as a science, and so emphasize the separation between the observer (the physician) and the object of his observation (the patient and his illness). Treatment is something the physician does to the patient's body. In the struggle between the physician and the illness, the patient is only a bystander.

However, even though Western traditional medicine has not abandoned chemical healing, refusing to admit that invading microbes could be affected by everything that affects our lives, in the United States we are experiencing a new approach to healing. The increasing influence of Asian and South American cultures provides us with a wide range of different worldviews and healing traditions, many of which recognize the existence of physiological and psychological factors and admit their importance in influencing the human body; there is an investigation of life circumstances rather than a frontal attack on a single "disease." These facts gave birth to an eclectic approach, sometimes called *holistic medicine,* that attempts to learn from a variety of healing traditions, combining the best of each. One of its main characteristics is a strong emphasis on the personal responsibility each individual bears for his or her own health.

One of these treatment programs—well known for having successful results with cancer patients—was developed by Dr. Carl Simonton, a Texas radiologist and the author of *Getting Well Again.* The principal technique he uses is visualization, in conjunction with other forms of therapy. He asks patients to visualize their cancer in whatever symbolic form they choose, and to visualize the treatment as successfully attacking and destroying the cancer. (One successful patient saw his cancer as a large hamburgerlike mass, and his treatment as ravenous dogs tearing chunks off the mass and devouring it.)

This sort of treatment is not something the healer does to the patient's body, like surgery or radiation therapy, but is something the patient does for himself, with the advice and guidance of the healer. For it to work, the patient must accept responsibility for his own health and must be willing to commit the necessary time and energy.

Simonton has found that the patients who were helped were those who devoted themselves wholeheartedly to the task with a positive attitude, while those who did it sporadically and halfheartedly usually did not improve.

I have observed many healing traditions and different healing techniques throughout the world. I have witnessed the amazing and successful healing of infected wounds, tumors, tuberculosis, and other illnesses. If some healers use herbs and similar remedies to treat their patients, others, such as African sorcerers, use dance and chanting. (Among the !Kung Bushmen, for example, healing takes place during ceremonial dances that cause the *n'um,* or healing energy, to flow.) Exorcisms—such as those performed by Voodoo priests—are a healing tradition for cultures that conceptualize illness in terms of possession by evil spirits, that throw people out of balance. Worldviews that place considerable importance on the role of deities or other spirits in the workings of the world tend to give those deities a central place in the healing process. Divine intervention in the healing process is also claimed by faith healers, whereas Gypsy witch doctors put their faith in the healing power of dead toads.

In examining the field, certain superficial features, as well as deeper structures, appear to be constant throughout the wide range of healing traditions found within the Fourth World, in spite of cultural diversity. The common thread is that these traditions are based on concepts of balance and energy flow, though specific ideas as to the methods used to rebalance the body vary widely. For some cultures, the energy flow is internal, part of the individual; for others, it is part of the life force of the universe, which flows through everything all the time.

The idea that health is related to some kind of energy or vital force that flows through us may sound archaic and naive, yet it is a belief that recurs in different forms in many cultures—even many that are not part of the Fourth World. If Hawaiians and other Polynesians call it *mana,* and the !Kung Bushmen call it *n'um,* the traditional Japanese medical perspective calls that energy *ki,* the Indian yogis call it *prana,* and the Russians, coming to it through parapsychological research rather than cultural tradition, call it *bioplasma*.

The Chinese healing tradition, for instance, views the body as a system of energy currents, which are extensions and reflections of the currents the Chinese see in the universe; the world within is the microcosm, reflecting the complexity and the variation of the external macrocosm. If the whole universe is subject to the law of equilibrium, man, being an integral part of the cosmos just like any other living being, must also be subject to these laws. He gets the fundamental energy, the life force, from two sources: the cosmos (the *Tsri* energy, represented by *yang*); and the earth (the *Siue* energy, represented by *yin*).

The vital force that allows the body to function, called *chi,* is thought to move along fifty-nine pathways known as *meridians* (the Hindu system has seven hundred meridians) and must be kept in balance by two opposing forces, *yin* and *yang.* Many civilizations understand nature in terms of opposing forces; for the Tao, the universe is the oscillation of the activities of yin and yang. In healthy individuals this flow is smooth, maintaining the balance between the receptive feminine yin force and the assertive, masculine yang force. Yin meridians are associated with such organs as the liver, kidneys, and spleen, while yang meridians are associated with the stomach, gall bladder, and intestines. Disease results from and reflects an imbalance of yin and yang forces, and manifests itself as an imbalance in *chi* somewhere in the body.

This imbalance may be corrected by stimulating appropriate points on the meridians—there are three hundred sixty-five juncture points, or acupuncture points—using finger massage, manual stimulation (acupressure), heat stimulation (moxibustion), or insertion of thin needles (acupuncture). Rebalancing the system may also be done through the administration of herbs or herb teas.

Basically, all the healing traditions practiced by peoples of tradition can be divided into three categories.

△ natural healing using plants
△ balance-way healing or rebalancing energies
△ psychic healing

Each category comprises various techniques and may interract with another category.

Despite the positive results they obtain, medicines of tradition are still rejected by Western medical science. Is this because, medically speaking, Western doctors cannot really understand what is going on during the process of "magic healing"? Or is it because our physicians want to be the only ones to hold the healing monopoly—medical studies being long and expensive? Or are their reactions dictated by the pharmaceutical and chemical industries, which would lose huge profits if patients were treated with plants and psychic healing? The plant that many peoples of tradition have used for birth control since the dawn of their existence could be easily proved to be as effective as the Pill, and without its side effects, but since we can grow that plant in our gardens, its use would cost drug companies billions of dollars of lost profits.

Many scientists claim that medicines of tradition are superstitions—ceremonies performed by charlatans using tricks to take advantage of their patients' naiveté. Others acknowledge that medicines of tradition may work, but not on us. And there are scientists who say that magic healing works due to coincidence or psychosomatic processes. And a very few are inclined to believe in the reality of medicines of tradition, but remain silent, waiting for more thorough reports.

It is certainly not true that all healings of tradition are fraudulent processes. However, one may sometimes find fraud during traditional healing processes. Some healers do use tricks during the ceremonies they perform, because they don't have the necessary powers or the knowledge to use them. Many Filipino psychic healers, for instance, have been caught out: the patient's supposed blood and organs were, in fact, the blood and organs of animals. But despite that, it seems they obtain successful results. Should we condemn Western medicine just because some of our physicians have made wrong diagnoses or performed unnecessary surgeries? And we could wonder to what degree it is really the Filipino healer's power that heals a patient, and to what degree it is the patient's belief in him. Or perhaps it is the patient's emotional and psychological reactions when he sees the blood and the organs that are supposedly his that lead to healing.

Some scientists claim that medicine of tradition works only because of coincidence or psychosomatic processes. However, the following summary statement from a seminar on psychic healing—including biotronic healing, bioenergotherapy, and bioenergotherapeutics—contradicts such conclusions. Organized in September 1975 by the Committee of Applied Cybernetics of the Czechoslovakian Scientific Technical Association, the seminar gave this summary, published in *The Realms of Healing* by Stanley Krippner and Alberto Villoldo:

It was agreed that bioenergotherapy is the capacity of one organism to transmit the proper energy to some other organism in order to improve its psychosomatic state. On the basis of the latest Soviet research, the mechanism is probably biological plasma. It can be presumed, therefore, that an interaction is taking place between the two biological plasmas— that of the bioenergotherapist and that of the patient. The bioenergo- therapy proceeds from the knowledge that the patient has the capacity for automatic regeneration and self-recovery, just as long as the limits imposed by the patient's state are not exceeded. When the patient's own reserves are quite limited, the bioenergotherapy provides an additional reserve, designated to restore equilibrium to the patient, bringing him back to health—both at an objective and subjective level.

Therefore, the bioenergotherapist can be conceived of as an indi- vidual with the capacity to transfer energy that has healing characteris- tics to individuals capable of using this energy. As early as 1956, there was a verification of these procedures in the USSR. Particularly striking results were found in the treatment of arthritis, asthma, poliomyelitis, tuberculosis, and of course, various psychosomatic ailments.

Scientists have also observed that in many cases a patient who is ill can, when receiving a placebo in place of medication, recover from his malady because he believes he is receiving medication that will cure him. This is called the placebo effect. Sigmund Freud realized the power of the placebo effect: "expectation colored by hope and faith is an effective force with which to reckon . . . in all our attempts at treatment and cure." Dr. Ted Kaptchuk noted in his book *The Healing Arts*:

> It must also be emphasized that when the placebo works it works like the drug—that is, it actually makes physical changes in the body. It isn't that the patient simply believes his ulcer is better—it actually heals; or that the arthritic believes he can walk—his inflammation is actually reduced. Virtually any organ or physiological system in the body can be reached by the placebo effect. . . . There is nothing in the "green pharmacy" or in the modern armory of drugs with such power and versatility. To see the placebo effect as simply an example of faith or the power of sugges- tion would be a mistake.

There are many ways to induce the placebo effect, one of them certainly being to instill in the patient trust and faith in the healer. The healer can then create medical miracles, even without having any real healing powers, thanks to this self-healing principle. (It is the be- lievers' faith in their preachers that allows some of those preachers to heal.)

I have personally performed many medical miracles over the years. I am aware that, because peoples of tradition are not used to Western medications, a single aspirin or dose of vitamin C can have a surprising effect, even on diseases that, in the West, respond only to drugs that are much more powerful. But the key to my success as a healer was the people's faith in me. No matter what I prescribed for them, what really healed their bodies was their belief in me and in my medicines.

My quickest results were produced by prescribing effervescent vitamin C or aspirin, because the thousands of small bubbles emerging as the tablet dissolved seemed magical to my patients. Also, whenever I gave a medication, I created a ritual to amplify its effectiveness. This not only accelerated the healing process, but enabled me to dispense substitutes when my stock of medication came to an end.

The first time I realized that people's faith in my healing powers could really cure their diseases was in the Sahara Desert. A crippled man was brought to me, carried in a stretcher. All his joints were so swollen from arthritis that he couldn't move by himself. I asked him what had happened. He explained that as a Tuareg's servant he had spent his whole life digging deep wells and trenches to carry the water needed to irrigate fields. I took one of his carriers aside and told him I was not sure I could help the man. He said that, having heard about my healing talents from other Tuaregs, the crippled man insisted on being brought to me. They had walked four days to reach the Tuareg encampment where I was. So I quickly invented a ritual, during which I applied wet rice to each of the cripple's joints. Then I said, "Now walk to your home!" I will never forget the expression on his face and the gratitude in his eyes when, by himself, he stood up and, slowly, walked away.

A strong religious belief system also provides fertile ground for miracles, even if only those due to the placebo effect. In Lourdes, France, at the place where the Virgin Mary is said to have appeared to the fourteen-year-old Bernadette Soubirou in 1858, there is a spring that is said to be miraculous. After long investigations of each case, even the Vatican has admitted that many miraculous healings have occurred in the pool supplied by this spring, where people who are ill bathe during the yearly pilgrimage to Lourdes. Yet biochemical analysis of the water shows that there is nothing special in it.

A repository of dead animals and other filth, the Ganges River in India is reported to be highly polluted with germs and bacteria of all kinds when it reaches the city of Benares. Yet millions of Hindus, each year, bathe in it and drink its waters. And to this day there is no evidence that any Hindu has been contaminated by this germ-carrying river—because for believers, the Ganges is sacred, a goddess. Just speaking its name erases all sins committed during the past two lives.

For whatever reason—whether psi plays a large or limited role, or none at all; whether some healing traditions really heal by a still-unknown process, or by activating some part of the brain that releases self-healing powers, or just by inducing the placebo effect—and no matter what techniques their healers use, medicines of tradition have a definite value and, in the right circumstances, can heal.

However, no healing tradition, including Western medicine, shows a clear superiority across the spectrum of human illness. And, despite their diversity and apparent incompatibility, all healing traditions work up to a point. Each seems capable of curing some illnesses and incapable of curing others. The reason, perhaps, lies in the fact that since one creates one's own illnesses, only one can really cure them. An outside agent—drug or healer—can aid in that process, can create conditions that make it easier to regain health, but the basic responsibility for healing rests with the patient. And the healing traditions of the Fourth World seem to recognize this more clearly than others.

Studies have shown that many illnesses are caused by our psychological attitude. Physiological and psychological factors are of great importance in influencing the body; and, according to Dr. Ted Kaptchuk,

> even invading microbes are affected by everything that affects our lives. . . . One is more likely to develop a disease after any stressful event, and in close correlation with the seriousness of the stress. A study of 5,000 British widowers published in *The Lancet* in 1963 showed that disease rates increased 40 percent in the first six months after their wife's death. . . . A special government medical task force investigating the determining factors for surviving artherosclerotic heart disease in Massachussetts reported that the most reliable prognosticator for surviving heart disease was not nonsmoking, normal blood pressure, or low cholesterol levels, but "job satisfaction." The second-best indication was "overall happiness." A nine-year study, reported in the *American Journal of Epidemiology,* made in Alameda County, California, of forty-seven hundred men and women showed that people who lacked social and community ties were more likely to fall sick and die.

Carl Jung noted:

> A suitable explanation or a comforting word to the patient may have something like a healing effect which may even influence the glandular secretions. The doctor's words, to be sure, are "only" vibrations in the

air, yet they constitute a particular set of vibrations corresponding to a particular psychic state in the doctor. The words are effective only insofar as they convey a meaning, or have significance. It is their meaning that is effective. But "meaning" is something mental or spiritual. Call it a fiction if you like. Nonetheless, it enables us to influence the course of a disease in a far more effective way than with chemical preparations.

Consequently, the ideal medicine of tomorrow would be based on psychophysiology, where practitioners would choose from among all healing traditions the one most adapted to each of their patients. It is amusing to note that what should be tomorrow's medicine is the ancient Western medicine that Hippocrates practiced.

This healing tradition was revived by the Arabs, who, later, brought it to China and India, where it is called the *Unani* healing tradition; *Unani* means "Greek" in Arabic. And now, centuries later, we are rediscovering the principles of this tradition. We are experiencing a return to Hippocrates, who said, "One shouldn't be ashamed of borrowing from the people what can be useful to the art of healing."

The cosmic repository of truth, wisdom, and knowledge lies within us, and it is up to us to reconnect with it, perhaps by once again using the parts of our brain where such skills originated early in our evolutionary history.

Many of us are experiencing an awakening to other orders of reality. Not knowing where else to go, we seek answers from science, but science has limits. And what science can't explain is often called metaphysics, so we are referred to theology. But long ago our official Western religions stopped being initiatory, metaphysical, and metapsychic. Instead, they became dogmatic and moral, proscribing the truths that could enlighten our lives. Our only solution may be to turn to the cultures that have not yet repressed those parts of their beings where these truths may be found.

In this book I am attempting to explore the secrets of the many peoples of tradition I have seen, and of the mysterious experiences I have witnessed. I hope to fashion some idea of where the truth may lie, and what these mysteries might indicate about our human powers.

I do not have rational explanations for the supernatural phenomena I have witnessed. Sometimes I will add some of my own speculations to the explanations I was given by the people who performed such feats. Also, I have no intention of insisting that the reader believe that these psychic phenomena really do exist—although I hope that skeptics will reconsider the reasons for their refusal to acknowledge the existence of paranormal phenomena.

This book is intended to assist those who will find, through my account, a means to renew their own faith in man's powers and to propel their conscious and subconscious forward. For, as Albert Hofmann, the Swiss chemist who discovered LSD, has written, "this renewal could lead to the renunciation of the materialistic philosophy of life and the development of a new reality consciousness."

2

The Cosmology of Peoples of Tradition

Humanity comprises many different cultures, each possessing its own logic, belief system, and reality. A culture regulates a person's system of thought and reasoning, filters his or her feelings and emotions, influences the way he or she sees and understands the world, and ultimately determines his or her perception of the world, thus creating its own reality.

Even within Western cultures there are vast differences in ways of seeing, understanding, and experiencing the same reality—and since seeing is believing, human beliefs are in accord with what our cultures have taught us to see. What Americans believe about love, death, marriage, children, and so on is often quite different from what a Frenchman or a German might believe. The reality of each of these issues may become many different realities as the logic of each culture diverges in its own way.

The same facts may be interpreted differently in different cultures, as in the classic story of the three blind men describing an elephant. The first blind man, who touches the elephant's leg, believes an elephant is something like a tree; the one who touches its trunk believes an elephant is like a snake; and the one touching its side believes it to be like a wall.

Our culture filters the information we receive and ultimately determines our perception of the world around us. Like a lens, it brings some aspects of the world into sharp focus, while blurring its other aspects. If we change cultures, we change the way in which we perceive the world. We then live in a different world, where different interactions become possible. What is impossible for us remains impossible as long as we live in the cultural world that formed our perceptions. Thus each culture creates its own limitations and its own limitless possibilities.

Another way of approaching the problem of multiple realities is through certain Eastern philosophies. These say that everything is illusion. If we believe in an illusion—say, that we have real bodies—then we *do* have real bodies. Belief creates that reality. Therefore, even inside a given reality one can easily create other realities, into which one fits more comfortably, by believing in the illusions that will create the realities one wants. (As you will find throughout this book, many cultures of tradition, like the Toradjas of Celebes, use that principle to create realities that will answer their need.)

In this chapter I would like to introduce you to the different modes of logic used by the peoples of tradition. Only from this starting point can we begin to understand their behavior, and consequently the beliefs that lie behind so many of the mysteries I have witnessed. Although generalizing about traditional cultures is just as difficult as generalizing about Western cultures, it is nonetheless important to at least sketch out the major cultural beliefs shared by the peoples of tradition.

Before giving specific examples, let me present the basic tenets of the peoples of tradition.

△ They believe in the existence of a main God who, in some cases, is the creator of all things.

△ They believe in the existence of an invisible world where their main deity lives and which is populated by lesser gods, goddesses, and divinities.

△ They believe in the existence of *invisibles*—invisible beings and spirits that may be active in the natural, visible world.

△ They believe in the existence of human souls that survive death.

△ They believe in the existence of magic.

△ They believe in the powers of their spiritual or religious leader.

All of these beliefs are interrelated and form an interdependent system of belief.

THE EXISTENCE OF A MAIN GOD

Every culture of tradition—in fact, every single human society—has something we could call a religion. (The term *religion* is used here to encompass a wide range of human religious institutions and belief systems, with as many significant differences among them as similarities.) But peoples of tradition do not live their religions in the same way we do.

We dedicate most of our week to a social life, reserving Friday, Saturday, or Sunday—depending on our religion—for the practice of religion (although we might dedicate more of our time to religion as we grow older). Peoples of tradition, however, do not have that separation between social life and religious life, for there is no separation between the profane and the sacred in their lives.

Through appropriate rituals and customs, they have made the world in which they live a sacred place—whereas the outer world, outside their domain, has remained profane. For peoples of tradition, the world—to which they have been sent to spend their physical lives—is chaos. By making the place in which they live sacred, they create order from chaos, linking themselves to the cosmic harmony. Everything they do in their everyday lives—eating, sleeping, making love, working, hunting, raising children, and so forth—is sacred. As the anthropologist Mircea Eliade said, "To be alive is to be religious."

Basically the religions of peoples of tradition fall into two broad categories. One of these is a form of monotheism. The creation myths of some cultures tell of a single god who created the whole universe, and this God-creator is the main deity of their religious pantheon, which may also include lower gods, divinities, angels, spirits, and so forth.

According to other cultures, the universe was created by someone or something other than a god. For example, according to the creation myths of the Apayaos of the Philippines, the Dayaks of Borneo, and the majority of Asian tribes, the universe began with the sexual union of two cosmic entities. From this act, two worlds emerged: the one above—an invisible one, represented by a god and his lieutenants—and the one below—the visible one, represented by another god and his subordinates. After this creation, there was a war between the two worlds. Although they were immortal, the lieutenants of the two divine groups killed each other. Their death symbolized the end of immortality. And in dying they gave birth to man and his universe—all that surrounds us. And through this new creation—human beings—

the two gods found oneness, a new or renewed unity and balance, and often became one. This second category of religions thus represents a unification of monotheism and polytheism.

The Existence of An Invisible World

Although one can find variations from one culture to another, peoples of tradition believe in the existence of an invisible world, often called the *primordial world*. This invisible world extends backward in time to the very creation of the universe; it is as old as the universe itself.

The invisible world represents the world above for some cultures; for others it is located all around us. Sometimes this primordial world corresponds to the Garden of Eden.

In many cultures one can find equivalents to the myth of the Garden of Eden, that tell of human beings originally living in the primordial world. Depending on the culture, this Eden may not be located on earth. For the Dayaks of Borneo, the Toradjas of Celebes, and the majority of Asian tribes, this Eden is the constellation of the Pleiades; for many African tribes it is Sirius, the Dog Star; for the Dogons of Africa it is Sirius B—a tiny planet gravitating around Sirius and discovered only in 1844; for some North American Indian tribes it is Venus.

Then, for whatever reason, people were sent to earth, where they have to spend their physical lives. But after death their souls return to the primordial world.

The Existence of Invisibles

It is in that invisible world that the primary god lives, as well as all the invisibles he governs, such as lesser gods and goddesses (sometimes referred to as divinities), the heroes of mythology who have been made divine, ancestors (one's own relatives) and other souls of the deceased, and other invisible entities.

Some lesser gods and goddesses may represent cosmic matters or astrological forms—the sun, the moon, the planets—or temporal symbols such as day and night, or archetypes like love and war. Others may represent natural phenomena and elements—water, rain, fire, wind, thunder, lightning, and so forth. For some cultures, certain divinities are energies that have been divinized—as is true of the *loas* of the Voodoo religion.

In certain cultures, inhabitants of the invisible world have the same needs and passions as do people living on Earth. For others, invisibles can materialize. But all peoples of tradition agree that invisibles can occupy the visible world of the living. These may be souls or divine energies that animate and inhabit matter, good and evil spirits, and other supernatural entities.

Although one can find variations from one culture to another, peoples of tradition believe that everything in nature, every single bit of matter, is alive. Each has a personal identity and emotions that are subject to influence. Anthropologists call this belief that the natural world is alive *animism* (from the Latin word *anima,* meaning "soul," or "that which animates, which gives life").

Many people ascribe a soul or spirit that generates the energy of life to trees, to mountains, to rivers, to everything. For some cultures, matter does not have its own soul, but is animated by disunited energies. A few believe that every element of nature is inhabited by the souls of ancestors. But the bottom line is the same: whatever their source, these souls, or disunited energies, or ancestral spirits can be worshiped or called upon for help, and people must deal with them whenever they harm anything in the natural world, for these spirits maintain the cosmic harmony of nature. As an Iglulik Eskimo told the Arctic explorer Knud Rasmussen,

> The greatest peril of life lies in the fact that human food consists entirely of souls. All the creatures that we have to kill and eat, all those that we have to strike down and destroy to make clothes for ourselves, have souls, souls that do not perish with the body and which must therefore be [pacified] lest they should revenge themselves on us for taking away their bodies.

The Dayaks who live in the jungles of Borneo adhere to a distinctive hunting ritual: after a chase that may last for days, a hunter will shoot his prey only after he and it have made eye contact. (Of course, the hunter runs the risk that the quarry may dart away; but it is in this way that the hunter honors his prey.) Then, and only then, is he allowed to shoot his poisoned dart or arrow. And, as the poison slowly destroys the nervous system of the wounded animal, the hunter invokes its spirit, which is linked with his own system of divinities, explaining the reasons for the killing and reciting prayers. Then, as the animal falls down, ready to die, the hunter hugs it, caresses it, kisses it, begging for forgiveness and imploring that this act of destruction will not disturb the harmony that reigns between men, nature, and gods.

Among the Papuan tribe of Asmats in New Guinea, a sago palm may not be cut down without a ceremony. As tribe members stand in front of the tree they intend to fell, the shaman gently beats a stick against the trunk to awaken the tree's spirit, while reciting invocations that beg the spirit for forgiveness. Then he drills a small hole in the trunk to allow the spirit to leave the tree. Only when he knows that the spirit has left it can the tree be cut down and emptied of its pith, which will be brought back to the village and used for flour. With the Capricorn beetle larvae that live inside the pith, the sago palm tree really is the Asmats' tree of life.

But the fact that it is a food source is not the only reason the Asmats venerate the sago palm. The word *Asmat* means "We, the tree-men"; they identify themselves with trees of whatever kind. According to their myth of creation, it is the primal tree of life that gave birth to the Asmat nation. Asmat women are directly identified with the sago palm for, as one Asmat saying has it, "life comes from inside of women as flour comes from inside the sago. Both allow the continuation of our tribe."

Failing to perform a ritual that maintains harmony can call for a lot of trouble. Spirits of trees, of animals, or of any other parts of nature, usually peaceful, can also become dangerous to the living, and those that do evil become harmless if the living respect them or know how to protect themselves. This dual nature of spirit is reflected in the population of invisibles that, for many cultures, surround the living.

One example of this good/evil duality can be found in Voodoo. Although some Voodoo spirits, or *loas,* are more inclined to produce evil than others are, and some more inclined to produce good, loas are generally neither good nor evil in themselves, and can be used for good or for evil. In the Voodoo religion, though, loas are never used for evil purposes. As a Voodoo priest told me, "Only loas representing good energies will contact us, because our mind creates positive vibrations." The many other sects that exist parallel to Voodoo, all dealing with sorcery, use loas for personal advancement in the visible world and for evil purposes—not for reaching the sacred.

The Tuareg of the Sahara Desert also believe in evil spirits. They believe that *djenouns*—imps who populate trees, mountains, and wells—are responsible for misleading travelers, among other things. They also believe in ghosts that haunt the sides of sand dunes, and in the evil spirit Efrit, who brings the *evil eye.* The Kel es Souf, a population of genies, live at the bottoms of ravines and inside caves; they are invisible during the day but materialize at night, often taking on a female appearance. They are responsible for making echoes and whirl-winds, and for causing dried-up rivers to flow; but they also perform evil acts, like dropping stones on travelers.

THE EXISTENCE OF HUMAN SOULS

All cultures of tradition believe that every human being has a soul that survives the death of the body. Funeral rituals are performed at the individual's death, and other rites as well, sometimes long after the physical death. Such rituals are intended to facilitate the separation of the soul from the body—for it is believed that no souls want to leave the world of the living—and to help the soul on its perilous journey to the afterlife, where it will join the ancestors and divinities living in the primordial world.

A belief in the existence of human souls has led to the idea that souls can be subjugated through specific rituals. One example of this cultural logic is embedded in the practice of headhunting, a ritual still performed in many areas of the world, including Borneo, Sumatra, New Guinea, the Philippines, Burma, the northeast of India, Southeast Asia's mountainous regions, the Amazon Basin, and some countries of black Africa.

We people of civilized societies have proven our unlimited capacity for repeated brutality; nevertheless, our feelings of repulsion about headhunting (and cannibalism and any form of human sacrifice) prevent us from approaching this phenomenon with understanding. When seen from within the cultures that engage in them, these practices cannot be considered savagery; the very logic of these cultures prompts such actions. Whatever the apparent reason—a rite of passage, revenge, a feud between two enemy clans, the need to express warlike values—headhunting has always had magical and religious components.

Headhunting is a ritual whose primary intent is the subjugation of an enemy's soul. When a tribesman attacks an enemy—never a man of his own tribe—the victim is beheaded while alive; otherwise his soul goes away. The head is wrapped in ashes, which are believed to create a magical envelope, stopping the soul from leaving the skull until specific rituals are performed that keep the soul permanently imprisoned in the skull. By retaining his victim's head, the tribesman becomes the guardian of this soul, and magically transfers to himself all of the victim's virtues and energies. He has power over the soul, which will protect him, his relatives, and his clan from evil. In exchange for this, the headhunter vows to venerate and care for the skull, adorning it with flowers and offering it meals to feed the spirit living within it. Headhunting is thus also a way to increase one's capacities as a warrior. The more heads a hunter takes, the more spiritual energies he gets.

In some cultures, the souls taken are not those of enemies but rather of their own ancestors. For example, although the skulls Asmat headhunters use in ceremonies such as initiation are those of their enemies, they always use the skulls of their male parents for personal protection. When a father gets too old to lead his family, he is sent to a friendly village, where he will be fed, decapitated, and eaten. His skull will then be sent back to his relatives so that they can maintain his soul at home. This allows the eldest son to take over the family. Disrespect toward this tradition would anger the deceased and deprive the living of an invaluable ally.

For the Asmats, a relative's skull shields the possessor from evil and malevolent spirits. It protects him from danger in the visible world, particularly during sleep, when his mind is open to curses, since his consciousness cannot protect him. Therefore, he uses his father's skull as a pillow. It is also a way for him to communicate with his dead parent during dreams, and to receive his wisdom. Whenever an Asmat goes on a headhunt or any dangerous trip, he carries the skull hanging around his neck.

Since it is difficult for a headhunter to carry around his cumbersome trophy, especially when hunting or fighting, some peoples of tradition wear something that symbolically represents, and is magically linked to, the heads hanging in their homes. For instance, some Dayak men wear wild boars' tusks in holes pierced in their ears, or on their necklaces. Warthogs' tusks hang around the necks of Papuans, and of the Nagas of India, who also wear them as bracelets.

Elsewhere in Africa, Asia, and South America, cut heads are represented by seashells or small red seeds, wild-animal or cat skin, gold plates, or feathers worn in the hair. For some tribes, body paintings or tattoos also mark the possession of human heads. (The Iban of Borneo wear small tattoos on their fingers and hands, each line or design representing a human head.) The Jivaros and Munduruku of the Amazon jungle have found an easier way to carry their victims' souls with them: they shrink their heads.

Scalps are even lighter than miniaturized heads. For the Maoris of New Zealand, and some native American Indians, these hanks of hair or scalp are trophies symbolizing the whole head.

As a substitute for a cut head, some tribes keep other parts of their victims such as the jaw, various bones, teeth, hands, ears, nose, lips, beard, or testicles. (The Danakil of Ethiopia wear the dried testicles of their victims around their necks.)

❦

Headhunting, like ritual cannibalism, also symbolizes human sacrifice, which intends to assimilate the victim's powers and virtues, courage and strength. Throughout mankind's history, all cultures have performed human sacrifices in one form or another, and it is still practiced in many countries today. However, for most tribes nowadays, fortunately, the sacrifice of an animal has become a substitute for a human kill.

Human sacrifice—or its substitute—reflects aspects of various creation myths and serves as a way to mark new beginnings in life. In creation myths it is always the death of a god that gives life to mankind. The god's death puts an end to immortality, thus engendering mankind's mortality. Something cannot start from nothing; something can start only if one puts an end to nothing. Consequently, something cannot start without being preceded by a death, a kill.

On the level of daily life, this myth tells its followers that to start something new, particularly something that does not belong to everyday life, a death is required. So, whenever a human being is about to create something, he must first perform an act of death—that is, the killing of a man. By sacrificing a human being, one becomes a god who kills another god. One lives the myth!

In Christianity, we have a similar symbology: only through the killing of a divinity—Jesus, the Son of God—could man be saved and reborn.

Also, the killing of humans—like animal sacrifices—is seen as a ritual of fertility, one that allows any new beginning, because of its symbolic link with blood. The idea that blood allows creation is connected to the belief that a woman can create a new life because she is able to menstruate. Therefore, the shedding of blood can call for the creation of something new.

Among headhunter tribes, headhunting, symbolizing the human sacrifice, is often performed to mark important events in the life of an individual or of a whole village: deaths, weddings, and other rites of passage, building a new house or even a canoe, planting a rice field, harvesting crops, or going on a big hunt.

For example, when the Iban build a house, they dig deep holes in which they place heavy tree trunks to support the building's structure. In the past, when they raised the first pole, they put a living woman into the hole first (generally a slave captured from an enemy village), crushing her with the tree trunk.

Even as late as the 1970s, during my stay in Sarawak, the Malaysian part of Borneo, I heard about an instance of human sacrifice. My informant—a Malayan who was educated at the University of Kuala Lumpur in Malaysia—at that time was in charge of building a bridge across a river for an engineering company working under government contract. He told me that he was managing a group of Iban workers. The tribesmen refused to begin construction until they could consecrate the place. Although they had stopped the practice of headhunting long before and were already part of the modern world, the workers' minds were still governed by their need of age-old rituals.

You can imagine my friend's surprise when the chief of the hundred or so workers requested a human sacrifice in order to proceed. Since they were his best workers, he tried to reason with them. Nothing worked.

"Building a bridge over water isn't like building something else!" said the workers' chief. "Building a bridge over water is creating a passage from one world to another. It requires a specific ritual; otherwise it will raise the wrath of spirits and our lives will be put in danger!" (The idea of bridging two worlds—visible to invisible—is a concept that still exists in spiritual tradition. The Pope is called the Sovereign Pontiff, which comes from the Latin *pontifex,* meaning "the bridge maker.")

"What do you need exactly?" asked my Malayan friend.

"A human sacrifice must be performed, and the head must be buried under the first pole that will hold the structure," replied the worker.

When the civil engineer made his report, his company had one answer: "Do whatever you want, but the bridge must be built on time. Otherwise we will lose the job!"

At his next meeting with the workers' chief, the engineer proposed using an old human skull for the ceremony, as a substitute for taking a human life. That suggestion was refused. Meanwhile, his company began pressuring him, suggesting that he was about to lose his job.

Once again he tried to make the Iban workers change their minds, but in vain. He never told me how he did it, but one night he managed to get a man who had been sentenced to death out of jail. That same night, the Iban performed their ceremony. The next morning the building of the bridge began.

C

Sacrifice also has another meaning. Like offerings of clothes, food, or beverages, it is intended to transform whatever is visible into something invisible, sending it into the world of the invisibles so that the inhabitants there can enjoy it. Sacrificing, or offering, liberates the essence or astral body, the level of existence, of what is offered, the part of things responsible for animating matter such as the physical body. Without this essence, matter ceases to exist. It is assumed that if the essence of something has been sent as food, the invisibles will actually be fed by it. A dress will actually be used as a dress; an animal will serve as an animal; and so on.

THE EXISTENCE OF MAGIC

Peoples of the Fourth World, like a large majority of the populations of Third World nations and even many who live in more developed countries in our modern world, believe in magic.

According to the *Random House College Dictionary, magic* is an art employing some occult force of nature. *Occultism* is the doctrine or study of the supernatural, magical, and so on. But the word *occultism* is a recent term, created by a magician named Eliphas Levi in the nineteenth century. It refers to *esotericism* without that term's sacred characteristics. Thus one must be familiar with esotericism to understand the theory on which magic is based, and to understand how much of magic may be a reality that follows principles of ancient sciences. (I owe much to Michel Mirabail's *Les 50 mots clefs de l'ésotérisme* for the definitions of esotericism and magic that follow.)

Esotericism is a wisdom. It means the secret doctrine that reveals the mysteries of the universe. It is a synthesis of the symbols and myths of all religions, and is based on self-knowledge. "Know yourself and you will know the gods' universe," wrote Socrates.

Taking as its field of study the symbolic common thread of religions, mythologies, initiations, and sacred sciences, esotericism covers a whole range of disciplines: astrology, alchemy, magic, numerical science (the Cabala), sacred science (Hermeticism), and the anthropology of the sacred, to name a few. Esoteric science is transmitted by a master to his adept to allow the adept to rediscover the ties that link him to the cosmic forces, to the superior entities of heaven and nature.

Generally, esotericism is transmitted orally, following the rules of oral tradition, so as to preserve the keys to the knowledge, which are entrusted only to the adept who has proven he deserves them. And if the secret doctrine has to be written down, the sacred text can be understood only through codes leading to interpretation—for example the Cabala, or certain passages of the New Testament ("only those who have ears can hear"). For esotericism refers to an oral tradition that God, or gods, have always possessed and which prophets and masters are the heirs of. Present among the Chaldean oracles as well as among Sufis in Islam, esotericism is as well known by mystics (Egyptian, Indian, Tibetan, Chinese, Japanese, Greek, Jewish, Islamic, early Christian, and shamans) as by men of science, like Hippocrates, Paracelsus, Kepler, Newton, and so forth, as well as some researchers in advanced sciences.

In having esotericism as its cultural background, one might say that magic is the power of the word, the power of imagination, the power of thought, the power of faith.

Whether used in a chant or incantation, the word exerts power as long as the word is born from man, who belongs to the duality of creation/creator. It has the power to act because the sound is a vibration, and the vibration is a creative energy. "And the Word has become Flesh and has lived among us," says the Bible.

To possess the Word is to be able to wake up the forces of the universe. God asked Adam to name beings; and the creation itself resulted from a Word used in the imperative tense. The Word is thus the reason of the world, and gives life to it. Also, the Word is the Son: Hochma in the Cabala, to whom "has been given all power over Heaven and Earth." The Word is, thus, science and power. Therefore, magic is "the science of the Word," says Piobb in *Formulaire de haute magie.* Magic is the esoteric practice itself, and not a mechanical constraint. If "Magic is authoritative, its sister, religion, is humble," wrote F. Ribadeau Dumas in *Histoire de la magie*—it is authoritative in the sense that Jesus talked of authority, the authority conferred on the Word by God.

Using the Word as a seed, man can impregnate the *nonexisting.* The emptiness that surrounds us consists of infinite nonexisting, not-yet existing, nonexistences, lifeless existences, non-energies, dormant energies, lifeless energies, non-conscious energies; all these different names try to define *nonexistence.* The nonexistence is like a womb that is capable of existing, that has the potential of existing. Without the seed of the Word, the "nonexistence" cannot exist, is unwrought, is like an egg without seed; so there is no creation. The Word is that spark that breaks the circle, the yolk of the non-conscious energy, and gives to it an image, an existence. The Word is what gives life to, what will animate, the non-conscious energy and gives to it an image, an existence.

We can't deny the power of man's faith, thought, and imagination. Frazer wrote, "Man's imagination can act on him with as much effectiveness as gravitation, and can kill him with the same certitude as a dose of prussic acid." Faith—which, according to the Bible, can displace mountains—can make a dream come true; it transforms into a reality whatever has been created by imagination and concentrated by thought.

On the orientation of the power depends the nature of magic: black or white. In black magic, the acquisition of powers is quick, but the subject is able to subdue the demons for only a short time before becoming their victim. (Remember the story of Faust, who sold his soul to the devil.) White magic always wins out over black magic, because evil is limited in its principle, and good is infinite.

Magic is a ritual, and the practice of magic requires the knowledge of various rites, chants, and formulas—to, for instance, open and close a ceremony, make gods and objects sacred in order to confer power on them, invoke a higher spirit, or command entities.

Magic is also a purely natural science that defies current scientific laws. It is the art of making possible what seems to not be. It is presumptuous of us to condemn magic as false just because it doesn't seem probable. One shouldn't deny what we can't understand with our logic and what our eyes can't see. To believe in magic is not necessarily a sign of lack of culture and civilization for, then, Ancient Greeks and Ancient Egyptians, who possessed an advanced moral civilization, would all have been barbarians.

Officially, modern Western science allows no validity to magic, first, because results that can be duplicated are impossible to obtain and therefore the effects of magic are considered a series of natural coincidences—and second, because magic is, theoretically, based on principles that defy our present understanding of many scientific laws. Yet a day will come when, thanks to further scientific discoveries, our scientists will realize that the laws that rule our natural and physical sciences are not immutable at all, and will acknowledge that magic is a true science for those who know how to use its fundamental principles. After all, electricity would have been considered a magic phenomenon if Maxwell hadn't proved that it follows the laws of physics.

There are obvious reasons why people of the modern world can't use magic. Our faith has been contaminated by a one-sided, rational, and materialistic worldview. We believe only in what has been approved by science. If we did try to do magic, we would wonder if it would work instead of concentrating the power of faith in what we were doing. The Word is used only to claim or pretend to express who we are, discuss business, and to comment on our advanced technology. As for our imagination, it has been shut down as we moved from childhood to adulthood by the materialistic society in which we live: "Concentrate on what you would like to do in order to become a part of society . . . Concentrate on your studies . . . Concentrate on your duties . . . Concentrate on how to climb the ladder of success . . ." and so forth, are the only subjects our imagination is allowed to explore. Only children are allowed to believe in fairy tales and Santa. Only children have the ability to have a conversation with a lifeless doll, and talk to invisible companions populating the adult emptiness.

Now that we have talked about what magic is in theory, let's look at the ins and outs, the particulars, of magic in the Fourth World and among other peoples of tradition.

Magic is found in all rituals peoples of tradition perform, for all are magico-religious rituals. Using such rituals, peoples of tradition keep their whole world in balance, in harmony with the cosmic forces. Magico-religious rituals allow them to communicate with the divine world. In calling the invisibles—gods, divinities, spirits, souls of the deceased—by means of prayers and rituals, peoples of tradition *capture* their energies, and those that animate the world and themselves. They can connect with these energies which are represented by supernatural characters. They can escape chaos and find order in the universe.

Among the Apayaos of the Philippines, for example, the shaman performs a small ritual at the end of the rice planting in order to keep the invisibles happy and to beseech their favors. He intones the following:

> I am calling the souls of the ancestors, I am calling the spirits of the eastern mountains and of the western mountains, I am calling [he enumerates all the gods, divinities, and spirits] so that they all will come and be present at our celebration marking the end of the rice planting.

And when the shaman assumes all souls and deities are present, he chants, "Today we are celebrating this feast, inviting you to accept these sacrifices of chicken and offerings of rice that we have prepared for you. Be the protectors of our children and of our brothers."

People can establish a link between themselves and the divine world by establishing, through magico-religious rituals, the center of their universe. This creates a magical axis between man and the gods, a conduit through which man's prayers reach the gods, and the gods' graces reach down to man, just as the steeples of our churches symbolize the magical axis linking the world of the living with heavens of the divine.

For instance, in each Apayao village, next to the *ato,* or ceremonial place, there is a wooden pole with chicken feathers attached to its top, beneath which an enemy's head is buried. This pole symbolically links the human world of the village to the divine one of the gods. This pole is the center of the Apayaos' universe, just as the totems of the Northwest Coast American Indians are of theirs. The so-called old trees of African tribes and the center poles of Haitian Voodoo temples serve similar purposes.

⊛

Using magico-religious rituals, people can create various techniques for coping with the fear of evil and for protecting themselves from malevolent spirits.

Foremost among these is the marking of the skin. It is believed that skin is the border between the individual's inner worlds—the conscious, unconscious, and subconscious worlds; the worlds of dreams, emotions, sexuality, beliefs, and so on—and the outer world, the society in which he lives. Whatever means are used to mark the body—mutilation, tattooing, branding, painting—the intent is the same: it is a talisman—the vivid language of cabalistic signs and magical designs that protects against malevolent spirits, exorcizes evil, and wins the favor of the gods. However, marking the skin also has other purposes:

△ It represents the death of the individual, which allows rebirth into another state, marked by a rite of passage.

△ It is a mnemonic device (a visual indication of the pain endured at the time of the marking of the skin, and a constant reminder of the teachings received and knowledge acquired during the initiation).

△ It marks the initiate's belonging to a specific sex and accepting the duties and responsibilities associated with that sex.

△ It expresses membership in a family, clan, tribe, or society.

△ It is a medium for the society in which the individual lives to send symbolic messages to his inner worlds that enable him to grow in wisdom, and to instill in him rules and codes of life that will, in some cases, limit his powers by restraining the freedom of some of his inner worlds—sexuality, dreams, and so on.

△ It carries messages expressing his individuality, which are intended for the society in which he lives.

Following magical principles, earrings protect the ears from evil spirits, nose rings protect the nose, while coloring or tattooing on the lips, chin, or gums insures a full-time protection of the mouth. Coloring finger and toe nails or coloring or tattooing fingers, hands, toes, or feet insulate the body from evil energies, as do rings, hand and foot bracelets, and specific hairstyles.

In our modern countries, many people wear a small crucifix or a star of David more from a conscious or unconscious desire to protect themselves against bad luck than to express their belief in a specific religion, in the same way that people display medallions of Saint Christopher or various statues of saints in their cars. (And who doesn't have a little fetish—a picture or an object, clothing of particular color—to protect against the evil eye and to bring luck and good fortune?) For peoples of tradition it is the magico-religious rituals that give powers and effectiveness to good-luck charms, talismans, and other gris-gris.

The Tuareg, for instance, wear many amulets, talismans, gris-gris, and small iron objects to protect themselves against *djenouns* and other evil spirits, and to win their blessing and mercy. They throw stones at certain trees to chase away evil spirits before sitting in their shadow. And to stop malevolent genies from entering their bodies through the mouth, nose, and ears, men wear a veil covering their face, which they never take off, even when eating; some Tuareg women have told me they have never seen the faces of their husbands.

Strangely enough, Tuareg women do not need to veil their faces, as if wearing their panoply of talismans were sufficient. Many peoples of tradition ascribe magical powers to women beyond anything imaginable in Western culture. Because of the magical symbolism of blood and its association with new beginnings, the feminine is venerated. In fact the Tuareg, like some other cultures of tradition have a matriarchal society, which some people believe to be the most ancient form of human society, one that goes back to the notion that women are endowed with the magical power of creating life, a power that men do not have. Also, menstruation can be seen as a woman's rejection of impurities— evil spirits that have penetrated her body—and women thus have the ability to cleanse themselves in a magical and physical sense.

As a result, the majority of the Fourth World considers a woman taboo, impure, during her menstrual periods, and members of the community avoid her. Often she must go away from the village and live somewhere else, so as to not curse any men, animals, plants, or other things that don't have the women's ability to cleanse themselves.

The belief that a woman has the power of creating a new life because of her ability to have menses is one of the sources of the notion that blood must precede any creation, which is also represented in various myths of creation. This is symbolized by the human or animal sacrifices performed during any ritual that is supposed to allow something new—something which doesn't belong to the everyday life—to be created.

☾

Magic rituals performed to chase away evil spirits can be found in certain customs of greeting a foreigner. Some Papuan tribes of New Guinea, for instance, have a very impressive and frightening ritual to chase evil spirits from outsiders who come to visit them. They perform a simulated attack, often called a *primal challenge,* which acts as a magical purification of the visitor. It is also believed that if the visitor has bad intentions, he will run away and be killed; if he stays, his intentions are taken to be pure, and the attackers in effect say, "We could have killed you; instead we are accepting you, but don't mess with us!" It is also a way for the tribe to test the courage and strength of the outsider. If he shows no fear during the simulated attack, he deserves respect.

Although some missionaries had warned me about this strange custom of greeting visitors, I must admit that experiencing it was far beyond what I expected, and very scary.

I was going down the Balim River in Irian Jaya, the Indonesian part of New Guinea, looking for Papuan villages. Although I usually try to get a native from the village I leave to guide me to the next village, I was alone this time since no natives of the last village were interested in hazarding a meeting with the Papuans living further down the river, claiming they didn't get along well with these tribes, which they considered to be savages.

As I began to see and smell the smoke of campfires, I knew I was near a village. I could also hear, carried by the wind, the screams of children, the shrieks of fighting pigs, and the clucking of roosters challenging each other in a wild opera of cock-a-doodle-doos. I decided to pitch my camp in a small clearing overlooking the river, some distance from the village.

Among the Papuans, as among the majority of peoples of tradition, entering a village or approaching too closely, without being invited to do so, is not considered acceptable behavior and can even be life-threatening. A funeral, initiation, or other secret ceremony could be taking place from which all visitors are forbidden. Also, if some member of the tribe were to become ill or die, the others might believe the visitor was responsible, directly or indirectly, for bringing on the illness or death.

I lit a campfire, not so much for my own use but to let the villagers know that I was there. And I waited for them. This waiting can last forever, but generally if after four or five days no villagers have come to greet me or to chase me away, I move on. I naturally prefer missing the opportunity of meeting the villagers to arousing their anger because of my presence; that's why I am still alive. But even for me, this waiting is not easy to endure because of all the excitement and dread that I experience.

As for the villagers, I know they, too, share my combination of curiosity and fear. Should they let the outsider enter their village? Is it a good time to do so? Is the visitor safe, is he friend or enemy, does he carry evil spirits with him? Will he disturb the harmony of the village? How will the divinities react to his presence?

To answer these questions, the natives hold meetings with the notables, wise men, chiefs of each family and clan, and the chief of the village. The shaman, or sorcerer, or some other religious leader then performs a ceremony through which he attempts to contact the invisibles to get an opinion and answers. It all takes time.

Then, depending on the divine decision, the tribesmen either accept the visitor and put him under the protection of their laws of hospitality, or refuse him by chasing him away, or by simply ignoring him. If the foreigner insists on staying, he will be seen as putting the villagers in danger, and he may be killed.

The first sign that Papuans are ready to welcome a visitor is the beating of drums, which suddenly extinguishes the usual jungle symphony of bird calls and swooshing trees. To an outsider, the drumbeats sound ominous; but they in fact can express various things.

Some wild beats are the voices of the divine, coming from the spirits, souls of ancestors, and deities that may inhabit the drums. The lugubrious beats are a magical call to the jungle's spirits and forces, or prayers to the planets, stars, and other cosmic energies. Repetitive beats are the clock of tradition scanning the rhythms of the seasons and of human life—weddings and other rites of passage, and initiations to the mystical and sometimes frightening world of magic. Drums beating mysterious melodies mark the passages and exchanges between the gods' domain and the land of men. Worrying beats are human lamentations calling for mourning. Savage rhythms are people's heartbeats, telling stories of love and war; they are music of joy, expressed through dance.

But drumbeats can just be a way to communicate—for example, to announce that a ritual is about to begin. The Papuan drumbeats proclaiming a simulated attack may go on for days, for it takes the warriors time to prepare themselves for the event: they decorate their skin with war paint; they adorn themselves with many-colored bird feathers and animal furs.

The drums started to beat two days after I pitched my camp. On the fourth day, at around 11:00 A.M., the drumbeats suddenly stopped, giving way to a heavy silence. But soon the ground began to shake, as if underground drums were starting to awake. At first the vibration was so gentle that it could have been the breathing of the earth and trees. Then slowly the ground shook louder and louder until, as it became very strong, about fifty, many-colored warriors—armed with long spears and bows and arrows—appeared from the thick jungle, hammering the ground with their heels. Then they stopped abruptly.

They were about thirty feet or so away. I don't remember how long they stayed there, silently staring at me, but I had the time to be tortured by thousands of questions. What if what the missionaries had told me about this ritual was wrong? What if the ritual of greeting was similar to the one of killing? After all, dead victims couldn't give proof one way or the other. Would my encounter with these fierce-looking men be my last meeting with destiny? Anyway, it was too late for me to think about running away. I had been warned not to move, whatever happened. And so I stayed frozen in place, perhaps just because I couldn't do anything else.

Putting a sudden end to my growing anguish and fear, the warriors, with piercing screams that quickened my own heartbeat, began running in my direction for the ultimate confrontation, with spears and arrows pointed at me. Stopping fifteen feet away, they shot their deadly weapons, which hissed as they passed over my head, and at my left side and at my right side. Some hit the ground just in front of my feet. I was literally surrounded by a circle of arrows and spears driven into the ground all around me. Immediately, the warriors' war screams were replaced by a deadly silence. I began shaking, the victim of an overdose of adrenaline.

I stretched my trembling hand out, holding a pack of tobacco leaves, wetted by my sweat. One of the men, whose face was painted red and black and who was wearing a long porcupine quill through his nasal membrane, approached and took the gift, and the others began chatting. Amid laughter and discussion, these ferocious men seemed to relax. Another man, wearing a kind of wig covered with mud and bird feathers, who looked like the chief, opened his bag of tobacco and offered me some.

My first contact with these people was thus a success. But as they were escorting me to their village, I couldn't stop a sudden chill from running through my body as I thought about what would have happened if I had just moved a little bit.

⚜

Certain things that defy elementary logic can be done through magic rituals that deal with supernatural energies, or energies of the spirits, or the cosmic force.

We members of so-called civilization are aware that the world, the whole universe, is composed of various positive and negative energies. Since we are basically energies ourselves, these outside energies can interfere, positively or negatively, with our own existence. The peoples of the Fourth World are also aware that, besides the elemental forces, there are positive and negative energies that govern the universe. Some cultures believe that the good energies were created by God and that demonic energies sprang from the devil; others believe that positive energies are good spirits and negative energies are evil spirits. Beyond these primary energies, there is the supernatural force that exists in the cosmos, in a free and untransformed state. It is the intent of the individual that determines whether the force will be used for good or for evil.

Through the process of magic, people try to connect with these energies or spirits—good or evil, depending on the nature of ritual and on its purpose—with the ultimate hope of being able to connect with the cosmic force. Peoples of tradition thus use their brains, creativity, and imagination to find elaborate ways—that is, magic rituals— to create what our reality considers impossible, and to deal with disunited energies, souls, spirits, and gods that inhabit the invisible world.

THE POWERS OF SPIRITUAL AND RELIGIOUS LEADERS

Every culture has its wise men and its heroes, those who can lead and teach, and those who seem to have the power to connect with God. So it is with most peoples of tradition. They, too, have their special people. Theirs are called shamans, sorcerers, medicinemen, witch doctors, and magicians.

The roots of the shaman go back before the earliest recorded civilizations. The practice of shamanism was probably born as human consciousness began to grow, giving men an awakening to realities more subtle than those of the everyday world, and leading, for instance, to the idea that everything in nature has a soul.

By experiencing a state of trance that induced metaphysical voyages, the shaman could connect with the souls of each element of nature and travel between man's world and the world of invisibles. He could metaphysically identify with each world, and intercede between gods and humans. He journeyed into the cosmos to master the supernatural force that exists there in a free and untransformed state, and to use it to reorganize the cosmic chaos and confusion, battle with elemental forces, and confront demons. To many, the shaman has the same power today. Mircea Eliade noted:

> Though the shaman is, among other things, a magician, not every magician can properly be termed a shaman. The same distinction must be applied in regard to shamanic healing; every medicine man is a healer, but the shaman employs a method that is his and his alone. As for the shamanic techniques of ecstasy, they do not exhaust all the varieties of ecstatic experience documented in the history of religions and religious ethnology. Hence any ecstatic cannot be considered a shaman; the shaman specializes in a trance during which his soul is believed to leave his body and ascend to the sky or descend to the underworld.

In spite of cultural and ethnic diversity, there are cross-cultural similarities concerning the shaman's role, function, and powers that connect all shamans around the world, even if—as in some cases, mainly in Asia and South America—the name *shaman* is given to a spiritual leader of a religion that evolved differently from traditional shamanism.

The shaman is the keeper of culture and traditions. He is the initiator of the mysteries and the secret knowledge—the aptitude to connect with the invisible world and the supernatural energies that derive from it. He is the repository of rituals.

By performing rituals, he protects or restores the multifaceted harmony existing within each of his people and in the relationship of each to his clan, the village, the tribe, their ancestors, their divinities, and nature. Having the responsibility to keep the invisibles happy or to beseech their favors means the shaman must also perform rituals whenever something very important is about to occur that could disturb the harmony between humans and invisibles.

The shaman can question ancestors and gods. While in a trance, he can reach them in the different realities where they live, and act as an intermediary between them and humans.

All these powers and abilities are essential to the shaman because peoples of tradition believe that all natural disorders—sickness, lack of rain, and so forth—are a reaction of the invisibles to a disturbance created by humans.

When someone is sick, the shaman begins restoring that person's health by exorcising the disturbance and reestablishing the balance between the person, the clan, and the cosmos. After performing appropriate rituals to appease the divine fury that has caused the malady, he will cure the patient with herbs and other natural medicines.

Because a mystical identification with fire is necessary during specific ceremonies, there are shamans in some cultures who also are blacksmiths. The ability to master fire in order to transmute minerals has always been linked to magical power. In fact, alchemists were called philosophers of fire. (In *Forgerons et alchimistes,* Mircea Eliade points out that the caster, the blacksmith, and the alchemist all claim a magico-religious experience in their relationship with metals.)

One of the greatest powers of the shaman—one that very few possess—is the ability to cross layers of time. It is believed that time stretches out in an infinite succession of layers. The present time is the layer of our conscious time, whereas the past (which still exists) and the future (which already exists) are held in layers of time that belong to other realities than the one we perceive.

The layers of time could be compared to the tracks of a record. The present time is the track on which the record player's needle is positioned, transmitting the music we hear; the music we have heard is held in the tracks on one side of the needle; that to be heard is in the tracks on the other side of the needle. When a record player has finished playing Beethoven's Ninth Symphony, does the music cease to exist? No, it still exists on the record tracks. You will be able to listen to it by playing it again.

In 1955, Albert Einstein wrote: "For us believing physicists, the distinction between Past, Present, and Future is only an illusion, even if a stubborn one." Today, quantum physicists and quantum mathematicians believe that, since infinity is a tangible fact, time by itself should be infinite. Therefore past, present, and future should exist at the same time, with past and future in different realities from the perceived reality of the present time.

"Some mainstream physicists now say that time travel, long the exclusive domain of science fiction, might be possible—at least in theory. All it takes is a rip in the fabric of the universe." So wrote David H. Freedman in his article "Cosmic Time Travel" in the June 1989 issue of *Discover*. The mainstream physicists are Kip Thorne of Caltech, and Michael Morris, a physicist and cosmologist at the University of Wisconsin in Milwaukee. Rips in the fabric of the universe are cosmic wormholes—wormholes and black holes are cousins—"that theoretically, at least, might tunnel from one region of space to another," halfway across the cosmos. And moreover, "a wormhole might turn out to be a time-hole as well."

Among the cultures of tradition for which the word *shaman* doesn't exist—in Africa, for instance, or where religions are different from shamanism, although based on the principle of trance and possession as a ritual performed to connect man to the invisibles and the supernatural forces that derive from them—the spiritual leader may be called a magician, witch doctor, or sorcerer. Elsewhere, he can be called a medicine man. However, such spiritual leaders may also co-exist with a shaman.

All have about the same role and functions as a shaman, but their powers may vary depending on the degree of knowledge they have received from their tribal initiations, and on their own talent for performing rituals. As in any discipline, knowledge without talent seldom produces results. And all spiritual leaders use magic and the supernatural during their magico-religious ceremonies.

Although they dedicate their lives only to doing good—because of their faith, moral principles, and their belief in the cosmic balance that predicts that if you give good, you harvest good; if you do evil, you harvest evil—shamans are not always paragons of integrity. As for other spiritual leaders—magicians, witch doctors, medicine men, sorcerers—if they are the sole religious leaders of a society, they generally allow themselves to perform some evil work—depending on the goal to be achieved, their believers' demands, and their own conscience. On the scale of integrity, it seems that magicians, shamans, and witch doctors perform evil works much less often that sorcerers do. Many are satisfied with using positive or negative primary energies, which are more accessible than the cosmic force, access to which requires a high degree of knowledge.

However, in most cultures of tradition, as soon as the spiritual leadership of a society is in the hands of a shaman or a magician who has chosen not to do evil works, there appears, parallel and in opposition to him, a black magician or a sorcerer who dedicates his talents to evil; this is true even in our modern societies. At that point, the differentiation between shamans, magicians, and witch doctors on one side, and sorcerers on the other, is made clear. (When in a village there is already a sorcerer, the name *witch doctor* or *medicine man* may be given to whoever has only healing powers.)

One can find an example of this in Haiti, where sects dealing with black magic coexist with the Voodoo religion. The spiritual leader of Voodoo is called a *houngan,* or a *mambo* if a woman. Often a houngan will initiate his wife as a spiritual leader if she has the aptitude for it. Those dealing with black magic are called *bokors,* which can be translated as "sorcerers."

Like the shaman, the houngan is the repository of rituals, the initiator of the secret knowledge and mysteries. He is a healer, an exorcist, and a diviner; and because he knows how to deal with the invisibles and enter their world, he can communicate with the souls of the dead. According to his degree of initiation to knowledge (the aptitude to enter the invisible world of energies—often called the Fifth Dimension—and to use the cosmic force), the houngan can manipulate supernatural powers; some houngans even have supernatural powers themselves.

Magic is the means used by the houngan to accomplish his works, but he never uses the cosmic force for evil purposes, nor will he use evil loas, because he dedicates his life and talents only to doing good. He leads a religion in search of the sacred, calling only upon loas representing good energies to possess the members of his community.

However, tempted by material comforts, some houngans fail in their principles. Then they stop being houngans, with all the principles and values attached to that sacerdotal function, and become bokors, dedicating their lives to sorcery and to the use of evil spirits and souls of the dead to accomplish evil works.

☾

There are various ways for a spiritual leader to select a pupil, whom he will initiate into his knowledge. In many tribes, mainly those in which sorcery is practiced, a neophyte is chosen because he has a physical defect; it is believed that the gods have so marked such a person as having special powers. And indeed, a physical handicap may cause a young person to develop some psychic powers.

In most cases, however, a neophyte is recognized by paranormal, psychic, and mediumistic talents and abilities. He will undergo trials; his personality and nervous resistance will be tested. It is only if the spiritual leader is completely satisfied with his choice that the neophyte becomes his pupil; and it is years before the actual initiation.

Becoming a shaman takes years of painful initiations. I have heard that many neophytes die from the hardships involved. The neophyte experiences the worst physical and psychological torments—even madness—in order to free his soul of the body, to be awakened to other cosmic realities, and to be open to knowledge.

In *Shaman: The Wounded Healer,* Joan Halifax writes that to become a shaman is to be aware that "all that exists in the revealed world has a living force within it. The knowledge that life is power is the realization of the shaman. Communion with the purveyors of power is the work of the shaman. Mastery of that power: this is the attainment of the shaman."

One can find women magicians and sorcerers only in the most ancient societies, where men continue to ascribe magic powers to women. Elsewhere men, jealous of women's magical powers, have slowly taken away women's prerogatives and have reserved the sacred functions for themselves; this is the case with Judeo-Christianity, for instance.

☾

There is no scientific or tangible proof of the existence of God, divinities, spirits, and other invisibles. But does that mean they don't exist?

Looking at the marvels that surround us and at the great sensitivity and humorous anomalies one can find throughout nature, it is difficult to deny the existence of a creator, in whatever form and by whatever name we use: God, the cosmic intelligence, the primordial energy, or the primal life breath. Consequently, I would not deny the existence of God as the creator of all things, chiefly because I believe in God's existence—not because of a religion (I don't have a specific religion anymore, for I have found no religions that satisfy my spiritual needs; I am my own religion, which is based on the universality of love and respect for myself and for others), but because that is the conclusion my reasoning has led me to.

If we accept the existence of God, we may speculate that divinities, spirits, and other invisibles, rather than being entities in themselves, represent all the different elemental and cosmic forces.

We are aware that the whole world, the whole universe, is composed of various positive and negative energies. These energies can interfere, positively or negatively, with our own existence, since we, too, are energies. Nothing was easier for man than to give to each positive and negative energy and each elemental and cosmic force a name and a divine personality, and through appropriate rituals to try to communicate with them.

But even if we assume that divinities, spirits, and other invisibles don't intrinsically exist, a second possibility is that they have been created and thus made real by man's faith, thought, and imagination. If man's faith can create miracles, if man's faith, thought, and imagination, with the creative power of the word, can do magic, they can certainly create divinities, spirits, and other invisible entities, giving them an image and his own sense of duality.

A third possibility is that divinities, spirits, and other invisible entities do exist, but within another reality. To reach that reality we must put aside our logic, which acts as a yoke that prevents us from expanding our minds and blinds our perceptions.

Drug-induced enlightenments produce mystico-religious experiences through which, as Albert Hofmann wrote in *LSD: My Problem Child,* "we realize that what one commonly takes as the reality, including the reality of one's own individual person, by no means signifies something fixed, but rather something that is ambiguous—that there is not only one, but that there are many realities."

It is possible to penetrate different realities through meditation. Again I will use Hofmann's words, which perfectly translate my own experience:

> Meditation begins at the limits of objective reality, at the farthest point yet reached by rational knowledge and perception. Not rejection of objective reality; on the contrary, it consists of a penetration to deeper dimensions of reality. . . . If it only advances deep enough, it inevitably leads to the inexplicable, primal ground of the universe: the wonder, the mystery of the divine—in the microcosm of the atom, in the macrocosm of the spiral nebula; in the seeds of plants, in the body and soul of people.

Meditation and, often drug-induced enlightenment are, among peoples of tradition, the tools used during initiations to help the neophyte move from a state of ignorance—the objective worldview—to the levels of a deeper reality where he will perceive the cosmic consciousness. It is through initiation that the tenets of a religion are made real, and consequently his faith is based upon a newly perceived reality—not simply an abstract idea. It is through active initiation that the individual is introduced to experience other realities. Only in that deepened and religious consciousness will he realize his creator-creation duality and acquire the knowledge transmitted by his master—shaman, sorcerer, or other keeper of his tribal culture.

The last possibility is to speculate that God, divinities, spirits, and other invisible entities do exist, but only for those who are aware of their existence and who know how to call them. Perhaps God and divinities become useless to whoever makes himself useless to God and divinities.

☾

3

The Philippines

In 1967, when I was twenty years old, I was hired by Gabriel Lingé, a French filmmaker, to be his cameraman. Our crew consisted of only two people: him and me. The goal of our expedition was to crisscross most of the 7,107 islands (7,110 at low tide) of the Filipino Archipelago, in order to make a documentary about the people and their way of life.

After several months of shooting, we completed the film. However, instead of going back to Europe with Gabriel, I decided to stay on and visit a few places he didn't want to see because they weren't relevant to his movie.

Two such places were the Sulu Islands, still ruled by sultans and pirates, and the deep jungles of the northern part of Luzon, which at that time still sheltered headhunter tribes that had not yet had any contact with the outside world. (I recounted both adventures in my book *Explorer.*)

On my way to the mountains of northern Luzon, I stopped in the town of Baguio, where I was hoping to find a missionary who could tell me where to find tribes still untouched by modern civilization.

A city two hundred miles north of Manila, Baguio is built in a crater at an altitude of forty-five hundred feet, in the mountain fief of a warrior tribe called the Ifugaos. The Ifugaos are now pacified: they no longer hunt human heads or chase away the rich people of Manila who come to Baguio during the summer for the cooler climate. Peaceful coexistence between the exotic mountain dwellers and the worshipers of wealth has made Baguio a city of remarkable contrasts.

I have found that one of the best ways to make new contacts and get the feeling of a country is to saunter through a local open-air market, the gathering place of those who come to buy, sell, trade or just meet each other, because it always reflects a people's state of mind. One can learn what religion they belong to, what their primary interest in life is, what their needs and tastes are, how interested they are in magic and alternative medicines, and what the characters of the different ethnic and cultural identities are. Walking through a market is also a feast for the ears, with the screams of animals, children, and vendors hawking their commodities; for the eyes, with the faces of people and the colors of clothes and goods; and for the nose, with the odors and perfumes left behind by people, spices, and food.

In Baguio's market the local Filipino population mixes with mountain tribesmen wearing either modern shirts that cover their tattoos or just their traditional dress of a long, thin piece of red cloth that is wrapped around the waist and passes between the legs and buttocks. On the back of their heads, they wear small straw caps ornamented with wild boars' tusks. Most tribal women go bare-breasted in their villages, but here in the city they cover their bodies with a many-colored, long, straight cotton skirt, and smoke a pipe that is always turned upside down. Some wear a kind of tiara made with the skeleton of a snake; others have golden bracelets around their wrists.

Between colorful alleys in which exotic Asian fruits are displayed alongside strawberries (which grow here in the more continental climate of the city) and cages filled with puppies, lizards, snakes, and other animals sold locally as delicacies, one can find the ingredients needed to chew betel nuts. These are seeds of the betel palm that are covered with quicklime and wrapped in tobacco and betel leaves. Betel nuts are astringent, and the quicklime liberates the alkaloids from the betel leaves and the nicotine from the tobacco. This mixture is a powerful stimulant that accelerates the heartbeat, cuts hunger and fatigue, and promotes euphoria. Betel nuts are for Asia what khat leaves are for Arabia, kola nuts for Africa, and coca leaves for some South American countries.

Along with different medicinal plants, vendors also sell an aphrodisiac called *balud,* which is a duck egg that has been cooked just a few days before it would have hatched. The baby duck is fully formed, with a beak and palmate feet but no feathers. The beak, feet, skull, and bones have the consistency of soft cartilage. (Sometimes the client gets an unpleasant surprise when the egg has been cooked a day or two too late!) One can buy *balud* almost anywhere, at any time of day or night, but mainly in the neighborhoods that shelter bars and dance clubs. At the shrill voices of vendors yelling, *"Balud! Balud!"* the older men rush to buy some, because it is believed *balud* will quickly *harden* their ability to satisfy their sex partners.

Besides providing a variety of tonics to overcome physical weakness, nature also provides psychedelics for peoples of tradition, who ascribe a sacred value to them. (They are often called "plants of the gods.") These plants usually remain the privilege of spiritual leaders and magicians, and of those who experience specific rituals of initiation.

As I learned which parts of the jungle to explore to find an isolated tribe called the Apayao, I discovered that Baguio was the home of a group of people known as psychic healers. These strange and mysterious people could plunge their fingers into their patients' bodies and tear out infected tissues and other causes of illness. At that time, they had not yet acquired their international reputation as psychic surgeons, and no foreigners were traveling to the Philippines to be treated by them. Their patients were limited to the locals. Intrigued by their mysterious powers, I decided that the jungle could wait for me, and began to investigate the psychic healers.

PSYCHIC HEALERS

I met many psychic healers in Baguio. Although their treatments seemed successful, since most of their patients really did get better, what many of them did as part of their healing tradition had not convinced me. Either they never permitted me to stand close enough to actually see the surgical details, or they performed the surgery in such an evasive way that detection was impossible, which left me questioning what I was supposed to have witnessed.

A surgeon-healer named Placido was among the very few who let me stay so close that I was able to follow, in detail, the entire surgery process and his other healing methods. A small, nervous man of about thirty, Placido was very secretive. Like other Filipino healers, he claimed that his knowledge was not human, but a gift of God. "God is healing, I am just his tool!" he would say whenever I questioned him about his talent. "I just do what God tells me to do through my intuition."

Since he performed his healings in the early morning, generally from 6:00 A.M. until 8:00 or 9:00 A.M. only, Placido awoke every day long before dawn, and spent hours reading the Bible, praying, and meditating before going to his chapel—his medical office, located near

the slums. He asked for no fees from his patients. They paid him whatever they could, or brought him a chicken, eggs, or something else to
eat. He lived in a simple house outside Baguio.

His chapel was just a small, very clean room, with a dozen pious
images representing Catholic saints hanging on one wall around a crucifix. Benches faced a long wooden table at one end of the room, opposite the entrance. This was the operating table. Behind it and leaned
against the wall was an old bench supporting a variety of thing—cups,
glasses, cotton pads, sheets of paper, several folded white sheets, a crucifix. An open Bible sat next to the operating table on a small pedestal
table similar to these used for spiritism sessions.

When Placido arrived, the chapel was crowded with patients and
their families—about twenty people—sitting on the floor and the
benches. The crowd was singing Catholic religious chants under the
direction of one of Placido's two assistants, a woman who also func-
tioned as his nurse. The other assistant, a young man, placed a basin of
water on the bench next to the operating table.

When Placido entered the chapel the crowd stopped singing, and
the first patient, a woman who had a great deal of pain in her abdomen,
was invited to lie down, dressed, on the operating table. As his two
assistants moved to his sides, the healer invited me to stand at one end
of the table. He crossed himself and closed his eyes for a short prayer.
Then, hardly listening to the patient's complaints, he slowly moved his
hands all along her body, without touching it. He was trying to locate
the pain and discover the cause and extent of the illness.

"Her left ovary is badly infected," he whispered to me.

The nurse removed the clothing from the part of the woman's
body that was to be operated on. The other assistant rubbed it with a
wet cotton pad. Then the healer began massaging the woman's body,
pushing his fingers down into it harder and deeper until they completely disappeared into the hollow they had formed in the body's surface. Suddenly, a yellowish liquid (it was pus, the healer told me later)
started to fill the hollow and flow onto the patient's abdomen. As fast
as she could, the nurse wiped away the liquid, which slowly lost its yellowish color and became red, like blood.

To see the liquid coming out of the hollow formed by the pressure
of the healer's fingers was in itself breathtaking, but what followed
was even more so. The healer plunged both hands into the woman's
body and removed something bloody that was still partially linked to
the rest of the inner organs; according to the healer, it was the left ovary
of the patient. He examined the organ; then, with a pair of scissors, he

cut away a small piece of it and put the rest back inside the body. After the healer pressed the skin together, his assistant again used a cotton pad to rub the affected area. And I saw the result: the skin had completely healed. There was not a single drop of blood, not the slightest indication of a wound; only a reddish spot on the skin due to the pressure of the healer's fingers.

The surgery had lasted only two minutes. The patient smiled and crossed herself, murmuring inaudible prayers; she kissed the healer's hands, expressing her deep gratitude and joy, got off the table, and walked away unaided. She showed no sign of illness; she had completely recovered. Her family prayed and cried and smiled—and left a chicken in return for the healer's services.

Afterward, using the same methods of diagnosis and surgery, Placido cut away part of a patient's intestine, removed an infected lump from the shoulder of another, and tore away a cyst from the throat of a third.

Another patient, whose face was very yellow, complained of vomiting a yellow liquid and of a deep pain in the right side of his abdomen. Placido removed a bloody piece of something from his abdomen; this, he said, was a tumor in the liver. After seeing the cause of his illness, the patient's complexion immediately returned to normal and he walked away, healed.

Placido healed a woman suffering from headaches by the laying-on-of-hands technique (which I will describe later). He also told a man he couldn't help him because his malady had gone too far. And he sent away a woman complaining about different illnesses, telling her that she was not sick but only imagining it.

It fascinated me how quickly the patients, once the healer had finished treating them, showed a visible physical recovery. Many of them came to Placido so weakened that they could hardly move without some help. And as soon the surgery was over, whether or not they had seen blood or parts of their own organs, they walked away as if they had never been sick.

Though the majority of Filipino healers ask very few questions of their patients, their methods of diagnosis and surgery vary. For example, Placido explained that the action of passing his hands over his patient's bodies allowed him to discover the place, the cause, and the gravity of the illness; he then knew how to treat it. Among the four other healers who convinced me of the truth of what I was witnessing, one said that while passing his hands over his patients' bodies he could, literally, experience the pain in his own body. Then he knew exactly how to heal the patient. Another could diagnose a patient just by looking at his photograph, or by concentrating on that person's name, age, and address.

The diagnostic methods of the two other healers were completely different. They never passed their hands over their patients' bodies, except when they were employing the laying-on-of-hands technique. One sat next to the patient and then went into a trance. Once in that state, the healer began writing down information about the diagnosis and healing process of the patient. Another method he was using with success was what he called "the spiritual diagnosis." He passed a Bible over the head of the patient and got by this means, from God (he said), the diagnosis and the knowledge of what surgery to perform. By looking at his patient, the last healer was able to see a glowing and pulsing aura. And depending on its shape and color, he could diagnose the patient and apply the correct surgical treatment.

(The aura is the field of energy, seen as a band of colored light, which surrounds all living things: humans, animals, and plants. Professor Harold Burr of the Yale University School of Medicine, called it the "L-field," the electro-dynamic field that surrounds every living thing. Auras are represented in religious paintings and statues in the form of an aureole surrounding the head. Although there is a lot of controversy about it, this invisible projection has been photographed in the United States and the Soviet Union—where it is believed to be bioplasma—thanks to the process of high frequency photography. Doctor Shafica Karagulla works with psychics who, by seeing auras, are able to read the physical, emotional, and mental states of individuals and diagnose illness. Their readings are accurate when compared with medical diagnoses.)

I witnessed still another method of diagnosis in a small jungle village in Gabon, Africa. By surrounding the patient with a white sheet, the sorcerer was able to see, or perceive, the internal organs of his patient on the sheet, much like an X-ray photograph.

The human faculty to perceive or see internal organs—which is called biofeedback, alteroscopy, or autoscopy—belongs to the domain of ESP. According to parapsychology, this faculty does exist. Psychical researchers have tested people whose perceptions were often accurate when compared with medical diagnoses.

Besides using different methods of diagnosis, the five Filipino healers I have mentioned, including Placido, also had different techniques for treating their patients. The six healing methods I observed were the laying on of hands, the healing of the aura's plasma, psychic injections, real surgery, penetration of the fingers into the body, and materialization of diseased tissues or organs on the skin outside the body.

The Laying on of Hands

The laying-on-of-hands method that I saw Placido use is often called *spiritual healing* by Filipino healers. I would be inclined to call it *magnetic healing,* because, before and after concentrating his healing powers on the disturbed parts of the patient's body, Placido would lay his hands over the spots where the *chakras* are located.

According to the Hindus, the *chakras* are the points where the physical body joins the astral body. They are the centers of psychic energies and life energies. A human being has seven main chakras. One is located outside the body, about four inches above the head; others are at the forehead, neck, heart, navel, genitals, and anus. (The one situated just below the navel is considered by the Japanese as the life center of the body. They call it *hara;* it is at this spot that they aim their sword when killing themselves by hara-kiri.)

The Healing of the Aura's Plasma

I don't have much information about healing the plasma of the patients' aura. But since it is acknowledged that one can diagnose a patient by reading his aura, I don't see why one couldn't treat a patient by healing the plasma of his aura—that is, concentrating the healing powers on the aura to restore all its colors.

Psychic Injections

The healer would stand about five feet away from the patient, with nothing in his hands. Each time he injected the patient psychically, the patient felt the pain of a pinprick, and at the spot where the patient had felt this one could see a drop of blood appear. At the end of the treatment, the patient would be visibly healed.

Real Surgery

Real surgery was performed on patients who were totally conscious. The healer made an incision in the skin with an ordinary knife and plunged his fingers, sometimes both hands, into the patient's body to extract sick tissues or a whole organ. Once he had cut out the diseased part, he put the organ back inside the body. Then he pressed the two parts of the incised skin together for a few seconds. When he took his hands away, there was a thin, healed scar.

Surprisingly, during the surgery, which never lasted more than one or two minutes, there was almost no blood; the patients felt very little pain, and always with a certain delay. Also, no infections were reported after the surgery, which was quite extraordinary considering that the hygiene usually thought necessary for such operations was lacking.

These kinds of surgery (perhaps similar to the surgery performed by the Egyptians a few thousand years ago, and by the Mayas, Incas, and other ancient civilizations) are still practiced in many places—for instance, in Brazil. In the slums of Rio de Janeiro I saw a woman, known for her magic healing abilities, making incisions with an old knife in the scalp of a male patient, who was supposedly suffering from a brain tumor. Then she made a hole through his skull, using an ordinary chisel and a hammer, and with her fingers reached into the diseased part of his brain. Not only was the patient perfectly conscious, but he was helping her by keeping his scalp away from the wound and wiping the blood away.

Alleviating the pain of a conscious patient during surgery, limiting the flow of blood, and accelerating the healing of the wounded flesh afterward are not considered magic phenomena any longer. The same results have been successfully obtained by Professor Berranger, a French surgeon and dentist and the author of many books, through a technique he calls *sophrology,* a kind of autohypnosis. (Professor Berranger was among the first people in France to study the techniques of self-healing.)

I knew him very well and worked with him many times. He once allowed me to assist him when he performed dental surgery on a woman whose heart condition couldn't sustain anaesthetics. Using his techniques, I was able to considerably lower the flow of her blood, to completely stop her pain, and to accelerate the healing process.

Now, Filipino psychic surgeons use neither hypnosis nor sophrology. So what is their secret? A surgeon-healer named Juan Blance (whom I actually saw on a trip some years later) used to make incisions in the skin, at a distance, without touching the skin. Standing one foot away from his patient, Juan, using only someone else's outstretched finger, would trace a small line in the air. While he did this, a cut would appear on the patient's skin. The rest of the surgery was performed in the manner of other Filipino healers.

I had to witness Juan's technique many times before I finally believed what I was seeing. Christian de Corgnol saw such surgery, too,

and described it in his book *Les guérisseurs philippins*. For him, this phenomenon was nothing other than *psychokinesis*—mind over matter: the
use of mind powers to affect or influence part of the environment, or
move inanimate objects. Although science has not yet given its final
verdict on psychokinesis, many psychic-research statistics point to its
reality.

Penetration of the Fingers into the Body

The surgery Placido was performing when he plunged his fingers
into his patients' bodies to extract ailing tissues or parts of organs,
without leaving any visible wound on the skin, is more difficult to understand and has raised many speculations. According to the most interesting hypothesis, a deep mental and physical relaxation of the patient, provoked by the healer's mental powers, could enhance the
patient's alpha waves, allowing a momentary disorder in the structure
of the skin, which could then be pierced, even by a finger, without
doing any damage.

Materialization of Diseased Tissues or Organs

I observed one case in which the healer made what was supposed
to be a part of the patient's stomach appear on the patient's skin. From
what I saw, there was no way the healer could have used a trick. One
moment the patient's belly was perfectly clean; a second later part of a
stomach was lying on his skin. The healer's hands were not covered
with blood—as they would have been had he put the piece of bloody
meat on the patient's belly. This phenomenon could perhaps be understood if we used a logic different from that of our scientific laws.

☾

Filipino psychic healers are not very helpful in explaining these
phenomena. When questioned, they always say, "It's a gift from God!
We are just mediums performing spiritual surgeries." And indeed, a
majority of them took up healing after having dreams and visions
about a holy mission. And for all of them, this call of God, to use their
term, came to them as they were experiencing a tragic event in their
lives. Those few who do try to understand the mechanism of their
healing methods say, "To heal a patient, we must rebalance his mental,
physical, and spiritual energies."

I would like, finally, to describe to you Mauricio X, who struck me by his personality and by what happens when he enters the state that allows him to use his psychic healing powers.

A small man in his fifties, Mauricio is a Brazilian physicist who works for his government in Brasília. That is how supports his six children. But three days a week, and sometimes more, he dedicates himself to going to hospitals and to visiting patients at home, treating them with his healing powers, for free. He has the reputation, acknowledged by the local medical faculty, of successfully healing patients suffering from cancer, even at a very advanced stage.

Mauricio treats many patients at the same time. They lie on benches or on a bed, side by side, in a dark room. From the speakers comes a religious chant, which, depending on the tape he has chosen, can be Catholic, Russian Orthodox, or Jewish. "The religion is not important," he says, "for as long as there is faith in it, there is a magic." Following is a description of one of his healing sessions I witnessed.

Mauricio asked his three patients, who were lying side by side and crosswise on a large bed, to close their eyes, breathe slowly, and relax their bodies. Then he started walking around the room, breathing faster and deeper, until he reached a kind of trance. And all of a sudden, a silent lightning, a charge of static electricity, moved across the ceiling and hit his forehead, illuminating the whole room for a brief moment. (He says it is a cosmic energy that has healing powers.) Mauricio touched his head, as if to stop a sharp pain, and moved toward the head of his first patient, while rubbing his own hands and breathing noisily. As he walked, his body released dozens of small lightning flashes that ran over his skin. Once he reached the patient's head, he suddenly discharged part of the cosmic energy he had received, directing it toward the patient. He touched different parts of the patient's face, massaging them, while his whole body sparkled with soft flashes. Then once again Mauricio's forehead was hit by a blinding flash of lighting coming from the ceiling. He touched the patient's heart and all the places where the chakras are located, releasing small flashes of energy from his body to the patient's. He then went on to massage the patient's feet, and other parts of his body.

When the first patient was treated, Mauricio began working on the second, using the same technique he had used on the first. Then he moved on to the third patient. And during the twenty minutes it took to heal the three patients, five or six powerful lightning charges hit his forehead, charging his body with electric energies that he released from different parts of his body onto the patients. Sometimes his eyes began to shine with a glowing, pulsing greenish light that grew in intensity until, suddenly, it silently exploded and, moving in a spiral, revolved all around his body before breaking into a dozen small flashes. Sometimes his whole body shone with hundreds of electric sparks running all over his skin.

When the treatment of the third patient ended, Mauricio took a short break, during which the three patients left the room and another three entered. Then he began another twenty-minute healing session.

Finally, his body overcome by fatigue and covered with sweat, Mauricio put an end to his healing sessions (which can last for hours). He had a burn on his forehead, at exactly the spot where he had been hit by the powerful charges of cosmic energies; the skin was red and swollen, and liquid was dripping from it. On his chest there were two spots where the skin was also red and swollen, and where the same liquid was present; it looked as if two designs had been burned onto his skin. The burn on his left side appeared to be a representation of the cross. On his right side, the burn resembled a cabalistic design that he has never been able to decipher. Within the next two hours, the burn on his forehead and those on his chest slowly disappeared, leaving no marks at all.

When I saw Mauricio's healing technique for the first time, I wondered what amazing electronic system the physicist had invented to produce such results. I asked him to treat me, so that I could see what he was doing at an even closer range.

During his diagnosis of my body, he was able to see that I have three kidneys (in fact I have an odd structure in one kidney called an unlining of the right upper calix) and the beginning of an ulcer. He had asked me to keep my eyes closed, but I cheated. While his head was over mine, I saw that his eyes were beginning to glow, and that through his shirt his skin was releasing a series of small lightning flashes that hit my body without my feeling anything.

Since I was his last patient, I was able to stay with him and see him in the light. When he took off his shirt, to show me the two burns on his chest, I saw that he was wearing no wires or anything that could have produced the flashes and sparks on his forehead, face, eyes, chest, hands, and fingers. Nowhere could I find evidence of trickery. I had to admit the reality of what I had seen.

"The lightning that hits me is a cosmic energy," Mauricio told me. "I am then able to see the internal organs of my patients. I can perceive everything that goes wrong. And I can heal patients by using this cosmic energy, which, since it is the cosmic life force, is a healing energy."

It all started for him many years ago when, during a tragic accident in which he came close to losing his life, he had visions and dreams about healing sick people with his *gift*. He found someone who was sick and tried to heal him without knowing what he was doing, and it worked: he was struck by the cosmic force, diagnosed his patient, and released the healing energies onto him; the patient was cured. "Everything happened as it had in my visions," Mauricio said. "Ever since, when I don't heal for a few days, I feel bad inside myself. Healing gets my inner balance back."

Mauricio is, in himself, a phenomenon. When he is not in the state that allows him to heal, this joyful man loves good wine and good food, and, at a party, rapidly becomes the center of attention because of his talent for telling funny stories and even dirty jokes. At the same time, he is amazingly erudite. Disposed by his scientific background to try to understand how his healing technique worked, he read everything he could about religion, philosophy, parapsychology, healing, and so on. A fervent Catholic before, he became more of a true believer in spirituality. "I made a mistake in my previous life, which I lived in one of the Pleiades," he told me. "Consequently, I have been reincarnated on earth, and condemned to heal."

When asked how he came to these conclusions, Mauricio replied: "I am sure of nothing. That's just my explanation. Every day I try to learn more about myself through meditation. Instead of moving out of one's body, the real meditation is to move into it. To decipher messages carried inside our cells. There one can find all the answers for everything; the whole history of God and of the universe is written there. That I know for sure because there are things I learned during my inner meditations and, later, found in books I never read before. So, when I say these are my explanations, it's because I learned them during my meditations, but have not yet found proof in books or in the knowledge of others."

DIVINATION

While exploring the northern jungles of Luzon Island, I met the tribe of headhunters called Apayaos, and lived with them for a time.

Like all peoples of tradition, the Apayaos believe that in order to avoid the invisibles' wrath, the invisibles should be consulted about any decision or action members of the tribe are about to take. This is done through divination rituals.

The shaman of the village where I was staying performed a most amazing divination using a technique for calling upon invisibles—one that I have seen nowhere else. He needed the help of the spirits to determine the correct healing ritual to cure a sick old woman.

The shaman filled a hollow half coconut shell with rice and wine. For about ten minutes he recited prayers while examining the surface of the wine, searching for the healing ritual he had to perform. When he was satisfied he had found the cure, he then used two other methods to confirm this with the spirits.

First he attached a stone to a thin rope hanging from the roof. When the stone was motionless, he started to enumerate all the possible healing rituals he could perform. As he pronounced the name of the ritual he had seen on the surface of the wine, the stone began moving in a circle.

As a second test, he took an egg and balanced the small end of it on the ground. Again he enumerated all the rituals, and, to my astonishment, the egg tipped over as he pronounced the name of the ritual the stone had confirmed.

Although the shaman's original divination technique (the surface of wine) is itself quite mysterious, what fascinates me the most are the two methods of confirmation. Let's examine these more closely.

The first technique used a stone attached to a thin rope made of woven palm leaves. The rope hung from the roof of the ceremonial house, where the divination session took place. The ceremonial house had no walls. It had a circular, conical roof, about fifteen feet in diameter, supported around the edges by five tree trunks used as poles, six feet tall. One taller pole stood at the center. The side poles and the center one were connected at their tops by a bamboo framework, to which the roof was fixed. The divination rope and stone were tied to one of these lateral bamboo beams. The other end of the rope was cut just after the knot. Although I did not weigh the stone, it was the size of an apple and should have been quite heavy.

You may suspect that the shaman, or someone else, did something, directly or indirectly, to mechanically restart the movement of the stone. Yet the shaman never touched the stone and was too far away from it to have moved it with his breath. Nor was he close to any of the poles supporting the roof. Since I was standing outside, it was easy for me to check that no one was on the roof.

A few weeks later, I was lucky enough to witness the same method of divination. This time, I sat next to one of the two poles holding up the bamboo frame to which the rope was tied. I was literally leaning against the pole. As the motionless stone began to rotate, I felt no shaking of the pole to indicate that someone else, by leaning against the house, had started the motion. The stone began to move in a circle at the very moment when the shaman pronounced the name of the ritual he had detected on the surface of the wine.

In the same way, I have twice seen the egg fall on its side without someone shaking the ground or being close enough to have started its fall. The second time I put both hands on the ground, to be able to feel any abnormal vibrations. No, the egg simply fell on its side as the shaman pronounced the name of the ritual to be performed.

What mysterious phenomenon could cause a hanging stone to start to move and an egg to fall on its side to indicate to a shaman that he was on the right track? When questioned, the shaman just smiled and said, "One day will come when, perhaps, you will understand the real powers of the spirits."

Near the end of my visit I wanted to become the blood brother of Kuru, a young warrior of that tribe. Informed of my intention, the native shaman told the two of us to join him in the ceremonial place before nightfall, where I was to perform a ritual in order to ask invisibles for advice about my request.

When we arrived, he was holding a live chicken. He asked us to be seated, and, crouching on the ground, he caressed the chicken and began to recite invocations. Then he beheaded the chicken with his knife and threw a few of its feathers into the air, noting the positions they took as they fell on the ground. Then, cutting open the body, he made a meticulous examination of the gallbladder and the liver. When he was finished, he announced, "The propitious time will be in three days. So the auguries have said!"

As I have mentioned, peoples of tradition believe that invisibles sometimes express their feelings about decisions people are about to make without being called through a ritual. Thus peoples of tradition carefully observe nature, searching for any signs that could be interpreted as good or bad omens, such as the spontaneous movement of stones as one passes by, or encounters with certain birds, snakes, and lizards, or cries of certain animals. If an Apayao warrior, for example, sees a blue bird moving from east to west, it is a sign that his hunt will be a complete disaster. And if as he begins a long journey he meets a lizard moving toward him, he will cancel his voyage and come back home. A Dayak of Borneo will interrupt whatever he is doing if a black bird flies in front of him, moving from north to south. A gecko that does not scream seven consecutive times is a sign of bad luck or danger for the majority of Asians. According to the Gypsy people, if your eyes catch sight of a toad while you are specifically thinking about doing something, it is considered a signal to do what you were thinking of doing.

If you think consulting such natural events as omens is something that only peoples of tradition practice, consider how many of us avoid walking under ladders and think a black cat crossing our path means bad luck.

Is divination a reality?

The issue here is not whether one particular divination session is genuine, but whether such a thing as divination is possible at all. To answer this question, we must realize that the art of divination deals with a number of different realities.

Let's start with the phenomenon of clairvoyance. Clairvoyance does not require any religious belief system, nor does one need faith to obtain a result. Perhaps it works only because we all have some kind of mental ability, as yet undiscovered by our science, that allows us to have a degree of knowledge about some aspects of the future, perhaps by connecting ourselves with a higher consciousness.

When you think of someone and he calls you that night, or you get a letter from that person soon after, it would not simply be a coincidence, but rather a real human ability to have some knowledge of the future. If we call this coincidence, it is because for most of us, such experiences happen only on rare occasions. This may be due to our not developing, or staying in touch with, this ability—often because we lack the faith to believe in our own powers of mind. Therefore we don't know how to use clairvoyance fully, on a full-time basis. Meanwhile, there are some people who can master this ability—as various experiments in the field of parapsychology have suggested.

Ritual divination may be just a means, a tool, for using this faculty of the mind that allows clairvoyance. Or perhaps we should consider the possibility that there really are ways to connect, using mediumistic talents, with invisibles or spiritual beings who know the secrets of the world and can reveal them to us. I have said that in calling spirits, people invoke energies that pass through the whole world as well as themselves. By their ability to link up with these energies, perhaps they can attune themselves to some kind of cosmic or universal harmony, of which each of us is a part. This harmony in turn guides us in such a way that our actions will not disrupt or interfere with it.

This view of the reality of divination remains valid with regard to omens as long as we consider them tools with which we connect with nature.

What is nature if not a part of the cosmic harmony? Any action we take against nature will be reflected in and disturb the cosmic harmony. Similarly, any actions that will interfere with or disturb the cosmic harmony will unbalance nature and put it in jeopardy. And this would explain why we get messages from nature, or omens, about some of our actions. By providing us with omens, nature tries to protect itself from those actions that could disrupt it; it tries to stop us from endangering the cosmic harmony.

Perhaps the success of peoples of tradition in using divination rituals and in interpreting omens is nothing less than a measure of their ability to be in sync with the wisdom of nature. Since all human beings are part of nature, it is a skill we all have a need to learn.

4

The Tuareg People

I went to the Sahara Desert purely by accident. In March 1970 I
finished a lecture tour and went off chasing Gypsies through the south
of France in order to make a movie about them. At the beginning of
the summer, some Belgian friends invited me to accompany them on a
four-week trip to Tamanrasset, a small legendary town in the Hoggar
Mountain region, in the heart of the Sahara Desert, in order to film
their expedition. (The Sahara runs from Libya to Mauritania, covering
the southern parts of Morocco and Algeria and the northern parts of
Niger and Mali; the Hoggar Mountains lie in the southern part of
Algeria.)

Although my movie about the Gypsies was keeping me busy,
within a week of getting my friends' proposition I found myself and
my girlfriend Danièle (who was later to become my first wife) following their Land Rover and two Volkswagen buses in my small car, on
the way to the Sahara.

Perhaps I followed my friends because I knew that in this desert
dwell a mysterious people called the Tuareg. And I couldn't wait to
meet these nomads.

At that time, trying to reach Tamanrasset with a small and fragile
car was a crazy idea. There were a thousand miles of rugged dirt road
that descended from high plateaus, crossed dried lakes of soft sand,
and climbed rocky mountains. Eventually, three hundred miles from
our final destination, a big stone hidden beneath layers of sand tore
away my car's front axle. My friends advised us to wait there until they
returned with spare parts.

Staying there was a good idea. A car left alone in the desert is soon pillaged and stripped of anything that might be valuable. However, we also made a big mistake: it was summer in the Sahara, and my friends didn't leave us a lot of water.

Thirst is worse than hunger. You think obsessively about how easy it is to obtain water by opening a faucet. You talk constantly about drinks and bars. You become parched to the point where the palate detaches itself and sticks to the tongue, which swells and becomes coated, and has an awful taste of salt. You lose your appetite and feel weak; your legs tremble at the slightest effort.

Aman iman—"Water is life"—says an old Tuareg proverb. These nomads know the implacable law of the desert. They know that when the human body misses water it begins taking it out of the blood plasma. Blood then becomes thick and begins to circulate with great difficulty, no longer able to maintain the body's normal temperature. The heart works harder. The brain begins to dehydrate, which leads to irreversible lesions. Finally, water is extracted from the tissues, causing painful convulsions. And if at that time the victim does get water, it is too late; it will just prolong his agony.

The process leading to death involves hours of horrible suffering. Thus the Tuareg, if they know that they have reached the stage at which nothing can save them, will lie down on the warm sand, their necks exposed to the burning sun. The heated blood begins to boil, and when it reaches the brain it brings an instant and quiet death.

Danièle and I thought about that while we waited. And hoped we would not be forced to do likewise.

During that wait, I also discovered that the Sahara plays with people's minds. Sometimes the sound of an automobile gave us the energy to leave the car and wait . . . until we realized that what we had heard was just grains of sand moving in the hot breeze. Sometimes the sight of heavy dust far away led us to hope that it was produced by a car . . . but we soon discovered it was just a whirlwind sucking up dust and throwing it high in the air. We saw what we thought were cameleers and jumped out of the car, stretching our trembling hands high in the sky to be seen . . . but then, as the sun stopped its burning brutality, we realized they were just stones—a little bit bigger than most, but just stones undulating in the heat that deformed the horizon.

The third day, we thought we saw a Tuareg riding a white camel in the distance. But this trembling image soon disappeared.

"Did you see that?" I whispered. Danièle nodded.

"That's it . . . we are hallucinating!" I continued. "I wonder how long we'll be able to make it." And we closed our eyes.

Suddenly, feeling that I was being watched, I opened my eyes. A few inches away, at the other side of the open car window, was the veiled face of a young boy. It took my breath away. His big, dark eyes contrasted with his pale skin. A few seconds later he turned away and disappeared into the bright nowhere. Danièle and I looked at each other and closed our eyes again—to stop our last hope for survival from vanishing forever.

A few minutes later we heard a noise. The veiled adolescent was there again, this time holding a half watermelon. He held it out to us. He was so silent that we were afraid to talk—as if our words might chase away the reality of what we were experiencing. Without a word I gave him our last bit of food, a biscuit. His eyes smiled. Then he turned back and slowly walked away, his long, blue robe undulating with each step. After walking a few feet he stopped and looked at us again, slowly raising a hand toward the sky in farewell. Without waiting for an answer, he turned back and rapidly disappeared into a mirage of water. His silhouette became transparent.

Yet the half watermelon I was holding in my hands was there to attest that Saint-Exupery's little prince had appeared again in the Sahara Desert, but this time with a Tuareg face.

The next day a Land Rover sent by our friends came to pick us up and tow our car. When we reached Tamanrasset, we learned that it would take a month or two to get the spare parts we needed.

Sooner than expected, our friends went back to Belgium. A few days later we met a young man, Eric S., and his sister, who told us their story. When their father died, they had emptied the home safe, bought a Land Rover, and headed for Africa in search of happiness. But happiness can't bloom on African roads if it is missing in one's heart. Now, two months later, they were on the their way home. Eric was still unhappy. However, he had agreed to wait in Tamanrasset while his sister pursued a new love affair with an urban Saharan.

So there we were, with a broken car but the will to explore the Hoggar region and meet the Tuareg, while Eric, bored by life and with a brand-new four-wheel-drive vehicle, was waiting around for his sister. It took me two days to break through Eric's solitude and one day to get him to agree to drive us around for ten days.

To understand who the Tuareg are and why they have been forced to keep some psychic faculties working, it is important to capture images of their environment—an awe-inspiring vastness of horizontal emptiness whose overpowering beauty and unfathomable depths of sky never fail to impress me.

The Sahara Desert is a state of mind. All the mineral beings of the desert move with the sun and change their signification. Behind every image quivering with heat appear illusions. One strains one's gaze by the constant irreality. Here and there one sees what appear to be layers of water floating over skeletons of camels, goats, and gazelles—and sometimes over the dried body of a bird who, exhausted by his migratory flight, landed for a rest, never to take wing again. Heated to over 120 degrees farenheit, the terrain seems to turn into water. Beneath each sand dune, each bush, is an upside-down image undulating as if it were a reflection on water of the object itself. As one approaches, the apparent water moves farther back, leaving in its wake only desolation.

Sometimes the mirage is not merely an optical effect. It can be a ghostly representation of real objects or landscapes that exist hundreds of miles away. This scenery is mirrored on high-altitude layers of heat, and then projected onto layers of heat floating three or four feet above the ground. Illusions in a land of mystery and anguish, mirages have always imparted an atmosphere of insecurity.

All around the Hoggar Mountain region are large stretches of sand—seas of sand of an infinite mobility on which the shivering of nature has drawn its impression. It is a pulverulent sand, as soft as the skin of a woman; as liquid as marshes and swamps, sucking in the wheels of cars, becoming in some places deadly quicksand. Large expanses of huge sand waves appear. Castles of wind. Hills where clouds do not dwell. Their colors cry in the silence, for the desert's palette is varied: rose at sunrise, yellow in the morning, white and bleached out at noon, brown and red at sunset. The dunes are made of a sand so light that when the scirocco blows, it can erase hundred-foot-high dunes in just one storm and build them again miles away.

Soon the large expanses of sand dunes give birth to stone pillars, basalts, and high plateaus—old witnesses of ancient volcanic activity. It's a broken landscape that seems to have been there since the beginning of the universe and which may well reflect how the end of the world will look. It keeps the memory of the time when fire and water fought together to build the earth, when the earth became hell within the time-space of eternity. Everything is painted with dead colors. Sinister set of rocks seems to be willing to tear the sky apart.

If water, which once shaped these forms, has disappeared today, the wind continues to erode the tormented shapes. It brings sand with it, which files, bites, and nibbles away with infinite slowness. At night, the erosion continues due to the difference in daytime and nighttime temperatures. The stones burst, crumble away, disintegrate, and are left sharpened like deadly claws.

And as the sun climbs ever higher, a stream of heat bathes the dried atmosphere. Life becomes a breath of fire; the ground, ashes not yet totally extinct.

Then comes the red and brown of the Hoggar—dry rocky mountains and peaks much like those of America's Monument Valley, but more massive and higher. Rocks stretch toward the sky, giant claws ruffle the clouds, and ridges are outlined on the horizon. Stone cathedrals and giant organs have been hewn for gods. Valleys tear high plateaus apart, and huge granite domes appear. Some formations look like giant fossilized books, the pages of which seem to be breaking apart of old age. There are monstrous flowers and forests of rock. There are dolmens and fierce volcanic peaks. It is an indescribable chaos of black, brown, and red boulders, of solidified tears, of lava spittles, of terrestrial slobbers—landscape hallucinated by inner fevers. Is ten-thousand-foot-high Atakor Mountain a stone prayer or a divine clamor?

As the sun goes down, giving colors back to the rock land, a great harmony begins to descend. Shadows are born from flat surfaces and penetrate everything, everywhere. The sky, now ultramarine, becomes more deeply infinite. The sand dunes appear to be made of gold, their shadows much like female organs opening to the setting sun.

The spectacle of the sun sacrificing itself is so grandiose that it arouses in one's heart a succession of sensations that bring on a longing to bathe, to drown oneself in the frenzy of the dying light. The sun's red ball is inserted into the horizontal emptiness. Then, slowly and majestically it descends beyond the horizon; the sky however, holds for a while the message of the day, with a rose backdrop before which yellow and red banderoles unfurl—as if a great display were necessary to assure the sun's return.

The motionlessness of these seemingly dead sands and stones and rocks becomes even more magical in the evening. And, looking at the desert stretching out and disappearing into the west, where nobody goes and from where nobody comes, I wonder what heady secrets are still kept by this cruel and loving mobility.

As night comes on, the air becomes cooler during summer, and freezing in winter. The Sahara is a cold land with a burning sun.

But most amazing, perhaps, is to be surrounded by stars. Their magical luminescent drawings cover the whole expanse of the sky, from one horizon to the other. They appear to be close enough to be caressed just by stretching out one's hands. When we lay down on the ground, it seems our bodies are attracted to this blue phosphorescent deep between stars.

And the silence is disturbed only by the throbbing of one's heart, filling up the immense emptiness. There is a Tuareg saying: "Facing the desert, don't say 'What a silence,' but say 'I can't hear.' "

℞

In this magical desert, where life seems merely a long, ultimately terminal disease, live the Tuareg—a people who always seem to appear suddenly, from a world that is not ours. They are the lords of this universe of desolation, sands, and stones. One doesn't know if they belong just to solitude or to these spaces from another time where anything can "be" or be anew. Their faces are covered with twelve-foot-long blue or white veils, of which one can see only the piercing eyes. Formerly pillagers, warriors still, they always filled our dreams with mystery.

They are called the blue men of the Sahara, for their clothes are dyed a deep indigo blue, and the color runs easily onto their skin. Their skin is thus well protected against the dry air, since the dye stops moisture from evaporating.

The Tuareg live under a feudal system. There are noblemen who have subdued vassal tribes; both groups have servants. The Tuareg are Caucasians. Scholars consider them part of the Berber ethnic group. (An *ethnic group* shares a racial heritage, language, and culture.) However, nobody knows with any certainty who the Berbers are or where they came from. As for the Tuareg, according to one of their legends, their motherland was in the middle of the Atlantic Ocean. Their ancestors used to sail up the African coast to the Sahara, where they sold, traded, and bought goods. One day their land disappeared under the water. Modern-day Tuareg claim they are the descendants of those who were in the Sahara on business when the catastrophe occurred.

Tuareg crisscross the Sahara, voyaging from the Hoggar to the Libyan desert, the northern Niger, and Timbuktu in Mali. And because the noblemen are warriors it is not easy to approach them. So, while we were waiting in Tamanrasset, Danièle and I spent time with various sedentary Tuareg, asking about their customs and language, called Tamahaq. Thus we learned a few things about their complicated greeting ritual, and about how to have a successful first contact with nomads.

An amazing divination session took place in the first Tuareg encampment we found in the Hoggar region. Stretching out on the soft sand of a dried riverbed, or *oued,* the encampment comprised only six tents, each quite distant from the others. A Tuareg tent consists of a large canopy made of thirty or more shaved animal skins sewn to-gether, and supported by a central pole. Its entrance is placed opposite to the direction of the wind.

We stopped the car about three hundred feet from the Tuareg en-campment. I veiled my face in the manner of Tuareg men and, leaving Danièle and Eric behind in the car, slowly walked toward the group of tents. As I approached, I began hearing the familiar noises of daily life, carried by the light wind: children's laughter, the screams of goats and camels, dogs barking.

When I was about one hundred fifty feet away, I saw a Tuareg man get out of a tent and look at me. As I continued to approach the en-campment, he began moving in my direction, walking very slowly and staring at me intensely. The dark blue robe surrounding his body and falling to his ankles undulated as he walked. The wind was playing with one edge of the veil that covered his face. The amulets hanging around his neck knocked against each other as he walked.

We were still staring at each other when the Tuareg stopped five feet away from me. His blackened eyelids gave him a fierce look. (The Tuareg blacken their eyelids with kohl, a dark powder that protects the eyes from flies.) I froze, too.

"*Ma t toulid?*" ("How are you?") he said, his piercing eyes driving deeply into mine.

"*Elrer râs!*" ("Only with the good!") I answered, knowing that these two words and nothing else were to be answered to all of his questions.

"*Ma d'oulan eddounet ennek?*" ("How are those of your family?")

"*Elrer râs!*"

"*Ma t toulid d asekel?*" ("How was your trip?")

"*Elrer râs!*"

"*Ma t toulid d oudouh?*" ("Are you tired?")

The litany of questions went on for about a minute. When he stopped, once again I said, "*Elrer ras!*" and then "*Tanemerd!*" ("Thank you"). Then my turn came to begin the same ritual of questions, while he continued to stare at me, trying to read my mind in order to find out whether I was friend or enemy. A nomad must decide this before ac-cepting a visitor into his camp. It can be a question of life or death, not only for him, but for his family and for the whole group of people camping together.

I finished my series of questions, yet the man didn't hold out his hand to greet me. Instead, he began the litany of questions again, ap-parently not yet satisfied with his first impression of me. Sometimes it can go on like that for five or six rounds.

Suddenly he offered me his bluish hand and told me his name was Brahim. I put my hand wide open against his, palm to palm, and our hands caressed each other up to the tips of the fingers. That is the Tuareg greeting.

Using French mixed with some Tamahaq, he said, "Let's drink tea together. You'll meet my family." According to the Tuareg laws of hospitality, the tea ceremony is the open door to friendship.

"*Tanemerd!* Let me get my friends."

We were sitting with Brahim in front of his tent, next to a small campfire, looking at him as he prepared the traditional tea ceremony. Sitting next to us were Zora, his wife, with their baby on her lap, and their other two children.

Following the Tuareg tradition, Zora wore no veil. With dozens of small braids in her hair, her clear but slightly bluish skin, her delicate nose, and her perfectly shaped mouth, she was beautiful. While listening to our conversation, she softly stretched her baby's nose to accentuate its thin shape—which for the Tuareg represents perfect beauty. Then she massaged her baby's skull with her hand in order to elongate it—an ancient custom that was standard practice among the ancient Egyptians and which is still performed, notably among the Peulh and some Massai tribes.

Set on the ground in front of Brahim were a decorated wooden box containing the raw green tea, and a large copper platter holding a two-pound egg-shaped piece of sugar, small tea glasses, a large glass, a copper teapot, and a bunch of mint leaves.

Brahim put a pinch of raw tea into the teapot. He took the kettle from the glowing embers and poured boiling water into the teapot. Using the hard bottom of a small tea glass, he cracked small pieces off the piece of sugar and added them to the teapot. Then, holding the teapot about two feet above the large glass, he slowly poured a long trickle of the steaming beverage into it which, in falling against the bottom of the glass, formed a foam that floated on top of the tea. When the teapot was empty, he refilled it from the large glass so that the sugar would mix perfectly with the tea.

After repeating this operation four or five times, he poured a little bit of the golden beverage into one of the small glasses, still holding the teapot high in the air. Almost religiously, he took the small glass, looked carefully at the color of the tea and without unveiling his face, passed the hand holding the glass beneath his turban, smelled the beverage and, noisily, sucked it rapidly, keeping it in his mouth to taste it carefully. After a few nods, he began serving tea for each of us, pouring it into the small glasses from high in the air. His measure was perfect: our glasses were filled up, and the teapot was empty.

Imitating Brahim and his family, I lifted my glass to my lips hidden under my veil, whispering, "*Bismillah*" ("To the grace of Allah"), and noisily took a sip of the hot beverage, which, being the first brew, had a bitter taste. And we began chatting in French, which he spoke with ease. (The whole Sahara and the countries north and south of it were French colonies for a long time. However, not all nomads speak French.)

When our glasses were empty, the second of the three rounds composing the tea ceremony began. Adding more sugar to the teapot, but keeping the old tea leaves he had used for the first round (he kept them to the end), and following the same principle, Brahim served us a second glass of tea. This one was lighter and sweeter. For the third round, he added even more sugar, and some mint leaves. According to Tuareg tradition, male guests do not have the right to refuse the three glasses of tea; women may pass on the first brew since it is often bitter. Children receive a fourth round, which is very weak and very sweet.

The heat had begun to abate, and the encampment began to come alive again. From a tent a young girl brought out a goatskin filled with milk, and attached it to a wooden tripod. Then she began shaking it, churning the milk to make butter and, later, cheese of it. A little bit farther away, servants were pounding millet in heavy wooden mortars. Everywhere children were playing, trying to outdo each other in screaming.

Brahim said we could stay with them for a few days. He allowed us to pitch our tent in the *oued,* among them. Then he left the encampment in search of wood. Zora and the two children went up to the well with two servants to bring some water.

From the car, we brought some food and our large tent. Very proud that Brahim and his family had accepted us with such warmth, we pitched our tent close to his. But when Brahim came back from his wood gathering, he suddenly looked unhappy.

"Is there something wrong?" I asked.

"We have a saying," he said. "Tents set apart get hearts together!" We moved our tent farther away.

Back at Brahim's tent, Zora began playing the *imzad*. Played with a bow, it is similar to a small violin, but with only one or two strings. It is made of an emptied half squash over which a goat or lizard skin is stretched. Her music soon called a gathering around her.

The *imzad* is the Tuaregs' most important musical instrument, around which has grown an absolute cult. It is for the Tuareg what the violin is for some Gypsy tribes. Women play it so skillfully that they are able to express their sorrows, their most intimate joys, their hopes, their avowed or still-secret loves. They can implore or punish.

Accompanying the *imzad's* melodious sounds are words of traditional songs or improvised poems, sung or recited by the musician or whoever else cares to join in. Anything and everything inspires them—the never-ending fawn-colored twilight; the sparkling of the night; the rising smoke that caresses the stars before kissing the moon; or the golden glance of a lonely gazelle, met on the way to the well, crying for love.

Poetry is part of the Tuaregs' education, and it soon becomes a need. In it they find a language full of visions and images. Their poetry, like their music, is melancholy, and deals mostly with love. For love is the most important thing in their lives. And, indeed, besides taking care of their tasks and watching the time pass by, one of the Tuareg's most important concerns during the day is to muse over music, to compose poems that will bring them success in the *tindi*—musical and poetic gatherings.

A thing that fascinates me is the seemingly contradictory way in which Tuareg men live. They are fierce warriors, always ready to fight with their *takouba,* a deadly sword, to protect their territory or their people, or to keep a would-be suitor away from their loved ones, and yet their only way to seduce women is through poetry. Since they are veiled, the men cannot rely on their physical beauty; instead, they must reveal the beauty of their souls and their hearts. This takes place late in the night, and is called an *ahal.*

Though it does not possess the high artistic qualities of the *tindi,* the *ahal* is also a musical, literary, and poetic gathering, but with a very licentious character. Always organized by women, it is a gathering where only singles are allowed to come and meet, to seduce and make love. Anyone free from a marital link is considered single.

It takes only a few single women in an encampment to organize an *ahal.* One is appointed as chairwoman, her role being to make the participants respect the rules of the occasion. She also serves as referee when a quarrel flares up between two jealous suitors, for the women's freedom to choose a lover sometimes liberates warlike feelings among rivals, which may even end in a duel with swords.

The event begins with music. The plaintive sounds of the *imzad* and strong beats of the drums glide over the sands. Like messengers, they are the women's call for love. And, coming from neighboring and distant encampments—some as far as sixty miles away—and traveling on the backs of their camels or donkeys, or by foot, wearing their nicest robes, and followed by the scent of their too-strong perfumes, the men hurry to be among the first to discover the beauty of the women who are waiting, to try to woo and seduce them.

Surrounded by men, the women, their faces made up, sit in a circle. One takes an *imzad* and, searching for musical inspiration, plays it slowly at first . . . then faster and more skillfully as she remembers the rhymes of a poem she composed during her nap. A young girl takes a drum and beats it, caressing its taut skin, beginning to sing verses, accompanied by men who mark the rhythms with *ho-hos* sung loudly . . . then ending softly.

The end of the song is marked by cries of joy from the crowd. One tells a joke. A woman laughs. A man begins a song he accompanies with drumbeats.

Already the positions have changed. Men have slipped between women. Three men surround the prettiest, while a fourth clings to her back, whispering verses into her ear. And she bursts out laughing. This seems to displease the other suitors, one of whom, very jealous, tries to remember some unpleasant details of his rival's life—in hopes of discrediting him.

But these verbal duels, in which the worst insults are given and the most violent accusations are exchanged, must be carried out with extraordinary chivalry. Adversaries must retort with good grace only, without scuffles or real disputes; rarely do these exchanges give rise to a grudge. Those are the *ahal*'s rules, and the chairwoman has the right to expel anyone who is not able to argue with dignity or uses coarse language.

Slowly, an atmosphere of sensuality begins to enfold the gathering. Men and women cuddle up to each other, gazing into each other's eyes. Hands and feet search for hands, for legs. Breasts and other intimate parts are caressed. A woman makes her *imzad* wail. Someone seeks out a rhythm on a drum. One jokes. Another gives out saucy hints.

Often, when a man feels that the woman he is interested in shares his warm feelings, he will continue to woo her, but while looking at another woman, to avoid a jealous reaction from any rival.

An *imzad* cries out again, at first uncertain. Then a melody takes shape and the cry becomes a sigh that a young woman's voice accompanies:

I don't want him to see my tears,
neither to know how much I love him;
even if, at the ahal, *I tremble like a gazelle,*
my imzad *slipping from my hands.*
I will wait until, such a hunter chasing after
his prey,
at last he discovers me.
But why are you not coming under my tent?
You'll find, to warm ourselves up,
a heart that burns for you
like the sand burns under the sun . . .

Suddenly there is silence. Not able to hide their passion, a newly formed couple search for darkness. There, hidden from sight, they breathe together slowly, nose against nose—this is the Tuareg kiss—then faster . . . until they are wonderfully intoxicated with love.

Confidences are shared. Eyelids lower furtively. Smiles reveal white teeth and lips swollen with desire. There is new laughter, new requests for the voice of an *imzad*. A woman smiles and plays again. Questions are posed to the women—in a whisper, for Tuareg are very discreet.

"Of the two of us, whom do you prefer, Lilla?"

"Who is the more handsome, the more valiant?"

A woman closes her eyes as a voice comes from the deepest part of her heart, a voice telling a story that she translates with music and a languorous incantation. Her low chant is disturbed only by whisperings and conniving caresses. The glowing embers of the fire start to darken, and soon die. But nobody cares. Nostrils breathe nostrils and the smell of the loved one. Those who are still alone, or for whom nothing is as yet sure, try hard to seduce. Perhaps they will make analogies: they will talk about the love existing between a stone and a desert plant—for stones and plants, and all the things in the desert that seem to be dead, have a heart, a story, a love to cry over, a happiness to shout about. And besides, now, in the *ahal,* one can hear the hearts of all things because they are beating almost as loudly as one's own heart . . . when fingers join together and squeeze, when a palm caresses, when one has the desire to give oneself so strongly that one's whole body shakes.

Warm hearts beat; and hands leave a message on another's skin. There is a sign language for lovers—a silent physical whispering. Palm against palm, fingers intertwined, thumb pressing thumb means "I desire you very much." A circle drawn on the skin, with a forefinger pressing its center, is a call for sex. If the other's forefinger answers in drawing a line from the wrist up to the fingers, this means a refusal. But if over that line, after a slight hesitation—which always makes the heart of the suitor beat faster—another line is drawn in the opposite direction, thus making a cross, that serves as a burning caress, a new communion of breathing, a primal contact with another's skin, heat arising from the genitals. It means, "Go away with your friends and, in a while, come back alone and join me at the place I will describe in my next song." And in the hollow of a sand dune, or on the soft bank of an *oued,* the perfume of love will mix with the smell of the warm sand. . . .

Thus, from puberty up until their wedding, boys and girls may have as many lovers as they want. But thereafter it is finished. (It seems we do the contrary.) And the more lovers a woman has, the greater will be the demand for her, perhaps because of her acquired knowledge in the area of sexual gymnastics. Thanks to such sexual freedom, men and women have the opportunity to try as many partners as they want, until they make their final choice.

One might think that this sexual freedom would lead to a great number of unwanted children. This is far from the case. Among the Tuareg birth control in necessary for survival. Tuareg women use a Saharan plant to accomplish this. A monthly infusion of it starts a menstrual period that would otherwise have been interrupted by ovulation. Similar natural techniques were used by some North American Indian tribes, and are still used in Asian jungles and wherever else people need to limit birth.

❦

The next night, just as we were about to finish the dinner we had all shared around the campfire in front of Brahim's tent, a cameleer approached the encampment.

"The *taleb* is there!" Brahim said, and went to greet him. A *taleb* is a respected person, a man of knowledge and wisdom. Depending on need, he acts as shaman, medicine man, or just adviser. He makes talismans that contain papers covered with magical signs—many of them from the Cabala—and verses of the Koran. They are believed to protect the owner from evil spirits and *djenouns*—imps whom the Tuareg believe are the source of maladies and misfortunes.

At the *taleb's* command, his camel knelt down on its front legs, sighing heavily. Then, screaming, it tucked in its back legs, allowing the cameleer to get down from the high saddle. The *taleb* untied and took off the saddle, and ordered his mount to stand up. Then he tucked in one of its front legs and bound it so that the camel could not stray too far during the night in search of food.

Later, during the tea ceremony (one traditionally follows each meal), I began asking the *taleb* questions about his duties and powers, using Brahim as my interpreter.

"One day, you will know!" he said, cutting short our conversation.

"How?" I asked.

"Your name means 'the one who knows.' You are aware of nothing yet, but when the day comes you will know!" I drank a sip of tea without answering, unable to understand what he meant. (I must add that merely telling them my name did open doors for me among the Tuareg.)

Later the *taleb* flattened about a square foot of sand near the campfire with his hand. Then he showed me how to make marks on the sand with the fingertips of my right hand, similar to the footprints of a cat.

"How many should I make?" I asked.

"As many as you feel like," he replied.

The *taleb* bent over the dozen or so marks I had made in the sand, and examined them conscientiously. As he was deciphering them, one by one, he drew a few signs beside him with his finger, and erased some of my marks. He drew more signs and erased more of mine, until the sand was covered with his small drawings alone. Then he started to talk. And as he was speaking to me, he erased some of the marks he had made. This is what he said:

> You left the land of your birth when you were a baby, and moved to another country, then to another one. You are a man of three cultures. Your mother died when you were a young boy. You travel a lot and will do so for the rest of your life, because you are searching for people of other lands, to learn their knowledge. Before you became a man, you almost died of a sickness. Then you almost died again less than one year ago. It happened in a small country in the middle of the water . . . the salty water. Your foot has been burned by something very hot. Boiling water or boiling earth . . . or something like that. You will come back here to the Sahara, and live with us. You will make pictures of us, and books. Then you will go all over the world to talk about our way of life. Many people will know about the Tuareg. Oh, oh, oh! You will move to another country beyond a big, big extent of water, salty water, and live there for a while. *Aywa!* [an expression of surprise].

He started to laugh, and, looking at the other Tuareg seated around us, he said to them, "This man will have four wives. *Aywa!*"

About half of the signs the *taleb* had drawn on the sand were still to be translated. But by this time he had already gone deeply into my future, telling me a few things that I still refuse to contemplate and others that I don't even want to mention. So I stopped him.

"Thank you, *taleb*," I said. "But I don't want to know more about what must come to me. I prefer to discover it by myself when the time comes."

"I understand," he said. "You are wise."

Yes, I got scared. Just by examining the marks I had made on the sand, he had told me things about my past that were true and that he couldn't have known. The people sitting around me that night were the first Tuareg I had met. And I had not told them a word about my life. I hadn't even had time to do so.

Now that twenty years have passed, I am able to evaluate the accuracy of what the *taleb* foretold. So let's review the whole reading, to get a better understanding of the correlation between the facts of my life and what the diviner told me.

The *taleb* said: "You left the land of your birth when you were a baby, and moved to another country, then to another one. You are a man of three cultures." Indeed, I was born in Czechoslovakia. For political reasons, my parents and I left that country when I was one year old, and moved to Africa. Then, when my father became seriously ill, we went to Belgium. So, effectively, I am a man of three different cultures.

He was also right when he said that I travel a lot and would continue to do so for the rest of my life. However, at that time I had no idea that I would dedicate my life to a search for the knowledge held by peoples of tradition.

"Before you became a man, you almost died of a sickness. Then you almost died again less than one year ago. It happened in a small country in the middle of the water . . . the salty water. Your foot has been burned by something very hot. Boiling water or boiling earth . . . or something like that."

Yes, I almost died at age seventeen of meningitis. And less than a year before I was with the Tuareg in that encampment, my left foot had received third-degree burns from boiling sulfur. Since the Tuareg have no word for *sea,* the *taleb* used "salty water" to indicate the ocean that surrounds New Zealand, where the accident occurred. Instead of using the words *boiling sulfur,* he said "boiling water or boiling earth"—an interesting detail. My injury happened in a volcanic area covered with solfataras, where boiling sulfur springs mingled with bubbling pots of mud on a treacherous shale crust. Therefore, it seems that the taleb tried to translate verbally the images he was getting— instead of deriving his knowledge directly from my memory, by whatever means.

"You will come back here to the Sahara, and live with us. You will make pictures of us, and books. Then you will go all over the world to talk about our way of life. Many people will know about the Tuareg."

In this case, there is no way that he could have used telepathy or any other form of ESP, since at the time of the reading I had no intention whatsoever of making a movie or writing books about the Tuareg. My mind was obsessed with the study I was doing on the Gypsies.

However, after that first experience with the Tuareg, I fell so much in love with their way of life that, a year later, I did indeed go back to the Sahara, with Danièle and an assistant. We spent almost a year and a half living with the Tuareg, wherever I could find them, all over the desert. And I wrote three successful books about them, and made a movie that was shown all over the United States and abroad, as part of my TV series *Explore.*

"You will move to another country beyond a big, big extent of water, salty water, and live there for a while." He was right again. Ten years later I suddenly decided to move from Europe to California.

When he predicted, in front of Danièle, to whom I was engaged, that I would marry many times, I felt in my heart and soul that it was nonsense. I was too much in love with her to imagine that after marrying her I would ever divorce her. Unfortunately, he was right about that, too.

It seems, then, that by reading those small marks I made on the sand with my fingertips, the *taleb* was able to get pictures from my memory. We could argue that this was due not to clairvoyance, but to telepathy. But he was also able to foretell events that were not in my mind at all. And that bothers me a lot. It even obsesses me. Was he able to capture images of my destiny? I don't like the idea that, whatever I do, I can't escape my destiny. Or, and I prefer this explanation, was he able somehow, by means of whatever phenomenon, to enter the layers of time, look ahead into the future and foresee what would happen to me years later? Perhaps he had this power, because, as I mentioned in chapter 3, even today time is not well understood by scientists—and I can't stop thinking about Albert Einstein who in 1955, wrote: "For us believing scientists, the difference between past, present, and future is an illusion, even if a stubborn one."

However, I must add that the *taleb* was totally wrong when he said that I lost my mother when I was a young boy. My mother is still alive; it was my father who died. However, as I write about that event, I feel a sudden chill. I remember that a number of my girlfriends, all through my life, have asked me if my mother had died. When asked why, they said that sometimes I was acting in an odd way, as if I had lost my mother. And thinking about that now, I wonder if those girls weren't right.

After my father died, my mother tried to be both a mother and a father at the same time, for the sake of my two sisters and myself. However, even after he died, my feelings for my father remained strong; I knew deep in my guts that he was staying close to me. Perhaps I always felt that by trying also to be my father, she had stopped being only and totally my mother. In that respect, then, the *taleb* was right. He had been able to capture emotional images from my psyche.

☾

A year later, in Timbuktu, I met another *taleb*. His special skill was the ability to predict, months in advance, during the dry season, how much rain would fall during the rainy season. According to everyone living in that region, he had never been wrong.

The *taleb* was part of a small seminomadic vassal tribe of Tuareg based in a small village about thirty miles east of Timbuktu. His house, made of reeds like all the other houses of the village, was built on the bank of an *oued*. He owned a small herd of goats, and was able to make a living from his two-acre garden, where he raised vegetables, thanks to an ingenious system of irrigation. A few times I helped him transport vegetables and goats to Timbuktu with my Land Rover. On another occasion, I gave some antibiotics to a patient of his, who was suffering from a bad tooth infection. So he owed me a favor. One day I found a way he could pay me back.

That day, someone from a nearby village had asked him how much rain would fall and when it would start. The *taleb* shared some tea with him, and then asked him to wait there as he left the room. I wanted to know the taleb's secret, so I followed him. He went to his garden, and looked at the sky, and at the trees and plants growing all around him.

When he came back, he said to the man, "The first rain should start in three months. We'll have about a foot of rain in all."

I waited until I was alone with him and said, "*Taleb,* tell me your secret."

"I will, but only if you use it for a good purpose."

I nodded. I think that writing about it in this book is a good purpose; in countries where people have lost contact with themselves and with nature, it will help awaken human consciousness to the truths one can read in nature.

The *taleb* took me to his garden and said; "My secret for predicting the amount of rain and when it will start lies in this garden. Look around you and find it!"

I looked everywhere and found nothing.

"Is it written on the trees?" I asked. The *taleb* shook his head. "Is it written on the vegetables?" He said no, smiling. For two hours I searched the *taleb's* entire garden for the secret, but in vain.

The *taleb* came to me. "The secret lies here," he said, pointing at some small nests that birds were building in some bushes. "How high from the ground are these nests?" he asked me.

"A foot!"

"These native birds know that they must build their nests just a little bit over the water level. Consequently, we will have a little less than a foot of rain at the height of the rainy season."

"They are never mistaken?" I asked.

"If they ever had been, there would be no birds!" he replied.

"I guess you're able to know when the rains will start by seeing how far along the nest-building has come. Am I right?"

"Only men make mistakes, nature never!" said the *taleb*.

For predicting when the rains would start and the amount that would fall, this *taleb* obviously used no ESP abilities at all. He had no need for clairvoyant talents. Instead, he knew the patterns of nature, and could read their messages.

It was in a small encampment in the Hoggar region that I witnessed another of the Tuaregs' mysterious psychic faculties.

We were the guests of a Tuareg named Oizek. Except for him and a few old men, there were mainly women in that encampment, for the fathers, husbands, and brothers had gone on a caravan to Niger to purchase cereal, clothes, and other goods in exchange for the salt they gathered in their region; salt remains the Tuaregs' only currency.

After I had been there about two weeks, Oizek told me, "The caravan is arriving soon!"

"How do you know?" I asked, surprised.

"It's Aicha who told me," he replied. "Aicha is the wife of one of the caravaneers. For two days she's been very nervous and has spent her time watching the horizon from the hill. She always knows these things in advance."

"How can she?" I asked.

"I don't know. I never asked. But she knows these things in advance," he repeated. "The *taleb* said that she is able to communicate with her husband mentally."

"When did the caravan leave?" I asked.

"More than three months ago," he said.

"When are they supposed to come back?"

"A few weeks ago or two months from now. Only Allah knows," he replied. (There is no fixed schedule for these long and exhausting voyages through the harsh and life-threatening desert.)

I left him, searching for Aicha. I found her sitting next to her tent, having her hair done by her sister. She wanted to be pretty for her husband's return.

"So your husband is coming back," I said as I sat next to them. She nodded. "How do you know?" I asked.

"I smelled him in the morning wind," she answered. I felt it wasn't the right time to question her about her mysterious faculties, so I remained sitting and watched.

Like women throughout the world, Tuareg women attach great importance to their hairstyle. As she untangled Aicha's hair with a small comb, the sister applied fine sand and soft ashes to her hair—the native natural dry shampoo. Then she deloused the hair. Once this was done, she separated the hair into small locks with a knife, greasing each one with butter to protect the hair from the dry air.

Then she began braiding the hair.

When half of her hair was done Aicha moved out of the encampment, and I followed her as she climbed a hill. From the top, looking south toward Niger, all one could see beyond the valley was miles and miles of sand dunes stretching to the far end of the undulating horizon. I watched Aicha. She was more than scrutinizing the open space; she was literally smelling the light breeze caressing her face. Standing next to her, I was able to see her nostrils quivering. Then she smiled, and slowly said her man would be arriving soon.

"How soon is soon?" I asked.

"Tonight!" she replied.

"How do you know?"

"I told you, the wind carries his smell," she said, laughing. And she turned away, running back to the encampment.

I looked at my watch. There was still more than an hour before sunset. I rushed to my Land Rover and drove as fast as I could, hoping to reach the far end of the valley. With powerful binoculars I searched the horizon, and saw nothing but horizontal emptiness. I climbed the slope of a rocky mountain and searched again for the caravan, until darkness had engulfed the desert entirely. But I saw no humans, nothing that could prove Aicha right.

It took me about two hours to return to the encampment because of the darkness. This gave me plenty of time to think things over. If, from where I was, and despite my powerful binoculars, I hadn't been able to see a human being approaching the encampment, Aicha obviously couldn't have seen anyone from where she was standing earlier that afternoon. And since no one can ever predict exactly when a caravan will return, I was extremely skeptical of her ability to foretell her husband's return. I decided to investigate further. Thinking about the possibility that Aicha had faculties of clairvoyance or precognition, I looked for her and asked if her husband was to arrive alone or with the whole caravan; and if so, if all the caravaneers were coming together or spread out in small groups.

"I don't know," she said. "But he wouldn't come back alone, traveling without his friends." I went to sleep, knowing that if the caravaneers were indeed to arrive during the night, the noise of their arrival would awake me.

"Douchan . . . Douchan . . ." Someone was whispering my name, softly and quietly at first, then gradually raising the tone of his voice, until I opened my eyes. (Tuareg do that so as not to awaken someone brutally. They are aware of the importance of the awakening, which decides the mood of the whole day. Many cultures of tradition use this technique of quiet awakening, for they believe that the human soul travels during sleep to other universes and other levels of time/ space—a dream being just a memory, a remembrance of such voyages. Calling someone's name quietly will give his soul time to get back into the body before awakening.) It was Oizek who was shaking me. "Aicha's husband is here! She was right; he just arrived."

It was about 5:00 A.M., and Aicha's husband had arrived alone. He had left his comrades in Niger before they had finished their business, and traveled with another caravan going to Libya, where he could get cheap silver. From there, he had journeyed alone back to the encampment.

If Aicha had clairvoyance or precognition faculties, she would have known that her husband was to arrive alone. Therefore, there is only one explanation: she had telepathic contact with her husband as he was approaching home.

The *taleb* was right; she has the power.

☾

The following story also belongs to the realm of telepathic phenomena.

Without telephones or other modern means of communication, news spreads rapidly throughout the Tuareg empire of wind and silence, despite the distances to be covered. Tribal news is transmitted when the Tuareg, practicing small nomadism, meet during their journeys. (*Small nomadism* consists of wandering from pasture to pasture within a tribal territory. When one pasture becomes exhausted, the Tuareg break their camp and move on to the next available pasture.) Saharan news is often exchanged around a well—often just a hole two or three feet wide, but very deep. There, those practicing small nomadism meet Tuareg practicing *wide nomadism*—caravaneers leading their long goods-carrying caravans across the Sahara up to Gao, Timbuktu, Agades, and other cities of black Africa; or driving massive herds of camels to, or back from, the green pastures of the Sahel, south of the desert. And when they meet, Tuareg drink hot tea and chat—about X who did this and that and met Y who will be going to the wedding of Z which will take place near the XYZ well, and so on.

Sometimes in parting two men will arrange for a rendezvous at a given place on a fixed date, which may be three months or a year down the road, but they always add, "*Inch Allah*" ("With Allah's will").

One day, in the middle of nowhere, away from wells and nomadic paths, I stumbled upon a Tuareg sitting in the shadow of his camel. Judging from the tracks on the sand around the camel, I knew he had been there at least one day. (He had moved around his animal to get into its shade.) After we exchanged the traditional greeting, I brought some tea from the car for the tea ceremony and, along with my companions, we drank with him and chatted.

"What are you doing here?" I asked.

"I'm waiting for a friend," he said.

"Since when?"

"Three days."

"When was he supposed to be here?"

"One of these days."

"How long will you stay here, waiting for him?"

"Perhaps two or three more days only. I am running short of water."

"How will your friend know that you were here, waiting for him?"

"I'll leave him a message on a stone, so we'll meet another time somewhere else."

The Tuareg tradition is oral only, and is passed on from one generation to the other. According to these people, nothing of great importance must ever be written down because anyone might read it. Yet the whole Sahara is covered with writings in Tifinah, the Tuareg alphabet. These are only messages, like the one this Tuareg was to leave for his friend; they can be deciphered from left to right or from right to left, from bottom to top or top to bottom, according to codes known only to the writer and the person for whom the message is left.

"When did you set a date with him?"

"About seven months ago."

"Where?"

"In Gao." (Gao is a city in Mali, about six hundred miles from where we were.)

I had to question him at length, and patiently, to finally learn that he was coming from the east and going south, and that his friend was traveling from west to north. This place was, indeed the best spot for such a rendezvous.

I looked all around us and saw only rocky hills, sand, and stones. "How do you know that this is the meeting place?" I asked. "Can't miss the place," he said, describing and giving names to everything that surrounded us.

Since sunset was approaching, our party decided to share our meal with the Tuareg and spend the night there. The next day, during the morning meal, I told the Tuareg I would leave him some water so that he could wait for his friend a few more days.

"I don't need more water, thank you. You'll need it for your long trip more than I will."

"I don't understand what you mean," I said.

"Last night, my friend told me where he was. Running short of water, he had to make a detour to fill up his *guerbas* [goatskins used to carry water] at a well. He is two days from here."

"How did he tell you that? Did you dream about him?"

"No, I didn't dream about him. He just told me where he was."

"But how did he tell you that?"

"He told me that in my mind. And in the same way I answered him that I will be waiting for him."

"How do you do that?"

"I just think about him, deeply, repeating what I want him

to know. And I know he is getting my message when I hear his answer."

"So you are sure that your friend will be here in two days?"

"*Inch Allah!*"

I turned to my companions and proposed that we wait two days, to see what would happen. They agreed.

At the end of the second day, a silhouette appeared from beyond the rocky hills, moving toward us. It was the friend for whom the Tuareg had been waiting.

After the traditional greetings and the ceremonial tea, I asked the newcomer if he knew that we were waiting for him with his friend. He said no. "My friend just told me he would wait for me." (If this Tuareg had used clairvoyance, he would have known of our presence with his friend.)

In conclusion, I offer another story, one that I find quite amazing.

We were in Djanet, an Algerian city not far from the Libyan border. I intended to drive from there to Timbuktu, in a straight line across the Sahara. It was a life-threatening voyage covering some eight hundred miles of rocky mountains, deep valleys, wide plains covered with sharp volcanic stones, and large extents of sand dunes and dangerous quicksand. Because maps of the area were not precise, it would have been ill advised to make this journey without the help of a guide to recognize landmarks and to lead us safely through the desert's many dangers—and to find wells in case we ran short of water.

Generally, all Tuareg nomads have an amazing faculty for finding their way in the desert. They always know where they are, even if they have never been there before. This is part of their cultural heritage; besides giving their children knowledge of their traditions and, through fables, their values, philosophy, and wisdom, Tuareg parents also teach them the nomadic life. They inscribe the desert in their children's memory: how and where to find water; how to recognize and use medicinal plants; how to get their bearings at night by looking at the stars and, during the day, by smelling the hot sand and caressing its grains, which are regionally distinctive, and by memorizing the colors and shapes of nature.

The head of the military outpost in Djanet told us where to find a man named Iken, who according to him, would be the best guide for our trip. As I was about to leave, the commander added that Iken was blind, but not to worry. I thought this was a joke and said so. He repeated that I shouldn't worry, that Iken was the best guide.

"The best you have, or the best one you have left?" I asked, trying to smile.

"Don't be worried!" he repeated, laughing.

"Was he born blind, or did he got this infirmity in his adult life?" I asked nervously.

"He became blind about ten years ago. Eye infection," he answered, stretching his hand to signify that the meeting was over.

Iken was a tall, thin man in his fifties. Talking with him, we learned that he had spent his childhood and adolescence with his father, who led caravans all over the Sahara. Then he became a caravaneer, working at that until he was hired as a guide by the French Foreign Legion when the French ruled Algeria. When he was thirty he lost his sight as a result of a poorly treated case of trachoma. (Many Saharan nomads suffer from trachoma. Owing to a lack of medication, the infection, which is spread by flies, progresses, making the eyelids swell so much that the eyelashes rub against the eye, inflaming and frosting the cornea, resulting in loss of sight. As a last attempt to avoid total blindness, members of Les Petits Frères de Foucault, a religious congregation dwelling in the Hoggar region, perform a minor operation—which I learned, and which I performed a few times—on the patient's swollen eyelids. It consists of cutting off, horizontally, a lamella of the swollen eyelids, to shorten the eyelids so that the lashes stop rubbing the cornea. With the aid of antibiotics for the wounds, the eyelids heal successfully.)

I described to Iken the trip I intended to take.

"I see. . . . I see." he repeated as I briefed him.

"Have you made this trip before?" I asked.

"Not exactly the same itinerary, but I see very well what you want to do. We can leave tomorrow night," he said.

"Why at night? I would prefer driving during the day so that I can film."

"As you wish, but once we get past the mountain region we must drive before 10:00 A.M and after 5:00 P.M."

"Why?"

"It is summer there already. It's a furnace, with sandstorms, and sixty-two, sixty-five degrees Celsius every day. Tires tear apart easily, and the engine will give out."

It may seem surprising, but despite his infirmity I felt confident with Iken as our guide, mainly because I have a blind friend who has made me aware that blind people, forced to deal with their lost sight, are usually quite in tune with some ESP faculties. Michel Delacroix is his name. He lives in Brussels. Despite his infirmity, he has been called to the bar and practices criminal law. He used to visit me often when I was living in Brussels, a block from his home; he loved spending time touching, caressing, and smelling each artifact in my primitive-art collection. He could easily tell whenever a new object had been added, without my saying anything. Besides knowing, from the amount of dust covering things, how long it had been since I had cleaned my place, he was able to talk for hours about an object he was holding, discussing its shape, features, and most amazingly, its colors—which, he said, he could literally feel through his fingers.

One day I was following the maze of never-ending corridors of the law court, looking for the room where I had to deal with a traffic-violation citation, when I heard Michel's voice calling me from behind. When I asked him how he knew I was there, he said, "You passed in front of me as I was moving out of a courtroom. I knew it was you."

"But how did you know it was me? My cologne? The sound of my footsteps?"

"The whole . . . and nothing in detail, really, but I knew it was you!"

"Can you recognize other people like that?"

"Only those I care for."

Amazed by what had happened, I decided, a few days later, to try an experiment to ascertain the elements Michel used to recognize me. I knew where he got off the bus and what street he took to walk home when coming back from the law court. I called the law court to check which days he was on duty. I replaced my usual cologne with another. And I waited for him halfway between the bus stop and his home, standing on the sidewalk he would use.

A dozen feet before he reached me, Michel, moving his white cane from side to side to assure safe passage, began showing signs of increased alertness. He slowed down, and his head began almost to follow the lateral moves of his cane, as if he were looking for something. I leaned against a wall to allow him a larger passage. As he passed in front of me, he instinctively looked at me, frowning and smelling the air, but continued walking slowly. Then he stopped as though waiting for me to say something. I kept quiet and remained motionless, feeling guilty about my little trick, and he left.

The following day I repeated the experiment, but this time I waited on the opposite sidewalk. Michel had the same reactions as the previous day. His dead eyes looked at me again; then he moved away.

I thought he would call me in the next few days. He didn't. I waited a week and paid him a visit, wearing my usual cologne. In the course of the conversation, he asked if I had changed my cologne lately. I said yes. "So it was you!" he exclaimed "I knew it was you. I was reluctant to call you because of the different scent I was smelling. I didn't want to make a fool of myself in my neighborhood by calling your name, but I was ready to bet it was you!"

I explained my motives to my friend, and he forgave me.

If he couldn't smell me or hear my footsteps, how had he been able to perceive my presence?

"I had an inexplicable feeling, an uncontrollable certitude!" said Michel.

Clairvoyance or telepathy?

Since we left Djanet, Iken had been sitting on the spare tire, which was strapped to the hood. "I need to breathe the smell of the desert," he had explained. "That tells me where I am, for each place has a particular smell. I can't do that from inside the car. And from here I can hear the different noises the tires make on the ground; that tells me a lot about the terrain.

"You must look carefully at the signs I will make to lead you. My left hand will show you what direction you must follow on the left side, my right hand on the right side. Two hands up tells you to speed up, two hands stretched laterally says you must stop, and to reduce your speed I will beat the air with my two hands. I also need help from all of you." (I was accompanied by Danièle and my assistant, Philippe.) "Don't talk while driving, but look carefully at the landscape all around you."

"Why?" I asked. I knew the answer, but I wanted to hear him give the reason.

"That, too, helps me to see where I am," he said.

It wasn't easy to drive with Iken sitting on the hood, blocking my sight. Following the directions he gave me, I had to zigzag carefully between a series of natural obstacles: quicksand, huge volcanic rocks, sand dunes, deep crevices dug by ancient rivers. To maneuver successfully, I had to drive with my head sticking out the window to see what was happening on the left side while Philippe, looking out the right window, gave me instructions about what was happening on his side.

Despite these technical problems, I felt confident with Iken as our guide.

One day, Iken's hands ordered me to stop the car. We helped him down from the hood. He sat on his heels and grabbed a handful of sand, which he smelled deeply and for a long time. Then he caressed the sand and played with its grain, carefully studying its texture. After a while, he stood up and, all anxiety released, said, "Now I know where we are. We should go more in that direction." His hand showed the direction to follow.

Another time, at night, running short of water, we were desperately searching for a well. Instead we stumbled upon a large dried-out bush, three or four feet high. Iken caressed the dead branches, smelled whatever was growing or dried all around, and finally gave new directions. And a few hours later we found water.

We reached Timbuktu as planned. We couldn't have missed it with Iken as our guide. Concerning his faculties, one could argue that they don't all belong to the realm of telepathy, some being more in the nature of claivoyance. But the point is that he was in tune with an aspect of the brain that allowed him to guide us through the desert.

"So, what will you do now, Iken?" I asked as we were getting ready to go our separate ways.

"Stay here and visit some friends I have not seen in years. Then I'll find a caravan going my direction and travel back home with them," he answered.

Some of the Tuareg we later used as guides also refused to guide from inside the car, but for a different reason. Accustomed to traveling on camels, they were unable to recognize landmarks from inside the car, because the configuration and the relief of the terrain were written in their memory as viewed from the perspective of a camel's back. So they traveled on the car's roof, since it was about the same height as a saddle on a camel's hump. But that caused a problem: I couldn't see the guide, and with the noise of the engine I couldn't hear his directions. Therefore Philippe had to sit on the spare tire fixed on the hood, acting as intermediary between the guide and me, transmitting his messages and directions.

The other problem I had with these guides was in driving at night with the headlights on. Because they were accustomed to traveling by the light of the stars and moon, they couldn't find their bearings at night because the car's headlights distorted the terrain's appearance. So I had to drive with the headlights off. However I must admit that it was an amazing experience, truly magical to drive by the light of the moon and the stars, with the feeling of being suspended between the human unknown and the mysterious—becoming, at last, a part of the cosmic reality, where anything could happen, even the impossible.

These are firsthand accounts of experiences that I had among the Tuareg. When I traveled through the Australian desert and in the Kalahari with the Bushmen, I also heard many stories testifying that people living in large desert expanses—where one has to travel long distances before meeting other humans—seem to be more in tune than others with that part of the brain that allows telepathy, because this is needed to insure survival.

I experienced many of these strange phenomena with peoples of tradition. They can't all be coincidental. I sometimes think, though, that some of them are the result of intuition, which these people seem to have a facility for because they are forced to use it for their survival. However, we shouldn't reject the possibility that many Fourth World peoples are skilled in telepathy. Many of us have had telepathic experiences at least once in our lives. But this faculty has a tendency to atrophy in us since we don't use it in our everyday lives. Picking up a telephone or writing a letter has become more common and easier than concentrating deeply to send someone a message.

I have noticed that most peoples of tradition live more in tune with themselves than we do. They have developed intuition and primal animal feelings more than reasoning. In living so closely to nature, intimately and deeply involved with it, they have learned its language. Perhaps because they don't have the choice to survive in other ways, they have been forced to be in tune with those aspects of their brain that allow them to have higher levels of consciousness.

5

Shamans and Sorcerers of the Andes

When my friend Michel Drachoussoff, a documentary filmmaker, came back from his yearlong trip to the Bolivian Andes, he told me so many amazing stories about men who cure with plants and secret prayer that I decided to go to the Andes myself, following his tracks.

My search for shamans, medicine men, and sorcerers began in La Paz, Bolivia, the highest city in the world. Anyone who gets sick there can go to physicians trained in the United States. But if modern therapy fails, people can try the native medicines, which the Indians always use. In the Calle Villares, the so-called magic market, there are hundreds of plant remedies for sale that will cure every disease known to man, and drive evil spirits away. Alongside native herbs such as *ayawasqua* and *estingo* you can find marijuana, tobacco, brightly colored wool, flamingo feathers, and mummified llama fetuses—very important in making magic.

It is not all superstition. Scientists from the University of Lima, Peru, have come to Bolivia, to conduct ongoing research into the effects of *coca, datura, quinua,* and other medicinal plants.

Up to the time of the Inca invasion, coca leaves were regarded as sacred and were used for religious and medicinal purpose only. During the Inca empire, coca was reserved for the imperial family, priests, and dignitaries. The people were given permission only to drink *mate de*

coca, a coca infusion that has a soothing and calming effect and effi-
ciently heals headaches, toothaches, and rheumatism; cooked with
honey, it cures mouth infections. Only miners were excepted from the
restrictions on coca. They were allowed to chew coca leaves because
this helped them endure the hardship of their work.

After the Spanish invasion, this miners' privilege became the
habit of a whole people. Indeed, millions of Indians who were suddenly reduced to slavery had only two means of forgetting their new
condition: alcohol and coca. At the end of the sixteenth century, about
a thousand tons of coca leaves were sold yearly in the city of Potosí
alone. Indians deprived themselves of food just to obtain a few of these
so-called leaves of oblivion.

Nowadays, the consumption of coca leaves is still very high
among the Indian population of cities and towns. Impregnated with
saliva and chewed with a small piece of *lejia* (*quinua* ashes that have
been solidified with other ingredients), coca diminishes feelings of
hunger and soothes pain. In the country, the consumption of coca is
much lower. There it is used mainly as a medication and for religious
and divination ceremonies. The philosopher Lopez Albujar wrote:

> Coca is the green bible made of thousands of leaves. In each of them lies
> a psalm of peace. Coca is a virtue not a vice; nor is a vice the glass of wine
> that the priest drinks every day during the mass. Coca is the seal of all the
> Indian's pacts, the sacramental deed of all his celebrations, the consola-
> tion of all his griefs, the incense of all his superstitions, the remedy to all
> his illnessess, the consecrated host of all his cults.

Since the dawn of mankind, even when illness was seen as having
to do with evil spirits and was dealt with in magical rituals, every culture has been aware of the healing properties of plants and other natural elements, and has used them to prevent or survive illness. And
these natural elements have been used to heal in both the homeopathic
and the allopathic healing systems. Natural healing has been used
alone or as a complement to other healing methods.

Several thousand years ago, the Chinese healer Kwang Ti wrote
about the medicinal properties of plants. Li Che Ten in his *Peng T'Sao,*
which may have been written as early as 2,500 B.C., gave the names of
eleven hundred medicinal plants divided into sixty-eight categories,
and eight thousand different recipes and formulas to prepare them.

Four thousand years ago, the Egyptians got from China, India,
and Persia the art of infusing plants, which had already been practiced

in those countries for thousands of years. And the Greeks got it from Egyptians.

But plants are not the only natural elements that can heal; there are also a great number of minerals and organic materials that have medicinal properties—bones, animal fetuses, horns, and so on. Visit any of the shops in your local Chinatown that specialize in natural elements that can cure diseases and you will get an idea of the diversity of the Chinese pharmacopoeia.

☾

The Indians of the Andes generally ignore the details of human anatomy and have no concept of the existence of germs. For them, illness is the result of an imbalance provoked by an *enemy*—a natural element or a spell—that one must fight.

According to the Indians, there are two categories of illnesses: those of God and those of the devil. Illnesses of God generally have a natural cause: cold, wind, heat, a fall, and so forth. Illnesses of the devil include the nervous maladies—epilepsy, nervous breakdowns, and so on. These are believed either to be provoked by angry gods or to result from spells cast by sorcerers, and are seen as being the works of demons who took away the sick person's soul or a part of his body, or who put something extraneous into the sick person.

Illnesses of God can be treated by a *curandero* with medicinal plants—that is, by a process of natural healing—or by a physician from the city. Illnesses of the devil, however, can be treated only by a healer who, to avoid the psychic and physical disintegration of the patient, must recover the lost element and put it back in the patient, or must chase away the extraneous matter; in other words, the healer must *rebalance energies.* To restore the psychic and physical balance of the patient, the healer must perform a sacrifice, which will ally him with the force of the most powerful divinities. He will give the patient medicinal plants as a complement to the magic treatment.

Living far away from dispensaries and hospitals, and too poor to afford them, 80 percent of the peasant population use the services of *curanderos* when they are sick. From a religious, social, and medical point of view the *curanderos* are indispensable to the physical and psychic balance of a community. Some are charlatans, of course, taking advantage of the peasants' credulity and naiveté to extract a few pesos from them. But in the majority of cases they are people of talent and integrity.

The function of *curandero* can be carried out by a shaman if he is a healer; otherwise it is a *collasiri* who does the healing work. A *collasiri* is someone who belongs to the religious clergy and devotes himself to medicine.

There is a fundamental difference between the shamans of the Andes and those of the Amazon. The shamans of the Amazon are endowed with all powers. The shamans of the Andes, though they, too, are the main spiritual leaders and are able to contact the supernatural world during a state of trance induced by drugs (cocaine or the San Pedro cactus, a powerful hallucinogen), may be endowed with all powers, but not systematically. And if they are not so endowed, they can surround themselves with others who have the powers they lack.

For instance a village can have, in addition to a shaman, a *collasiri* who devotes himself to medicine, a *yatiri* who masters the art of divination, a *pako* who does white magic, and a *laika* who performs black magic to do evil work. Consequently, shamans can be a combination of *collasiri, yatiri, pako,* and *laika,* but none of these individuals is a shaman.

Also, some of these members of the clergy may have more than one power, and take on more than one function. For instance, in some regions of the Andes where no medicinal plants grow, the *collasiri* will often also serve as sorcerer and magician and will treat his patients using magic healing techniques.

In the villages on the northeastern slopes of the Andes live the Khallawayas, who are considered the elite of the Andes' healers. They are shamans whose repute in the art of healing was known five centuries ago, at the time of the Incas.

When, in the fifteenth century, the Incas invaded the Bolivian high plateaus, they discovered a valley, east of Lake Titicaca, which they called Quollo Suyo, meaning "the land of remedies." The inhabitants had a deep religious knowledge, and their art of healing was much superior to the one practiced by the doctors and diviners of the imperial family based in Cuzco, the Incan capital. The discovery of these people, with their advanced medical, astrological, and magic culture, so impressed the Incas that they called them Khallawayas (in Machchaj Juyai, the secret Incan language, *khalla* means "priest," and *wayai* means "libations"), and invited them to exercise their art and talent in Cuzco. The Khallawayas adopted Quechua, the language used in this region, and learned the sacred language of the Incas, which they still use during their ceremonies nowadays.

The sudden arrival of the conquistadors forced the Khallawayas to move back to their original valley in the Charazani region, where they survived, and still do, impervious to the vagaries of history.

The origin of these people and of their culture is still a mystery. Their name may actually be derived from the Aymara *quolla waya,* meaning "medication" and "carry on the shoulder." Their medical knowledge is quite elaborate and has been scientifically recognized. During the 1900 Universal Exhibition in Paris, Bolivia presented the most important collection of medicinal plants ever gathered—the Khallawaya pharmacopoeia. Nowadays, some Khallawayas considered masters in the science of medicinal plants are regularly invited to lecture at the medical faculty of Lima, Peru. Two examples of their knowledge are their use, over the centuries, of penicillin and oxytetracycline. They discovered penicillin during the Inca period. They mix ferment from banana trees or mold from corn or grease with spiderwebs to form a blackish paste, which is applied like a pomade to infected wounds. Extracted from black mud, oxytetracycline is used as a cold or warm poultice.

The Khallawaya pharmacopoeia comprises hundreds of plants that healers either cultivate or gather on slopes that range in altitude from one thousand to ten thousand feet, offering different microclimates and therefore a large variety of plants.

The prestige of these people is not limited to their art of healing. Even the Incas were impressed by their philosophy and their concept of the divine, which they had been developing since the dawn of their existence. In order to better understand the esoteric side of their art of healing, it's worthwhile taking a brief look at their religious principles.

For the Khallawayas, there are three main divinities: Tutujanawin, Pacha Caman, and Unaru Khochaj. Tutujanawin is the supreme being who rules the whole of visible and invisible existence. He is the energy that fuels the universe and gives life to beings. He is the personification of the cosmic reality, which shows itself in the fusion of what exists and what does not exist. This principle is the basis of the Khallawaya doctrine of opposition. For the Khallawayas, the concept of existence lies in the balance produced by opposing forces. The world couldn't exist without the forces that create its stability in opposing themselves: good is opposed to evil, day to night, health to illness. Some stars and planets broadcast beneficent emanations, others malignant.

Pacha Caman ("supreme light") created human beings. He is the father of the sun god Pacha Tata (or Inti, the Inca sun god), the earth goddess Pacha Mama, and the moon goddess Occlo. Inti impregnates

Pacha Mama permanently so that she can give birth to human beings, animals, and plants. Pacha Caman is in fact the god who manages the world.

Unaru Khochaj is the son of Inti. He symbolizes purity and justice. He has been sent to earth to preach love and banish envy and rancor from people's hearts. (Note that the Khallaway religious pantheon existed long before Catholicism was brought into South America by the conquistadors.) He corresponds to the god Wiracocha of the Amayara people, and has similarities with Pachacamac, the god of the Indians who lived on the Peruvian coast.

The religious pantheon of the Khallawayas also consists of many saints, demons, gods, and goddesses. Following are the main ones:

△ Purun Runa is the mythical man living in the mountains, who captures young women to seduce them.

△ The goddess Achalay dwells in jungles and isolated places; she subjugates young men.

△ Pachagargarey is the goddess of dawn and hope.

△ Ekeko is the god of happiness and well-being, who with lavishness dispenses favors to humans.

△ Illapa is the god of thunder and lightning; he takes the rain necessary to humans from a river that crosses the sky (the Milky Way).

△ The woman Chchasca is a paragon of beauty; she is the personification of the star Venus.

△ Supay is the genie of evil; he holds all the wealth of the world. (One can compare him to the Hindu goddess Shiva.)

△ Yawar Chchonga is a vampire-sorcerer.

The Khallawayas also worship spirits, ancestors, and *achachillas,* the souls of those who belonged to past generations. Living in mountains, rivers, and valleys, *achachillas* influence people's destinies and are invoked during some religious ceremonies.

For Khallawayas, a human being is composed of three vital elements: the body, the soul, and the spirit. The body, the only tangible substance of the being, cannot live without the soul, which is the divine breath of Pacha Caman—life, sensibility, movement, the faculty of thinking. When the soul goes away, the body dies. The spirit is the fluid that gives consistency to the body; it is in charge of the pathological control of the body, without causing life or death. When the spirit moves away from the body, the body does not die, but suffers an abnormal state that constitutes illness. However, during sleep, the spirit also can get out of the body and wander in the external world. Sometimes it leaves the body and refuses to return; this can be caused by a curse. A Khallawaya will then need to call the spirit back to the body by performing a series of magical and religious rituals.

Each time my party reached a new Khallawaya village, we had to go through the same ritual. First I had to ask the chief for permission to stay in his village. Then we had to discuss the reasons for our request with the council of elders. Finally, since the decision about our staying would ultimately be made by the spirits (for only the spirits knew if we were good or bad people, and could foresee the results of our behavior with the villagers), the village chief called the local shaman to perform a *kapita*, a ritual of divination with coca leaves. What follows is a detailed description of one such divination session similar to those performed in other villages throughout the Andes.

The shaman joined us. He sat on a bench, stretched the *kapita*—a small piece of colored, woven wool—on his lap, and unwrapped a bunch of coca leaves from another piece of fabric. (Throughout the Andes, these leaves are the tool most often used for divination.) He selected a dozen leaves that had a perfect, regular shape and a nice green color, put them on the *kapita*, and began chewing the others.

When he started to sweat, visibly entering another state of consciousness, a kind of trance, he picked up the selected coca leaves and rubbed them gently between his hands while invoking his favorite divinities as his allies; they were to be involved in the decision about our staying. Then he brought his mouth close to his joined hands, still holding the coca leaves, and whispered, "Coca, little mother, you who know everything, tell me everything in the name of ancestors; can we accept these foreigners?"

Then, maintaining his deep concentration and keeping his eyes closed, he half-opened his hands to the sky and blew three times, to give life to the coca leaves. They would be the intermediaries between him and the divinities. He questioned the coca leaves again to insure the communication and again invoked the divinities. Then he opened his hands and let the leaves fall one by one to the *kapita*, conscientiously studying how they fell and positioned themselves.

He repeated this procedure three times. Then he picked up the leaves from the *kapita*, began to chew them, and took them out of his mouth to see how they looked. Their appearance and good taste confirmed the divine answer: "Yes, you may stay as long as you wish." In every village we visited but one, the answer was always the same.

Using a lot of patience and a complicated network of contacts, I finally succeeded, with my companions (one of them spoke the Quechua language, used throughout the Andes), in finding a village where a Khallawaya healer was living. His name was Don Florentino, and he was reputed to be able to heal diseases like tuberculosis and polio. After many days of suspicion, he allowed us to accompany him in his daily gathering of medicinal plants in his garden and on the steep slopes of the valley. And he told us the story of his training.

"When I was twelve," said Don Florentino, "my uncle gave me a secret mixture of plants to eat. And I saw a jaguar, as tall as a man, with steel claws about to rip me apart. Then the jaguar changed into Pacha Mama, and she let me suck her breasts while she sang a song. Later, when I awoke, I sang the song to my uncle, who said that was the right song, and he agreed to teach me about healing and plants. That was thirty years ago."

A week or so later what I was hoping for happened: Don Florentino was called to heal someone living in a nearby village. And he agreed to let us watch him treat the patient.

We went into the village ahead of the Khallawaya healer and his apprentice in hopes of being able to examine the patient and question his family. The house where the sick man lived, with his wife and his sister, was at the end of a pathway edged with San Pedro cactuses— which have powerful hallucinogenic properties. We were welcomed into their courtyard, which had been carefully swept by the patient's wife and his sister.

The patient, a man in his forties, was lying on one side of the courtyard. He was very weak, and had a high fever—almost 103 degrees—and had great difficulty breathing normally; he was delirious. His wife explained that he had had pain in his chest for many months, but had started to cough blood only recently. She said he had gone to a dispensary a month before, but despite the medication the doctor gave him, his health was growing worse. We believed the man was suffering from a severe pulmonary infection, probably a bad case of tuberculosis.

The two women, who were wearing their prettiest mantles, stood up when Don Florentino and his apprentice entered the courtyard. While the Khallawaya healer was exchanging words with the two women, his apprentice set on a small stone altar a *chusilla,* a kind of tablecloth made of alpaca wool, which he covered with an *istalla,* a richly decorated cloth. Then the healer took out of his bag the basic elements of the *mesa,* meaning *offering* in this case. And that was the start of the ceremony, where the two primordial healing elements were mixed:

religion and science—that is, magico-religious rituals and the science of medicinal plants.

"Healing plants are the least important part of the ritual," explained Don Florentino. "The universe is made of opposing forces: good and evil, wrong and right. It is the balance between the opposing forces that makes something exist. Over the years I have collected objects of good and objects of evil, and I use them according to what I want to produce. Today, before I consulted with the patient, I put a llama fetus on the *istalla,* along with two wrong things, rotten eggs and wool that was woven in the wrong way; and two right things, coca leaves and copal resin. When I arrange these things on the *istalla,* it becomes a battle ground. This tells Pacha Mama that I want to reestablish the balance between wrong and right for this man. Then I can manipulate the forces of sickness and the forces of health for him."

"What is the meaning of the mummified llama fetus?" I asked, knowing that such an item costs more than anything else in the markets.

"The llama is a semidivine animal. A miscarriage is an abnormal birth. So a llama fetus is evidence that even the gods of fertility can make mistakes. It generates very strong magical forces. This object in the hands of a sorcerer can be a powerful weapon for doing evil. But now I must pray; Pacha Mama is sometimes very unpredictable."

Don Florentino kneeled down and began to concentrate, whispering prayers to Pacha Mama. Meanwhile, the patient's wife and sister sat and, like the healer, placed on their own *istalla,* which was set on a small bench, the elements of their offering to Pacha Mama: amulets, coca leaves, copal resin, tufts of wool, an egg, and a llama fetus.

When his prayers to Pacha Mama were over, Don Florentino stood up and went over to the two women's *istalla* to take their offerings. While reciting sacred invocations in the secret language of the Incas, he mixed the women's offering with his own. "To travel in the invisible universe," said Don Florentino, "I need to be in the center of this one. I invoke the seven directions: north, south, east, west, the above, the below, and the center."

Then he threw everything he was holding into the fire. He closed his eyes and remained motionless for a long time, as if his spirit had left the living.

"To remind Pacha Mama to keep everything balanced," he eventually said, "I burn the two *mesa.* We breathe the smoke and Pacha Mama breathes the smoke. When the world is rebalanced right here on this spot, only then will I diagnose the patient's illness." One first heals the soul and the spirit by rebalancing opposing forces, and then treats the body.

Don Florentino approached the patient and began the next step of the healing process: the *limpia,* or cleansing. He pulled a live guinea pig out of his poncho and rubbed the man's body with it, asking him to breathe on it regularly. While doing this, the healer squeezed the guinea pig's neck, eventually choking it to death. The animal's death had to coincide with the end of the operation. Now the patient was free from the evil influence that had caused his sickness; it had been transferred to the animal. "The patient couldn't breathe," explained the Khallawaya healer, "so I made a transfer between him and the guinea pig. Now he can breathe easily and the guinea pig is the one who is choking."

The apprentice cut the throat of the guinea pig and put its blood and viscera into an empty shell. (Among all methods of divination used in the Andes, examining viscera is the most widespread.) Don Florentino looked at the contents of the shell and said, "The trouble with doctors in the city is that they diagnose the patient by dissecting him. We dissect the guinea pig instead, and carefully study the way its blood coagulates and the consistency of the excrement in its lower intestine. In this case, since everything is loose, he only has tuberculosis. And the man is lucky: the omen says that the divinities have accepted our prayers. I won't have to fight any supernatural demons to treat him."

Then Don Florentino took from his bag the plants that, with the help of divinities, were to treat the bodily damage caused by the illness. What we would call the medical part of the treatment was very brief. Eucalyptus leaves were wrapped around the patient's head, and he was given a diluted drink of coca leaves and *quinua* ashes boiled in water. Soon his fever broke and he started talking rationally. When we saw him a month later, he was working like a healthy man, with neither pains in the chest nor bloody coughs. He said he hadn't felt so good in a long time.

It is only after an apprenticeship that can take up to twelve years that the Khallaway healer's son, or a member of his family, gets from the assembly of elders and notables the authorization to exercise his art. The sometimes-amazing results obtained by these Khallawaya healers seem to be proof of the efficacy of their science. Functioning simultaneously as psychologists, psychiatrists, herbalists, homeopaths, and physicians, they practice a complex art, yet they claim that without the help of divinities, they would have no healing power.

The Khallawaya healers' methods are hard for us to understand, but Don Florentino insisted that the most important part of his cure is supernatural, especially if the sickness is a manifestation of demonic spells sent by black magic.

It was among the Sicuyas that we were able to witness the healing of a patient suffering from an illness of the devil; he was the victim of a spell cast by a sorcerer.

Feared by their neighbors because of their fierceness in fighting, and considered savage and anthropophagous by the other Indian tribes of the northern Potosi region, the Sicuyas have kept their ancient magico-religious, agricultural, and artisanal traditions intact. Using Quechua, spoken throughout the Andes, only for commercial purposes, among themselves they speak Aymara, which they consider the language of intimacy, feelings, and poetry, as well as secrecy and magic.

The divination session that was to decide the question of our staying in the village was performed by the local sorcerer-healer, a man in his fifties named Sylverio. He was born with his left hand deformed. He told us later that all sorcerers have some physical defect, that this is the way the gods mark them as having special powers. Once we had a positive answer from the divinities, it took us only two days to become friendly with the *hilankho,* the tribal chief. (This title is reassigned every year. The *hilankho* presides over the council of the elders, whose members remain on the council until death.)

And we rapidly developed a very warm relationship with Pamphillo, the schoolteacher. His son, who was five, had epilepsy, which the doctors in La Paz had been unable to cure. I asked Pamphillo if he would consider asking the sorcerer-healer to try to cure his son.

"No way!" he answered. "That's just a bunch of superstitions." The schoolteacher's convictions were congruent with his governmental duty: to teach the Indians to change their way of life in order to move them into the modern age. The process begins by the teacher's advising the children to mistrust the traditional medicine performed by sorcerers and instead to turn toward chemical medications given by physicians in dispensaries and hospitals. The teacher exalts science and modern ways of living—such as wearing clothes that come from the city. The children learn math, geography, and Spanish.

One day, however, Pamphillo was ready to try anything to help his son, whose health was growing worse. To my surprise, he asked Sylverio to try a ritual cure for the boy. The sorcerer, seeing an opportunity to prove to the schoolteacher that he had real powers, gladly agreed to perform a magic healing ritual that night.

At 8:00 P.M. we gathered in the teacher's house, with his wife, their son, Sylverio, and the *hilankho.* The door was locked from inside so that nobody—neither human beings nor spirits—could enter or leave during the ceremony. We assembled in the main room, which was lighted only by candles and a small fire burning in the hearth.

Coca leaves, *chicha* beer, *cuti* (corn grains to be used for divination), and several medicinal plants were set on the table, along with the heart of a llama that had been sacrificed few days before for another religious purpose.

Sylverio distributed coca leaves and *chicha* beer to everybody except Pamphillo's son. And everyone began drinking and chewing silently. (I disliked *chicha* beer once I learned how it is made: old women chew corn and spit it into a bowl, where it ferments. It is said that when sorcerers drink a lot of *chicha,* they sometimes have a vision of Pacha Mama nursing all the animals of the field, giving them enough life to last another year.)

The silence was sometimes interrupted by the whispered words of the sorcerer, who began to perform the *cuti* divination, reading the way the corn grains were positioned in his palm after he took them from the table. Four hours later nothing had happened, except that we all were quite intoxicated. The effects of the coca and alcohol had created an unreal atmosphere. The sorcerer continued to whisper the same word, *suerte,* which means "luck."

All of a sudden, the sorcerer and the tribal chief, each took a censer, and filled them with small pieces of glowing charcoal from the hearth, over which they dropped copal resin and other incense. Sylverio prayed: "Pacha Mama, Holy Earth, you shall protect this house. Do not allow its inhabitants to be overcome with illness. Protect them from all misfortune. Pacha Mama, protect me from evil, and next year I shall serve you even better."

When the room was filled with the smell and smoke of burning incense, the sorcerer and the tribal chief, each still carrying a censer, moved out of the house to pray to Pfarsi Mamay, the moon goddess; hands stretched toward the bright orb, they also implored the Holy Virgin of Copacabana. (Better to put all chances on one's side; there are more powers in two divinities than in one.)

When they came back into the house, the sorcerer began chewing more coca leaves and a small piece of San Pedro cactus to help him go into a trance, a state that would enable him to communicate with the supernatural.

After an hour or so, we could see that the sorcerer was entering a trance: his face began to look many years older, and his voice changed to a whisper. He began to strike two sticks of wood, called *hantis,* against each other. *Hantis* are the magic batons that create a passageway or bridge to the other world. Thus he could use them to awaken the occult powers. And it is through these *hantis* that the voice of the spirits can be manifested.

While still hitting the *hantis,* the sorcerer approached the schoolteacher and whispered something in his ear. Then he suddenly dropped the *hantis* and kneeled at each of the four cardinal directions. Then, keeping one knee on the ground, he started turning himself, faster and faster, while invoking divinities. Without transition, he began insulting demons, running all over the room to chase them away. Then he moved out of the house, screaming. For a while we could hear his screams as he ran away, disappearing into the night.

We were petrified.

I asked Pamphillo what the sorcerer had told him.

"He said that my little boy's epilepsy was caused by the unconscious conflicts he has with us." And he admitted that his son had epileptic fits whenever he and his wife quarreled.

Then he added, "But Sylverio told me that there was another problem here. A man from a nearby village has sent a curse into our son's body that has broken his inner harmony, and this is what allowed his body to suffer from the unconscious conflicts with us. First Sylverio has to perform the ultimate rebalancing by sending the curse back where it came from, to the man who created it. Then he will heal my boy. And because this curse would now be even stronger, deadly on its way back, he doesn't want us to witness that part of the ceremony."

Thinking of all of that, we had a sleepless night.

The next morning we awoke very early, for according to the healing ritual, Sylverio was supposed to offer the llama heart to the rising sun. We joined the teacher and his wife, who were gathered around their little boy sitting next to a table set in their courtyard. On the table were all the ingredients of the previous night's offering: coca leaves, *chicha* beer, *lejia, cuti,* several medicinal plants, and the llama heart.

Soon we were joined by the tribal chief. But the sorcerer was still missing. We waited for him for a long time. We were beginning to worry because dawn was breaking. Then Sylverio appeared, smiling. He greeted us with a laugh, as if nothing had happened the night before; he sat down at the table next to the boy, and began chewing coca leaves and drinking alcohol.

While chewing and drinking without stopping, he took a metal bowl, and in it he ground the grains of corn he had used the previous night. He mixed in a few clots of llama's blood, and then examined the mixture carefully for a great while. He added a small piece of the lower part of the llama's heart and a few coca leaves.

Once the mixture was ready, the sorcerer stood up and, while whispering magic incantations, moved the bowl around the boy's head three times, and then skimmed the surface of the boy's body with it.

Afterward, he took a few grains of corn in his hand. Smiling, he stretched this hand to us, showing us the divine message, and said, "*Suerte! Suerte!* The child shall heal!"

Then he took the bowl, still filled with the mixture, out of the house and walked to the church. (It had been a long time since a Catholic priest had officiated in the little church, and, in the holy tabernacle, the ciborium had long since been replaced by a statuette of Saint John, the patron saint of the Indians.) The sorcerer-healer kneeled in front of the church's main porch. Then he stood up, turned to the sun, and kneeled again. He stood up and threw the contents of the bowl toward Inti, the sun god. This marked the end of the healing ceremony.

Later we learned that someone in the nearby village had suddenly died the previous night. And the teacher told us his son has been a lot better since Sylverio's treatment. Was the cure psychological, or did it result from what the sorcerer described as the ultimate rebalancing?

Thanks to my many experiences with sorcerers, I know that an evil curse cannot be broken. Instead, it must be driven back to the original sender. I had always wanted to witness this kind of ceremony, but the sorcerers I asked always refused, explaining that it could put me in danger, because these kinds of rituals force them to create an even stronger and much more powerful curse. And doing this is like playing with lightning.

Only once did a sorcerer allow me to observe such a ceremony, but even then I was allowed to watch only until he put a small cross, made of two long thorns tied crosswise, on a doll that was supposed to represent the man responsible for having cast an evil spell. And a few days later, I heard that the magic had worked: the man had mysteriously died.

Although we did not witness the ceremony Sylverio performed to kill the person responsible for the schoolteacher's son's affliction, I imagine he used an evil doll.

One day, however, elsewhere in that part of the Andes, a sorcerer allowed us to attend a ritual where he used the powers of an evil doll. It was a ceremony of bewitchment.

This sorcerer, who was the local specialist in black magic, was to work on behalf of an old woman who wanted an evil spell cast on a man of another village, whom she hated. So one night, lighting our way with flashlights, we followed the sorcerer up to the village's old deserted Catholic church, where the ceremony was to be held. The church had not be used for services in years, due to the lack of true believers, but there was still a huge cross hanging over the altar.

The sorcerer settled himself in a corner of the church, took two candles from his bag, set them on the flagstone floor, and lit them. He placed a small multicolored ritual cloth between the two candles, thus establishing his *mesa* or altar in this context. He emptied onto it the contents of his small bag: rags, grass, long cactus thorns, and various other small ritual objects. Then he moved to the other corner of the church, lifted up one flagstone covering a hole and, to our surprise, took from it three human skulls, of which one had a circular section removed, and set them on his *mesa*. Then he began whispering prayers and incantations.

An hour or so later, the door of the church opened and a silhouette appeared: the old woman for whom the sorcerer was performing the ritual. Upon entering the church she saw us and seemed fearful. She was about to leave when the sorcerer called her back and assured her that we, being his personal friends, would say nothing of the ceremony. Thus calmed, she approached and gave the sorcerer a small rag containing a piece of cloth belonging to her intended victim, a lock of his hair, and bits of his fingernails—enough things to cast on him the most redoubtable evil spell.

With the grass, rags, and the elements brought by the old woman, the sorcerer made a doll that represented, magically, the old woman's personal enemy. Then he began insulting and spitefully cursing the doll, while pricking its head and body with the cactus thorns. Again he lambasted the doll with maledictions and insults full of hatred. Then he sent the old woman away.

Thanks to the knowledge his master had passed on to him at the time of his initiation, the sorcerer knew that, when it reaches its apex, the will to do evil can effectively reach out and hit its designated victim. At that point, the sorcerer calls his client to him, puts the doll and evil charms on his *mesa,* and begins the final ceremony of black magic. All sorcerers who cast evil spells keep their clients next to them during such ceremonies, for, according to them, their own role is to amplify the hatred their clients generate toward the designated victim, and to transform it into evil forces, which they then send to the victim through a ritual.

Charged with evil forces, the sorcerer will then bury the doll next to the victim's house. And to increase the effectiveness and power of the doll, the sorcerer will find ways to let the victim know that an evil spell has been cast on him; his terror will be such that it will bring forth the first symptoms of evil. Indians dread such practices so much that when they learn that an evil spell has been cast on them, they generally let themselves decay, convinced of their powerlessness in the face of evil forces.

❦

A day or two after we arrived in Sylverio's village, the tribal chief and Sylverio told us a disturbing story. Just three weeks before our arrival in their village, two brothers came hurriedly back from the high plateaus, where they had gone with their herd. They had abandoned everything there, and looked absolutely terrorized. They claimed to have seen the devil and described something much like a vampire. The following day, the eldest got sick; he died a few days later. His brother became ill in his turn and died too.

Their young brother had gotten ill just before our arrival. The tribal chief swore that one night, when there was a full moon, he had seen the third brother's white and transparent ghost, who was crying. According to him, this was a very bad omen announcing the boy's possible death.

"Can we see him? Maybe we can help with our medications," I said, worried that if the boy were to die, we would be seen as being responsible for his sudden sickness and death, and driven away from the village, if not killed.

"No!" answered the tribal chief. "Although the divinities said you could stay among us, some villagers here believe you are *likitchiris* and therefore responsible for the boy's sickness." (A *likitchiri* is a malevolent spirit that transforms itself into a white man and, during the night while people sleep, comes to take fat from their lower backs—the symbol of the vital force. This pre-Columbian belief got new strength with the Spanish invasion, when some monks supposedly took advantage of Indian's sleep to cut off a piece of the lower part of their back, in order to use it for making the oil used to anoint bishops.)

The tribal chief went to talk to Sylverio. After they met we were asked to stay within our house until further notice. We knew that the sorcerer-healer would perform a ceremony that night to treat the young boy.

Around noon the next day the tribal chief called us out of our house. Standing next to him was the young boy. His face was pale, but he was alive. The sorcerer's magic healing had worked, proving to the villagers that we were genuine white men, not *likitchiris*. Thank God!

❦

As these examples have shown, the Indians of the Andes place a great emphasis on what they call balance. If people do something wrong or in some other way upset the balance in their lives, it throws their energies and inner harmony out of balance, which in turn throws the gods and the cosmic harmony out of balance; consequently sickness, and sometimes storms and other natural disasters, follow. A whole village or even a whole region may suffer because of one individual's mistake. So, even if the harmony between his village and the cosmos has not been broken, a sorcerer may perform a rebalancing ceremony as a kind of preventive medicine to calm the divinities in advance.

Following is a description of such a rebalancing ceremony that Sylverio performed. Its intent was to calm the destructive fury of Apu Illampu, the god of thunder and lightning—for the next harvest depended upon his goodwill.

The day of that ceremony was July 25, Saint James's Day, and in the majority of Andean villages the same ritual was being celebrated. Apu Illampu has been associated with Saint James ever since the Indians saw conquistadors shooting their arquebuses at the army of the Incas, and shouting, "*Santiago!*" The association of thunder and lightning (produced in this case by arquebuses) with Saint James thus was formed and has survived over centuries despite intensive Christianization.

The village's main square was filled with people as Sylverio, conversing with the gods, studied falling coca leaves. "*Sumarr*" ("Everything is all right") said the sorcerer-healer, whose shriveled face and hoarse voice testified that he had reached a state of trance. With his finger he pointed to one of the coca leaves spread out on the sacred cloth. Its position and features predicted that the god of thunder would accept the sacrifice.

"Will you bring rain in abundance, O Apu Illampu? May your voice order the water of the sky to join Pacha Mama, our holy earth, to grow crops!"

Sylverio's hand opened and a dozen coca leaves fell on the sacred cloth. The crowd surrounding the sorcerer was silent. No one would have dared interrupt the dialogue between Sylverio and Apu Illampu, who was answering through the sacred leaves.

Afterward, four men stood up and grasped a llama, who had no idea that its blood was going to serve the villagers' cause. Without resisting it allowed itself to be laid on its flank and, resigned, made just a small recoil when the sharp blade touched its neck. Sylverio approached, holding a large wooden spoon that is used only for rituals. The blood spurted out of the llama's jugular and instantly filled the sacred spoon.

"The coca leaves told me that Apu Illampu accepts the offering of a llama. The sacrificed llama is not a gift to him; rather, since the souls of the dead are sometimes reincarnated in llamas, we are sending one of our ancestors to talk with Apu Ilampu and work things out. We need rain for crops, but hail is a disaster. If the llama blood coagulated quickly, rain will coagulate to hail," explained the sorcerer while carefully examining the llama's blood in the ritual spoon. "In this case the blood is thin, a good sign, a very good sign. *Suerte! Suerte!*"

While whispering prayers and magic invocations, the sorcerer went to the edge of the square, which bordered a small valley, and threw the blood down to impregnate Pacha Mama, Mother Earth.

Meanwhile, the sorcerer's assistant had opened the llama's chest and had torn apart its diaphragm. And, as the Incas had done five centuries before, he tore the heart away with his hands.

The atmosphere relaxed and the crowd became noisy as cans of alcohol were distributed to everybody. Before drinking, everyone poured a few drops on the ground to honor Pacha Mama. And soon everyone became talkative, commenting on Apu Illampu's transmitted messages and on the llama sacrifice. A few men carved the llama, and the meat was cooked in huge pots, to be eaten that evening.

Meanwhile, the sorcerer disappeared with the llama's heart, which was to be used for other magic rituals. (That was the heart Sylverio used in the healing ceremony for the schoolteacher's boy.)

*

If the energies of a whole village can be rebalanced as preventive medicine, so, too, can the energies of an entire region. "Once a year," said Sylverio, "Indian tribes and sorcerers come from all over the Andes and gather in one village, whose name must be kept secret. It is one of the highest inhabited spots in the mountains. There, we rebalance the entire Andes. First the axis of the world is set, for if the world spins on a bad axis, everything goes wrong; we would have earthquake, sickness, starvation. But if we do the right ritual for three days, our villages will survive the rest of the year." This festival is held at the vernal equinox.

We arrived in that secret village on the first day of the three-day festival. More than one thousand Indians were already there, dancing, eating, drinking, and having fun. Some Indians had walked for days to reach this place; other had come on donkeys or in trucks.

Each arriving group first stopped fifty yards from an ancient calvary, which was built about one hundred yards from the village.

There, the men put on whatever costume they were going to wear throughout the festival. Some dressed as conquistadors, with iron or leather helmets, holding shields and swords; with small round copper bells attached to their ankles, they beat the ground with their heels. Others wore traditional tribal dress. The Laime and Jukumane tribes, for instance, wore magnificent headdresses made of pink flamingo feathers. Other tribes had headdresses of condor feathers.

Musicians prepared their instruments: drums, trumpets, pan flutes of different sizes, as well as *sicu* and *hullas hullas,* which are bamboo tubes of various sizes, sometimes reaching five feet in length.

After the women unfolded their tribal banners, the whole group approached the calvary. Everybody kneeled at the foot of the cross— which existed as a symbol for the Indians long before the conquistadors' arrival, and which represents the tree of life—and crossed themselves in the Indian manner (they touch their fist to their forehead, chest, and mouth). Then they began playing their instruments, which they continued to do for the entire three days.

Then, with each group holding a cross from its own village, and each sorcerer carrying a pole from a tree struck by lightning, they moved toward the village, walking in a long single line and playing music. The women walked ahead, shaking red and white flags. A white flag marks a tribe at peace; a red flag marks a tribe at war with its neighbors. Showing the colors was very important since the majority of the tribes gathered at the village—the Laimes, the Jukumanes, the Chullpas, the Sicuyas, the Machas, the Pocoatas—were warriors, and each tribe had its enemy. But this day even blood feuds were set aside so that the sorcerers could create harmony and balance.

Each group, as it arrived, was greeted in the main square by the villagers, and everybody kneeled down. Then they exchanged boughs of *molle* (a low-valley shrub), a sign of renewed life. Afterward, still playing their instruments, they moved to the church's porch, where the men kneeled, sending a prayer to Señor de l'Exaltacion de la Cruz. Then they went to eat, and to drink *chicha* beer served with a wooden spoon, symbolizing fertility.

Indians continued to arrive. About two thousand were gathered in the village by the third day. And for all three days, it was a colorful feast for the eyes, with purple dominating. Women were covered with necklaces of pearls and mirrors. Some people wore masks depicting bears, condors or rabbits; others wore headdresses made of condor feathers or of a whole stuffed condor. Here a man played a very rare flute carved of condor bone; there Indians, dressed as conquistadors, parodied the Spanish invaders, giving their dance a brutal and destructive air reminiscent of those who had destroyed the Inca empire. For three days these people prayed, played music, danced, ate, and drank. It was a cacophony as different instruments—drums, trumpets, various flutes—played the same piercing tones all day long. The atmosphere was a mixture of faith, exaltation, and intoxication.

The third day all the sorcerers began dancing around a pole erected at the center of the square, which symbolized the central axis of the world. Musicians beat drums and blew trumpets made of bamboo tubes a foot and a half long with a gourd attached to one end to create resonance; these strange instruments, which produced a deep sound, had been used only a few years before as war trumpets.

Then the most respected sorcerers gathered all the lightning-struck poles they had carried from their villages and stood them around the pole in the center of the square, creating a symbolic temple. We felt a strange chill in the air. Was it only imagination?

"It is important that all gods work in harmony," explained Sylverio. "We pray to all of them. Apu Illampu, god of thunder, give us rain, not hail. Pachachillas, spirits of the mountain ridges, give us the north wind that blows vitality, not the south wind that blows diseases. Condors, messengers of the sun, take our prayers on your wings to Viracocha, creator of the sun and its sister the moon. Keep heaven in balance and we will keep our towns and families in balance, and we will all have a good life for another year."

6

Gypsies, Namibians, Shamans of Java, Howling Dervishes, and Kataragama

This chapter contains descriptions of strange things and mysterious rituals I have witnessed among Gypsies, a tribe in Namibia, the Shamans of Java, Iranian Kurds, and people of Sri Lanka.

GYPSIES

Since Gypsies are reputed to excel in the art of divination, some information about these people, still considered mysterious, may help clarify their divination techniques.

In studying the customs of the Gypsies, I have spent a lot of time with them over many years. I have shared their everyday experiences wherever they roam, from India to North Africa, passing through the Middle East and Europe. And I have learned a great deal, both from and about them. Once I became accepted among some Gypsy tribes, I was even able to witness some of their witchcraft ceremonies, which use age-old rituals that come not only from India, their motherland, but also from those countries they have crossed.

More through linguistics than anything else, anthropologists have been able to establish the ethnic origin of these nomad people. Their language, Romany, still spoken among themselves wherever they live throughout the world, comes from an old form of Sanskrit used in about the ninth century in the Rajasthan and Indus regions of India.

It is believed that around the tenth century, for reasons still unknown, some Gypsy groups left India and started roaming toward the West, many settling in the different countries they crossed. Never—or rarely—mixing with the other peoples they came across, whom they called *gadje,* the Gypsies learned the local languages and the native music, which they mastered thanks to their skills as musicians.

It wasn't always easy to be accepted among Gypsies, even when I was introduced to them by one of their clan. I often had to undergo a simulated attack, a kind of primal challenge much like those Papuan tribes issue, to test me. The first time it happened, I was shocked because I was unaware of that custom; nobody had told me about it, and I never read such a thing in all the books I had read describing the Gypsies. That event took place in a small Greek village, where Muro, a Gypsy friend, was to introduce me to the chief of his clan.

The chief was drinking Greek brandy and playing dominoes with his friends, sitting around one of the tables set outside a small bar next to the Gypsy encampment. Muro asked me to sit at a table nearby and went to talk to the chief, explaining to him my reasons for wanting to stay with their clan. As they were talking, the chief continued playing, glancing at me two or three times. I answered each of his glances with a smile, but he didn't respond.

Muro sat behind the chief. And I waited. I waited for about twenty minutes, watching Muro and the chief, looking for a reaction. But both appeared to be so concentrated over the game that I no longer existed.

Suddenly, the chief stood up and started to yell at me. His screams alerted the whole encampment, and everybody gathered around us. I stayed in my chair, looking at Muro, waiting to read his reaction, then staring at the chief, trying to maintain a relaxed attitude, with a smile hanging on my lips. Believe me, it wasn't easy!

Now the chief grabbed his chair, menacing me with it. All of sudden he threw it in my direction. The chair landed on the table where I was sitting and ended up against my arm, which I had put in front of me to protect my face. The Gypsies reacted with laughter. The chief threw a glass, but missed me. He threw another that broke when it hit the table. Then, as if nothing happened, he sat down, emptied a glass of brandy that was sitting in front of one of his friends, and continued playing dominoes. Muro indicated with his hand that I should come closer.

Shaking a little and trying to keep my smile, I approached the chief. Without looking at me, he ordered two glasses of brandy, we shook our glasses, and he said, "Welcome."

☽

Almost every Gypsy woman claims to be an expert in palm reading. As in the Chinese culture, for Gypsies palm reading is the most widely used method for seeing the past and the present, and for foretelling the future. Many books claim to teach one how to decipher the complicated patterns of lines crossing the palms. However, as I learned from the Gypsies, physical contact between reader and subject has a lot to do with how well one can use this divination method. The palm reader tries to interpret body waves—sensations and energies she feels coming from the subject's body as she holds his hand.

Although I have undergone palm readings that revealed some interesting things about my past and present, I have never learned more about my destiny than I already knew. And, frankly, I would be very careful in considering as true what a palm reader said about my future, even if she gave me an accurate reading about my past and present. I suspect there may be many charlatans offering readings, because a person need have no ESP abilities to be a good palm reader. With a bit of psychology and practice, anyone can feel a subject's subtle reactions as his hand is read. Knowledge of human morphology—how to recognize the body types that are typical of various kinds of character—also helps in discerning characteristics of an individual.

I have more trouble understanding the other divination method in which Gypsy women are considered to excel—examining the coffee grounds or tea leaves left after the subject has drained the cup. Here there is no physical contact with the subject that could lead the reader in a definite direction. Sometimes the reader looks carefully for symbols: for example, coffee grounds that lie close to the handle indicate the beginning or the end of the year. But it seems that this technique is used more as a tool for focusing attention and concentration, much like a crystal ball. Perhaps the reader uses another part of her brain to mentally *read* the subject.

Many Gypsy women also excel in the art of telling fortunes with cards, or *cartomancy*. For some readers, a normal pack of playing cards is good enough. But many prefer to use a tarot deck because the twenty-two Major Arcana that it contains represent archetypes that are relatively easy to interpret.

Reading tarot cards is believed to date back to the Egyptians. The Gypsies supposedly brought this technique to Europe around the fourteenth or fifteenth century. Modern playing cards evolved from the original Egyptian tarots. The zero became the fool or joker; spears or swords became spades; pentacles or disks are diamonds; wands are clubs; cups are hearts.

In this divination technique, the role of the card reader is to capture the psychic energy that the subject has put into the cards by shuffling them. The reader pulls the answers into conscious form from the unconscious mind of the subject.

I have had some interesting surprises in this field. However, don't put your trust in the first fortune teller you meet. Reading cards is not a technique one can learn from books, unless one is also a psychic. And I believe this is also true for such methods as the Chinese I Ching or the casting of runes.

According to the Gypsy people, if you catch sight of a toad while you are thinking about doing something specific, it is considered a blessing—a divine signal to encourage you to go ahead and do it.

When I asked my friend Yarko, a Gypsy witch doctor living in France, about this, he replied, "Have you ever seen a dead toad?"

"Yes, many times. Why?"

"Nothing caught your attention?"

"Nope."

"Next time, look more carefully. A dead toad never rots. Instead, it dries up."

"Why?"

"Because a toad possesses energies. Powerful energies. We use toads for magic healing, but also for casting spells. A toad is the main ingredient in evil charms that are left beside victims' houses. But most of all, toads are good omens."

Seeing my incredulous reaction, Yarko smiled. "Try it. You'll be surprised," he said. His smile uncovered his teeth, all covered with gold. He was a goldsmith, and made most of his money by going from church to church, covering sacred ritual objects with gold. Since he was licensed by the French Académie des Beaux-Arts, he was welcomed in all Catholic churches of France.

Remembering Yarko's words concerning toads, I was often surprised to find that he was right. In one case, what happened was particularly amazing.

The event took place in a small seaside city in the south of France during the winter, after a lecture I had given in the city's main theater. Around midnight I finished storing the sound and projection equipment in my car, which I had left for safety in the theater's garage. The rain, which had been falling the whole evening, had just stopped. There was a full moon. When I walked up to my hotel, I found two people, a woman and a man, waiting for me at the door, to ask questions about my lecture. She was the head of a small manufacturing company; he was a teacher in the local school.

We sat on a bench overlooking the large cement patio, which was lit by a lamp hanging over the hotel's entrance. The schoolteacher asked questions first. Then the woman began to talk. She was in her thirties, quite fat, and average looking.

She told me that she was born in Casablanca. When she was seven her grandmother gave her a ring that changed her life: she started to feel that she wanted her parents to hate her. She forced herself to eat in excess, and became fat and ugly. ("I now have a four-liter air pocket in my stomach," she said). She stopped feeling hungry or thirsty, cold or hot; she felt no emotion whatever, for herself or for others. But interestingly enough, she could get everything she wanted from a material point of view. "When I desire something, it comes to me immediately. If I want a job, I am hired. If someone else has the job already, the person is fired and it's offered to me," she said.

"What do you want from me?" I asked.

"I don't really know. Maybe you can help me to change," she replied in a sad voice.

"Is there something special about your grandmother, the one who gave you the ring?" I asked.

"She was celibate, ugly, and we feared her. Everybody in the family feared her. We used to call her the witch. She died suddenly the day she gave me the ring. And she herself got the ring from a relative who had the same kind of life, projecting the same fear all around her, and who also died the day she gave her the ring."

I asked to see the ring. She took it off and put it in my hand. I don't know why—perhaps it was the spooky story she had told me—but I felt something like an electric shock as the ring touched me, and I was so shaken that it fell to the ground. She looked at me without surprise.

"Put it on your finger, so that I can look at it," I said.

At this point, her companion began acting nervous. She put the ring back on her finger and stretched out her hand. It was a massive gold ring, engraved with strange designs and inscriptions.

"It must be very old," I said, still holding her hand and looking carefully at the ring.

"Once, someone wanted to buy it for a lot of money, and told me that it was Catharist. But I couldn't sell it."

I told her that the ring was probably possessed wth evil energies passed on from generation to generation, and that the best thing would be to get rid of it. After a few beats, she took the ring off her finger and threw it away. I told her that we needed to destroy it, because whoever found it would likely also get the evil energies of the ring.

The three of us began looking for the ring. Suddenly we heard the sound of a toad. In the middle of the cement patio, sat a huge toad. "That's an omen. We need to destroy the ring!" I almost screamed, shaking nervously as I remembered what my Gypsy friend had told me.

To our great surprise, the toad moved back a few inches, uncovering the ring, and remained there motionless. I asked the woman to pick up the ring. She did. And the toad slowly left the patio.

I don't know why, but I said that we should burn the ring—that fire would destroy its evil energies—and that we should then throw it into the sea. The teacher said he knew of a beach where we could light a fire. He proposed to take us there in his car.

On the way to the beach, we passed through a forest. I told him that we needed dry wood, paper, and matches. "I have some at home," he said, and began slowing down to make a U-turn. As the car stopped, I saw on my side of the road a large cardboard box. I got out, opened the box, and found that it contained paper, matches, and dry wood—which was surprising since it had been raining the whole evening.

He parked the car at the top of a cliff. "The beach is down below," he said. "It's a steep path. Be careful."

He walked ahead. The woman—who up to this point had said nothing—walked behind him, and I followed. The path was slippery because of the mud.

There was no other way to reach the beach—which was enclosed on both sides by high cliffs—except by sea. We gathered all the small pieces of wood we could find on the beach. I set the paper and the dry wood, along with the rest of wood we had collected, in the middle of the beach, and we sat side by side—the woman between us—with our backs to the sea to protect the fire from the breeze. The teacher and I were trembling, due as much to nervousness as to the winter's cold.

I warned the teacher that I didn't know what would happen to us when we put the ring into the fire. He said nothing.

When the fire was burning nicely, I asked the woman to throw the ring into it, and began reciting whatever silent prayers came to me. The ring produced flames of different colors. Then I began seeing strange faces in the smoke, formed by the smoke itself. The teacher interrupted my thoughts, whispering, "Douchan . . . do you see that?"

Before I could say anything, the woman, who was sitting cross-legged, staring at the ring, began moving her head and upper body toward the fire, slowly at first, then faster and faster, as if attracted by the fire. She would have fallen into it if we had not stopped her.

Suddenly the teacher and I heard a strange noise behind us, a kind of splash. We turned and beheld a huge, powerfully built man, with a large stomach. He wore a swimming suit. Soaking wet, he approached the fire, and stood on the other side of it, across from us. The two of us were speechless; the woman continued to stare at the ring, which was still creating colored flames.

"I was born in Casablanca," the huge man said. "And I wanted to be hated by my parents. I wanted to become ugly, so I ate so much that now I have a four-liter air pocket in my stomach."

We were petrified. Try to picture the situation—2 A.M. in the middle of winter, and this man appears from the sea and tells us the same story the woman had told. In conclusion, he said, "Well . . . I see that I can't do anything to stop you. So, there is only one thing left for me to do."

He moved to the side of one cliff, picked up a huge tree trunk as if it were weightless, and looked at us. The schoolteacher and I froze, scared as hell. The man slammed the tree trunk against the cliff. The wood exploded. He picked up the pieces, put them on the fire and, after a last look at us, slowly moved back into the sea.

Still praying, I picked up the ring with a small stick and threw it into the sea. The woman began shaking and said. "I am cold, I am hungry." Then she burst into tears. "It's so good to feel the need to cry," she said.

A year later I received a letter from her. She was working in New York with a religious institution that takes care of the homeless and those who need help and love.

NAMIBIANS

In Namibia, in southwest Africa, I met an interesting tribe. Like all peoples of tradition, these tribesmen believe deeply in the power of the supernatural, and often consult their *sangoma,* or witch doctor, in order to learn their destinies. I wanted to meet this *sangoma.* When I contacted him he told me to meet him at the new moon. (I learned later that this tribe believes fortune is governed by the lunar cycle.)

The *sangoma* and I were sitting face to face outside the village, next to a small campfire set under a huge old tree, which symbolized the magical axis that links the visible world to the invisible one. He unwrapped a small leather bag and asked me to open my right hand, into which he emptied the contents of the bag: his set of divination bones.

A witch doctor's set of bones comprises six chicken bones, four small colored stones, and two small, flat, strangely sculpted pieces of tree bark. The twelve objects are paired, symbolically, as male and female. The larger of a pair represents the male.

△ The two longest chicken bones (those that join the knee to the foot) represent the central characters: man and woman.

△ The four smaller chicken bones (parts of the feet) represent the children: members of the family unit.

△ The two pieces of tree bark represent the ancestral spirits: the positive forces symbolizing vigilance and protection.

△ The two red stones represent crocodiles: the negative forces of the underworld.

△ The two golden brown stones represent the *seeing* eyes of man and woman: wisdom and perception.

Thus a witchdoctor's bones symbolize human characters and the positive and negative forces influencing their lives.

The *sangoma* asked me to blow on these objects of divination, and to chant with him the spell that would start the spirit flowing between me and the bones: "I breathe my soul and the soul of my guiding spirit upon you."

Then he took the bones from my hand, threw them on the ground, and carefully examined them, for destiny is read according to their relative positions. This throwing of bones is a way of foretelling romance, fertility, health, and prosperity. The forecast applies to the current month—from new moon to new moon—only.

The state of health of each family member is determined by the position of the appropriate bone—face up indicating good health for the month, face-down denoting illness and distress. Romance and fertility are indicated by the position of positive and negative forces lying between the man and the woman. To foretell prosperity, two imaginary lines are drawn, one joining the two positive forces, the other joining the two negative forces. Should these lines cross any of the characters, those fall under the influence of either good fortune or bad.

Characters under negative influences are able to perceive and counteract the forces only if the *seeing* eyes lie closer to them than to the negative forces.

SHAMANS OF JAVA

What is the source of man's powers? They come from his mind—whether the mind is their actual source or acts only as a transformer of energies coming from the cosmos. This explanation is based on the fact that the mind has complete control over the body. Evidence of this can be found in an amazing ceremony of shamanism I witnessed in a small village in central Java, Indonesia, where the shaman's neophytes, in an effort to discover their oneness with nature, bend to the will of their master and, for a time, become wild animals.

In central Java, shamanism survived Islam, and people worship both religions equally. So inhabitants of these villages, though Moslem, have a deep and unshakable faith in the absolute power of their shaman. They believe he alone can travel between man's world and the invisible, nonmaterial world of the spirits. The ceremony I witnessed was intended to display the shaman's powers. Although he couldn't show the villagers his ability to travel between the two worlds, he was to transform his two neophytes into wild animals. The shaman knew that once he demonstrated his visible power over men, the villagers would believe he had powers over spirits.

The ceremony began in the early morning. A group of musicians—equipped with native xylophones called gamelons, drums, and a kind of native clarinet—gathered on one side of the village's main plaza and began to play. The music called the villagers to the square. After a few dances by male transvestites (women are not allowed to take part in these ritual dances), the shaman's two novices appeared, riding hobby horses, which symbolize transportation to the invisible world.

The shaman drew a magic circle with ashes. It was in this circle, about fifteen feet in diameter, that he was to cast his magic spells. As he finished drawing the circle, a man jumped into the middle of it, wearing a tiger costume. The tiger is a symbol of power, strength, and courage all over Asia. The shaman began fighting the tiger in order to draw all his mythical forces from him, and to prove his power over this most powerful animal. With the tiger's defeat, he would show himself to be the most powerful of all humans, for no ordinary man could survive a battle with a tiger. Once he had subdued the tiger, he was ready to lead his assistants into a world they had never known—the world of wild animals.

The shaman then prepared magic powders, which he combined with bits of tiger skin and whiskers to make three amulets, tying one around his wrist and the others around the waists of the neophytes. Thus he established a link between the young men and himself. Then, with one hand on each head, he slowly put them into a deep trance, replacing their human consciousness with that of an animal. His purpose was not to have them regress to a wild state, but rather to help them experience the most primal and original aspect of their being—perhaps a return to using the ancient reptilian brain that goes back to the time of the Garden of Eden, when humankind shared the language of all creatures. Through that ceremony—part of their long initiation to become, one day perhaps, a shaman in their turn—the neophytes would begin to experience being the channel for interspecies communication.

Suddenly, the men pawed the earth, snorting and grunting. They had been psychologically transformed into wild boars—not merely acting like them, but thinking, feeling, and being wild boars. Like those of a beast, their eyelids became motionless, their stares restless and savage. Driven by hunger, the wild-boar men hurled themselves toward the fields, going on all fours, desperately searching for manioc roots—the favorite food of boars. Carrying his small drum, the shaman followed them, staring at them with his hypnotic eyes, for they were under his control and would remain so for as long as he wanted.

The men dug up manioc roots and ripped at them with their teeth, eating earth along with the roots. But there was a terrible danger here, for raw manioc contains arsenic—deadly to men, but not to wild boars. If their bodies were not deeply enough under the control of their animal consciousness, they would be poisoned.

The shaman finally beat his drum, calling the two wild-boar men back to the magic circle, where the most delicate part of the ceremony began: bringing them back to being human again. Placing one hand on each head and staring at them, he first disconnected the neophytes' animal consciousness, and they fell into a deep coma: except for shallow breathing, they were, in effect, dead. He cleared the manioc from their mouths to prevent poisoning and suffocation when they again became human. Then, gently, carefully, he began giving them back their human consciousness. He knew he held their most precious possession in his hands: their minds. One slip and they would remain unconscious forever. Slowly he brought them out of the coma. For them it was like being reborn into the world of humans. The men rose slowly, shaking their heads. The spell was broken.

Over and over the shaman transformed his two novices into different animals, so that they would identify with all the wildlife around them. They were monkeys, and like monkeys they ripped the husks from coconuts with their teeth. They were transformed into foxes, stalking the chickens that ran all over the village; when they caught one, they ate it live.

They became otters. Led to a pond, they sniffed the air for danger. Then, following their animal instincts, they entered the water. Slithering and sliding, they searched the pond for food. Many times they disappeared into the pond for a long time—between five and ten minutes. Finally one came up with his prey, a fish he had caught with his teeth, just as an otter would. The second did likewise.

Called by the shaman's drum, the two otter-men returned to the magic circle, fish still flopping in their mouths. Again, the shaman began the slow process of return. He disconnected the otter consciousness. Then, before bringing them back to the human world, he slowly removed the fish from between their teeth, and, with his fingers, cleared from their mouths and throats the fish bones and pieces of fish that were already half swallowed. Gently, as with a baby, he used his mouth to draw the water out of their lungs, so they wouldn't drown when they became men again. Then he gave them back their human consciousness.

Afterward, before moving on to his next destination, the shaman asked all the men of the village to follow him to a nearby forest. Then he instructed them to stretch out a sixty-foot-long net, about six feet high, in a V shape. The men, armed with machetes and strong sticks, positioned themselves at either end of the V. The shaman crouched outside the V at its apex and disconnected his human consciousness. He then connected with the consciousness of a wild boar, transforming himself in order to attract wild boars to the hunters. The result was beyond belief. Called by the wild-boar shaman, more than twenty wild boars, in small groups, moved out of the deep bushes, rushing toward the shaman crouched on the other side of the net. As the boars were caught in the net, the men jumped in and killed them.

That was the shaman's farewell gift to the villagers.

HOWLING DERVISHES

For some cultures, the trance phenomenon leads the believer into a state where he can be possessed by a divinity and, thus, become himself a divinity. For other cultures, trances lead worshipers into a mystic experience through self-inflicted pain as a means for experiencing a contact with the Divine.

It was in Mahabad, Iran, that I had the unique opportunity to observe a most unusual ceremony of a secret sect that called themselves Howling Dervishes. Its members were Kurds, an oppressed minority that once had its own land, called Kurdistan—since taken over by Iraq, Iran, Turkey, and the Soviet Union.

The origins of the Howling Dervishes go back to the fourteenth century. Their rituals can be completely understood only by those who have undergone secret initiations. Like Sufis, Dervishes are Islamic mystics. During the day, these men lead average lives; they are landowners, shopkeepers, civil servants. One sign of membership in their society is long hair, which they normally keep hidden under their turbans. They say, "When Allah is ready to pull us out of this world and into paradise, he will be able to grip our hair."

They claim to be Muslims. But since most branches of Islam forbid self-injury, the Dervishes are outcasts. They worship once a week, in secret, in the dark of night—the time of shame for Muslims. On the walls of the secret room where they gather is a painting of Ali, the son-in-law of the prophet Mohammed. Some Muslims believe that Ali was the incarnation of God.

The caliph—the master and spiritual leader of the dervishes— starts praying. He is joined by his assistants, and then by everyone in chorus. Afterward, chanting to Ali and Allah begins as the caliph beats out a rhythm on a tabor. The Dervishes remove their turbans to free their hair and, throughout the long hours of chanting that ensue, move their heads in hypnotic circles, calling upon God to witness their attempt to overcome pain. This helps those who are trying to achieve communion with God.

Only when the Dervishes are transformed by faith can they leave the human condition and come closer to God. What these men are about to do to their bodies is not pleasant to watch, but it is their way of expressing a deep faith. And it must be understood without religious or cultural bias. If their faith is not strong enough, accidents can happen: lost eyes, perforated intestines, bleeding, infections.

In the frenzied atmosphere of chanting, drumbeats, and heads moving in a circle, the Dervishes reach a state of trance, their faces covered with sweat. A man takes a foot-long iron skewer—similar to those we use for grilling meat—and drives it into his flesh, pushing it across his abdomen until its end appears on the other side of his body. There is no sign of blood, the Dervish having gained complete mental control of his body. Another drives a skewer through his cheeks and tongue, without showing signs of pain, and again no blood appears.

A man steps barefoot onto a razor-sharp sword, which two other Dervishes are holding; he lifts his weight onto the blade and then stabs his feet many times. One of the fatter Dervishes leans over another razor-sharp sword, lifts his hands and feet from the ground, and then, invites another man to stand on him. He should be sliced in two, but there is no sign of blood.

A man pushes the deadly blade of a knife under his eye. Another, who was blinded some years before by a momentary loss of concentration while doing the same thing, now chews up several drinking glasses. Swallowing sharp-edged broken glass would normally bring a slow agonizing death, but this man, having made up for his earlier lack of faith, now has control over his body.

At each meeting these men push their bodies further and subject themselves to ever more violent trials, always testing their own faith, proving they are ready to meet God.

It has been estimated that there are still two hundred thousand to three hundred thousand Dervishes in Kurdistan. And once a week each will stand alone, calling God with a scream of pain that he believes will help him penetrate the divine kingdom. Through the purification of self-inflicted pain, Dervishes aspire to a state of ecstasy, a contact with the Divine, and many succeed.

KATARAGAMA

In Sri Lanka, there is a yearly ten-day festival dedicated to the god Kataragama, during which worshipers inflict unusual tortures on themselves as a means of being filled with the sacred. Some even roll their bodies all the way from their faraway villages to the festival, which is shared by Hindus, Buddhists, and Muslims.

The Amahadva temple is dedicated to the god Kataragama, who is also called Supramanya, Kandakumara, Handsome Youth, Born from the Eyes, Came from the Pleiades, Born from the Ganges, Fire Born, Six Faced, or Seganda. Inside the temple is hidden something called *Yantra*. No one knows what it is because only two priests in each generation are ever allowed to handle it, and when they do so it remains under a sacred cloth.

The festival opens with a ritual called the cutting of the water. In the shallow part of a nearby river, the priest, completely concealed by leaves, bows and slices the water once with a large sword to separate good from evil. This ceremony takes only a minute, but the crowd spends the next several hours joyfully bathing in the cool river.

Then the day arrives for the self-mortification to begin. Elaborate heavy wooden structures are carried on the shoulders of men, women, and children who are desirous of being purified by overcoming the pain of physical effort.

All of a sudden, people stop talking. Their eyes become much brighter and have a vacant stare. Intoxicated by chanting, dancing, and music, they begin to fall into trances. Their faces show happiness; their bodies are in perfect harmony. Possessed by another force, they are preparing their minds to accept the pain to come.

The trials begin whenever the people have achieved a state of transcendance. I wait and watch. And here they are, those whose faith can overcome pain. There are many with hooks in the skin of their backs that are attached to cords. They pull forward with great effort as people at the other end of the cords restrain them, as if controlling some wild animal. Small silver lances, shaped like the legendary lance that Kataragama used to kill an evil enemy, are inserted through people's cheeks. A young woman standing next to me also consents to have her cheeks pierced. A long silver needle is carefully inserted through one cheek. Then a silver cobra is hooked in the middle before the other cheek is pierced. It takes several minutes to adjust the lance and the cobra, and the woman seems to be in pain but nods for them to continue. People who later talk about this experience say they feel the pain in all of its intensity, but are so filled with thoughts of God that the pain becomes almost trivial.

As the ceremony reaches its high point, some men are standing on deadly sharp needles; others are being lifted into the air on four hooks attached to their flesh. They have become puppets of the gods. And since they are in contact with the sacred, they become divine themselves. People surround them, asking questions and listening to their prophecies.

I came to this festival searching for explanations and hoping to be enlightened. But when we are confronted with a state of consciousness beyond reasoning and logic, the *why, when,* and *how* suddenly seem meaningless, for even if we receive explanations in exhaustive detail, we still cannot fully understand what they are experiencing because these people do not live according to our logic. A man in a trance is possessed by powerful forces. The cause of his trance may be music, drugs, prayer, or pain; or you may call it mass hysteria. But what is important is the result: ecstasy. Here gods talk with creatures they have created in their own image. And to hear the voices of the gods you need to accept the gods' logic. According to that logic, in order to become a puppet of the gods, you must overcome pain; to overcome pain you must forget your human belief that you have limited powers and possibilities; only when you forget you are human will you remember that you are a god.

7

Voodoo in Haiti

Some words have an amazing power over the human imagination. *Voodoo* is one of them. The word alone conjures up images of black magic, savage bloody ceremonies, and mysterious deaths. One can't help but picture dolls pierced with needles, and zombies awaiting commands from their masters.

And why not? Everything we know about Voodoo is derived from horror films, late-night television shows, and cheap literature. If someone enters a Catholic church during the Mass and hears the priest saying, "This is my flesh, eat it; this is my blood, drink it . . . ," and if he doesn't understand this portion of the ritual and its context, he will probably claim that he has attended a cannibalistic ceremony.

Yet Voodoo is real, and exists today in Haiti—where it was born. It even exists in the United States, brought with Haitian immigrants. No longer do doctors and psychiatrists in Florida rule out Voodoo spells as possible causes for their patients' illnesses. No longer is the New York Police Department puzzled over the mysterious remains of animal sacrifices in their parks. And in New Orleans, there are markets that sell animals for sacrificial slaughter, in much the same way kosher markets sell meat to those of the Jewish faith.

However, it took me years of investigation in Haiti to understand that under the umbrella of Voodoo there are many different realities, none of which is a superstitition, and all of which can produce results.

When slaves were brought into Haiti—the majority came from Nigeria and Dahomey (now called Benin); others came from Guinea, Senegal, Mozambique, and the Congo (now known as Zaire)—they took along with them their religious belief systems. Once in Haiti, they were confronted with the religion of the last Arawak Indian survivors (the Arawaks were a Caribbean tribe of the Amazon Basin who migrated to Haiti around the seventh century, and were later decimated by the Spanish) and that of their Catholic masters.

Slowly, with the passing of time, the different African ethnic groups in Haiti, united by their tragic destiny, focused their religious beliefs on the sacred rituals of Benin. To those, they added some beliefs of the Arawak Indians and Catholicism. This mixture became Voodoo. (Although also based on rituals leading to trances and possessions, *Condamblé* in the West Indies, *Quimbois* in the French Antilles, *Macumba* in Brazil, *Santeria* in Cuba, *Tromba* in Madagascar, and so on, are based on the ethnic and regional differences of the African slaves brought to these places, on which African rituals became predominant, and on how much was borrowed from Catholicism and indigenous beliefs.)

In a parallel development, hundreds of sects practicing sorcery and dealing with vampirism, spiritism, satanism, werewolves, flying witches, and so forth flourished throughout Europe in the Middle Ages, mainly in France, and these beliefs were brought to Haiti by the first French settlers, by pirates, and, later, by Catholic priests who had been driven out of France by the clergy because they had become Freemasons or were performing black magic (and thus had signed a treaty with the devil). These priests introduced treatises on alchemy and esoterism, occultism, the Cabala, Theosophy, and high magic.

The Voodoo religion encompasses many aspects of Freemasonry, as well as esoterism, the Cabala, occultism, alchemy, astrology, metaphysics, and Theosophy. In its rituals it uses principles of high magic, and deals with the mysteries and secrets of the Knights Templar order, whose presence can be seen in the ceremonial dresses worn by *houngans* (Voodoo priests) during certain ceremonies.

So, basically, the Voodoo religion draws its inspiration from African religious belief systems and practices, but the rituals of magic that it uses—including those performed by sorcerers—are based on the principles of French and Indo-European magic.

Voodoo was a strong force in unifying the Haitians in rebellion against their masters, which led the country to become, in 1804, the first black independent nation. And Voodoo has kept them spiritually and morally alive since, providing them with hope, perseverance, and a kind of fatalism concerning their lives on earth, which are seen as being only temporary, their own most important task being to develop their spiritual lives. Despite their misery, these people have a *joie de vivre* derived from their deep faith in their religious system.

So far, misery there has the languorous rhythm of meringé, the smell of feast and celebration, and the color of naive paintings. Their faith is written everywhere. Walking through the cities is like moving through art galleries, or being in the middle of a religious procession. Naive paintings cover buses and taxis, which carry names like "Ave Maria," "Pater Noster," and names of saints and apostles, or slogans like "God is my master," "Be patient, the Lord is taking care of you," "A powerful soul in a clean body," "God is love," and so on. Here a shop is called "The Glory of Jesus"; there a bakery's name is "Happily God loves me, bakery messenger of Happiness."

Even cemeteries are works of art, not only in their colorful architecture—tombs often are more sophisticated and luxurious than houses—but also in the mystic paintings covering the tombs, as in the cemetery of Saint-Soleil, where people often gather to play cards or dominos or chat, Sundays after the Catholic mass.

Ninety percent of Haitians are Voodoo worshipers; the great majority of them are also devout Catholics.

For decades, Catholic priests fought against Voodoo, trying to abolish it. When Papa Doc (François Duvalier) took power in Haiti, he declared Voodoo an official religion, as valid as all the Christian religions of the country, but he forbade sorcery, including all practices of black magic, the making of zombies, and so on. Consequently, sorcery went underground; it continued to be performed, but secretly, in temples similar to those dedicated to Voodoo, so that it would be perceived as another form of Voodoo rather than sorcery. Thus it isn't easy to dissociate Voodoo from sorcery. In this chapter I will limit my discussion to true Voodoo.

Theologians have begun to consider Voodoo as more sacred and solemn than they had previously thought. More than a religion, Voodoo is a mysticism, a culture, a philosophy, a way of life. And because it is a living and dynamic religion, which, instead of being dogmatic and moral—as most Western religions are—is based on initiatory, metaphysical, and metapsychical principles, it is impossible to describe Voodoo in everyday language. One can only experience it.

I remember what a houngan once told me as I was questioning him about the mysteries of his religion: "You are always questioning me, but there are no more words I can use to answer you. I have used them all. But words have different levels and values of comprehension as one moves into other realities; it is time for you to experience the words within other realities."

The Tuareg, also known as the Blue Men, roam across the Sahara Desert. (See Chapter 4.)

Gypsies of Golubinci, Yugoslavia. (See Chapter 6.)

Ninety percent of the Haitian population are Voodoo worshippers. (See Chapter 7.)

A Voodoo initiate covered with the blood of a sacrificed animal. (See Chapter 7.)

Magical drawings (vévés) used to call the loas. *(See Chapter 7.)*

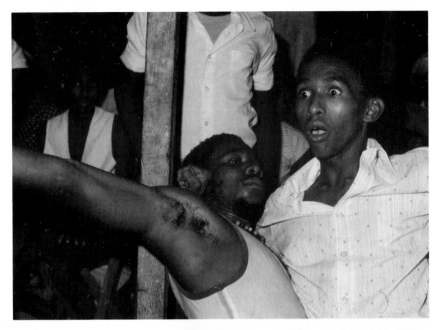

*Voodoo worshippers
often resist the*
loa *who wants to
possess them.
(See Chapter 7.)*

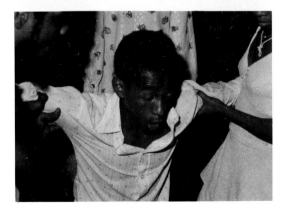

Cemetery of Soissons,
Haiti, where tombs
are covered with
paintings that
resemble Miro,
Picasso, or
Modigliani.
(See Chapter 7.)

The man who levitated climbs down from the tree where he landed. As a woman worshipper reaches up to help him, she is suddenly possessed by a spirit. (See Chapter 7.)

Inside a houmfort *sanctuary. (See Chapter 7.)*

A loa *can possess a worshipper at any time or any place. (See Chapter 7.)*

A houngan *performing an exorcism. (See Chapter 7.)*

Cemeteries in Haiti are guarded by crosses symbolizing Baron Samedi, the loa *who is "Lord of the Dead." (See Chapter 7.)*

Two assons *greeting the* loas *who possess the drummers.*

A houngan *beginning a Voodoo ceremony. (See Chapter 7.)*

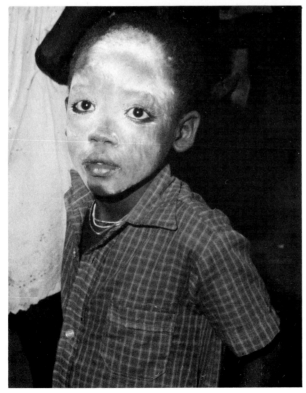

During the guédé *ceremonies, anyone who is possessed by the soul of a dead person has his or her face covered with white ashes. (See Chapter 7.)*

Ceremonies dedicated to the guédé loas *call for violent possession by the spirits. (See Chapter 7.)*

A Voodoo worshipper going into a trance during a ceremony dedicated to the guédé loas. *(See Chapter 7.)*

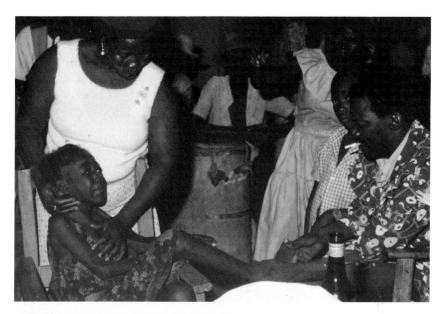

Exorcism of a child who was suffering from an advanced case of tuberculosis. (See Chapter 7.)

The front of a houmfort *in the Haitian countryside. The paintings and epitaphs express the dedication of the community and the powers of the* houngan. *(See Chapter 7.)*

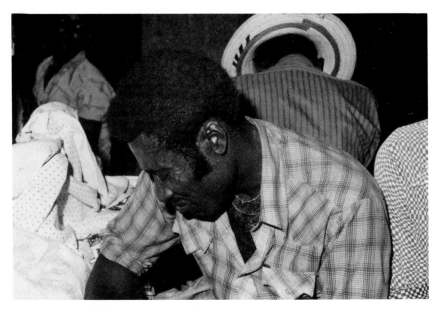

A Voodoo worshipper entering a deep trance during an exorcism ceremony. (See Chapter 7.)

A cross representing Baron Samedi guards a cemetery. (See Chapter 7.)

The altar of a
sanctuary in which
black-magic
ceremonies are
performed. (See
Chapter 8.)

Human skull on a
black-magic altar.
(See Chapter 8.)

Detail of another altar dedicated to black magic. (See Chapter 7.)

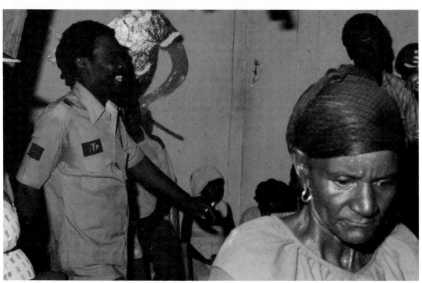

A bokor *leading a black-magic ceremony in Haiti. (See Chapter 8.)*

A woman participant in a black magic ceremony in Haiti. (See Chapter 8.)

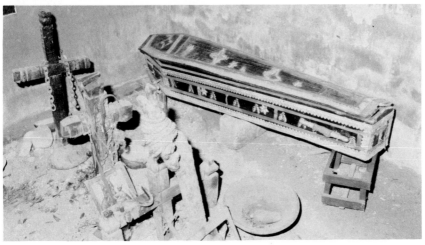

Inside the black-magic sanctuary: the coffin contains the body, stolen from the cemetery, of a person whose soul the bokor *uses to work black magic. (See Chapter 8.)*

A houngan
performing the
ceremony of "calling
the soul out of the
water" on the tomb
of the dead man, as
part of a Voodoo
ritual in Haiti.
(See Chapter 9.)

I couldn't help thinking of P. B. Randolph, who wrote, in *Magia Sexualis:*

> The word is anemic, the thought is full of blood. The word has a muffled resonance, the thought vibrates like metal. The word is a motionless image, the thought is a dynamic being.

My intention is not to give a complete report of my study of Voodoo in Haiti—I would need a whole book for that—but to familiarize you with another way to perceive the world.

☾

It is generally accepted that the word *Voodoo* comes from *Voundoun,* which in the language of Benin means God. Other scholars propose that it comes from *Vodun* a word in the language of the Fon tribe that means God, ghost, or supernatural.

According to Voodoo, there is only one God, who is the creator of the universe. He created the visible world and the invisible one—sometimes called the spiritual world. After he did this he retired, giving to humans *loas,* who serve as intermediaries between the living and God, and the freedom to use the cosmic force that he put at our disposal. This force is neither good nor evil. We are to use it as we wish: for good or for evil. Therefore, its consequences may be positive or negative.

The invisible world is all around us, among us, behind the cosmic mirror. This world is like a reflection of our visible world. The inhabitants have the same needs and passions as we do. It is populated by the souls of the deceased and by an infinite number of loas, who are the original inhabitants of this world. Sometimes called spirits or angels, loas are energies or entities that have been made divine. They are divided into different families, groups, and sub-groups. Some have great powers.

Because Voodoo is a living religion—from one community to another, believers deal with a varying number of loas—it is impossible to make a complete classification of loas.

The main families of loas, those with the greatest powers and prestige, come from the African religious pantheon—mainly from the Yoruba and Fon tribes. They are symbolized by the elements of nature, and each has a specific responsibility.

Legba is the father-protector of main entries, thresholds, and doorways.

Djamballah-Wedo is the energy of fecundity, symbolized by a snake.

Aida-Wedo is his wife.

Calfou (from the French word *carrefour*) is the ruler of crossroads.

Ogoune-Feraille is the energy of war, symbolized by a piece of iron.

Shango is the energy of thunder and lightning.

Ezili or *Erzulie* is the energy of love and sex.

Ogoué is the energy of the sea, symbolized by a boat; he is considered the Voodoo Neptune.

Another powerful family of loas are the *Guédés,* the guardians of the deceased. Their chief is *Baron Samedi* (Baron Saturday), also known as the Brave, symbolized by a cross or a grave. He is the keeper of all the knowledge of the dead; he controls the passage between life and death, and is the energy of the soul's life. His two assistants are *Baron la Croix* (Baron Cross) and *Baron Cimetierre* (Baron Cemetery).

The less-prestigious loas take their names from African tribes, such as Ibo, Bambara, and Nago; and from African regions, such as Congo and Siniga (Senegal). Some loas have their origins in the beliefs of the Arawak Indians. Others are of more recent origin.

Loas can be represented by Catholic pious images. Since Djamballah-Wedo is symbolized by a snake, he is represented by Saint Patrick crushing a snake. Djamballah-Wedo does not *become* Saint Patrick but Saint Patrick *is* Djamballah-Wedo. This is no substitution, but a transfer from Catholicism to Voodoo. Saint Peter is Legba; Saint James is Ogoune-Feraille. Saint Theresa is Erzulie, Moses is Ogoué, and so on. This explains the presence of Catholic religious images and objects outside and inside Voodoo temples. The mixing of Catholicism and Voodoo is also evident in the fact that in order to be initiated into Voodoo, a believer must be a baptized Catholic.

The main purpose of Voodoo ceremonies is to allow each believer to enter into communication with loas, which will act as his guides in the visible world and intermediaries with God in the invisible world—something like the guardian angels of Catholicism. Loas have various ways to communicate with believers. They can enter dreams or possess believers during rituals. These phenomena are quite common in Haiti and can occur at any time. More rarely, there are reports that loas can materialize and appear visibly.

Loas are endowed with the good/evil duality. Although some are more inclined to produce evil powers—these are called Petro loas (the word *Petro* comes from Don Pedro, an eighteenth century Catholic priest, who was known as a powerful sorcerer and who used the cosmic force and the loas for evil purposes)—and others to produce good—these are called Rada loas (the word *Rada* seems to come from Arada, an old kingdom of Benin)—loas are generally neither good nor evil in themselves, and can be used for either good or evil.

But Voodoo is a religion in search of the sacred: it uses the cosmic force only in a positive way, and loas are never called for evil purposes. "Only loas representing good energies will contact us, because our mind creates positive vibrations," a Voodoo priest told me. So, within the context of Voodoo, all rituals are Rada rituals.

The many other sects that exist parallel to Voodoo, all dealing with sorcery, use loas for personal advancement in the visible world and for evil purposes, not for reaching the sacred. Rituals performed outside the Voodoo context are thus called Petro rituals. (To mark the distinction between Voodoo and these other beliefs and rituals, Haitians sometimes say, "There is Voodoo left hand [sorcery] and Voodoo right hand [true Voodoo]," or "There is Rada Voodoo [true Voodoo] and Petro Voodoo [sorcery])."

A spiritual leader of Voodoo is called a *houngan* if a man, a *mambo* if a woman. The word *houngan* can be translated as "Voodoo priest," but the real meaning is "healer of the mind and body." The mind is seen as being what animates the body; if the mind is out of balance, the body will be out of balance and therefore sick. The principal role of the houngan is to keep in balance the energies that flow between the body, the mind, the soul, and the loas of the initiate, in order to create harmony between the physical and the cosmic, between the individual and the sacred or to restore the balance if it has been upset. To do this, the houngan uses plants or other natural ingredients to repair the damage done to the body by illness—the cosmic imbalance.

Like a shaman, a houngan is a keeper of the ritual, an initiate into the secret knowledge and mysteries. He is a healer, an exorcist, and a diviner; because he knows how to deal with the invisibles and enter their supernatural world, he can communicate with the souls of the dead. According to his degree of initiation into this secret knowledge (that is, the aptitude to enter the invisible world and to use the cosmic force), a houngan can use his psychic faculties and manipulate supernatural powers. A houngan may use magic in his works, but he never uses the cosmic force for evil purposes, nor does he use evil loas. He dedicates his life and talents only to good, since he leads a religion in search of the sacred.

However, tempted by material comforts, houngans sometimes fail in their principles. They then stop being houngans with all the principles and values attached to that sacerdotal function, and they become *bokors,* dedicating their lives to sorcery and to the use of Petro loas, evil spirits, and souls of the dead to accomplish their evil works. (Chapter 8 deals with bokors.)

A houngan is an autonomous patriarch, in the biblical sense of the word. He is absolutely responsible for the well-being of all the worshipers he has initiated; they become members of the community that belongs to his temple, or *houmfort*. But besides being their spiritual adviser and protector, a houngan also has the obligation to help the members of his community in their social lives: finding them a job, feeding those who are hungry, sheltering the homeless in his houmfort. In exchange, the community members obey him, pay for his services in whatever way they can, and help during the ceremonies he performs.

Some houngans own commercial enterprises—cattle, pig, goat, or chicken farms, sugar-cane plantations, and so on—but always set aside some animals for ceremonial sacrifices and to feed the community. In these cases, the community members work on the farm and are paid for their services.

I have lived in many houmforts. Besides the warm and friendly atmosphere that prevails in them, what touched me the most was that the community members call their houngan *father*, and their mambo *mother*.

In Voodoo, there is no pyramidal hierarchy as in Catholicism. From his first initiation into Voodoo until the day he becomes a houngan, the neophyte belongs to the community of the houngan who initiated him, and is at his beck and call. The day he himself becomes a houngan, he is freed of that duty and becomes independent and autonomous. Different reasons may lead a Voodoo believer to become a houngan: faith, vocation, a calling by a loa, the discovery by another houngan of spiritual and psychic abilities in him, or a houngan father or a mambo mother.

It takes years of study and apprenticeship, following a long, harsh path of humility that leads to wisdom and enlightment, to become a houngan. The *lavé-tête,* a kind of baptism performed when the neophyte is *invested* by his first loa, which will be called the *loa-tête* (loa head"), constitutes the first degree of Voodoo initiation. With the second degree of initiation, a neophyte becomes a Voodoo initiate—a *kanzo* or *hounsi.* He can assist a houngan.

The third degree of initiation makes him a freemason, in order to understand and manipulate symbols of the occult tradition. It introduces him to the esoteric knowledge of alchemy, astrology, the Cabala, metaphysics, metaphysic principles, and Theosophy; he is able to converse with loas through states of possession—his own or others'—and it gives him the right to possess his own houmfort and become the leader of his own community, for he has become a houngan. He then gets his *asson,* a small gourd filled with snake vertebrae, to which a bell may be attached. The *asson* is a kind of magic baton, a symbol of his sacerdotal profession, the sceptre of the highly initiated, an instrument of power over the invisibles. Used like a rattle, it gives him the power to call the loas into the houmfort.

A houngan often pursues more studies in order to get higher degrees of intiation and knowledge. Some become disciples of greater houngans; others get higher knowledge from their loa-tête. The fourth degree of initiation, for instance, leads a houngan to a secret ceremony called *la prise des yeux* ("the taking of eyes"), during which he acquires clairvoyant powers. He gets the ability of reading past and future through various means. (A houngan once very accurately described my past and present, and foretold a few events that did indeed happen years later. He did this just by examining the surface of water in a bowl, over which I had to blow.)

At this point the houngan becomes a psychic healer and a magician, able to enter the mysteries of life and of the universe, and to converse with the souls of the dead through a *govi,* a little pitcher.

Voodoo worship can be conducted at home, in front of the family shrine, where, on a daily basis, the head of the family may perform small rituals to salute the family's loas and the souls of dead relatives. Although they may consist of food offerings and, sometimes, animal sacrifices, these domestic rituals seldom induce trances or possession phenomena.

The major Voodoo ceremonies take place in the houmfort, where they can be performed according to the local religious calendar, and as often as community needs dictate.

A houmfort is composed of a *peristyle*—a large room where ceremonies take place—and of many smaller rooms, called *sanctuaries,* with shrines dedicated to the specific loas honored by the community. Depending on its importance and on the community's wealth, a houmfort can be just an open place covered with a palm-leaf roof and surrounded by small huts made out of dried mud, or it can be a group of small houses sheltering the sanctuaries, built around a larger structure.

A houmfort is often recognizable by magical designs and writings and by colorful mystical paintings or pious representations of Catholic saints covering the walls both inside and out. The paintings are reminiscent of Chagall, Miró, and Mondrian. To the initiate who can decipher it, Voodoo art reveals which loas are honored by the community, and indicates what kind of magic and rituals are performed there. The art also describes the houngan's powers, the magical forces he has mastered, and the occult worlds he can penetrate.

A large wooden cross is always erected near the houmfort's main entrance. This is not a Christian cross; rather, it symbolizes the *tree of life*—the intersection between the visible or physical world and the invisible or spiritual world. The horizontal bar marks the separation between the visible world below and the invisible world above; the vertical pole is the magic axis, the mystical passage that links the two worlds. In a sense, the cross is the point of convergence of all energies.

We know that this symbol existed long before Christianity, which in fact assimilated it just as it did many sacred principles from other, more ancient religions. But in Voodoo the cross has kept its original, mystic values.

Sometimes the cross is driven into a small false grave. This grave symbolizes Baron Samedi, the head of the Guédés. Not far from the cross, a piece of iron driven into the ground represents Ogoune-Feraille, the energy of war, (and also symbolizes the power of life). Every tree, large stone, or small pond, or other element of nature near the houmfort is a place where loas may dwell.

At the center of the houmfort's peristyle is a pole, called the *poteau-mitan,* which joins the ground to the roof. Like the totems of North American Indians, it represents the axis of the metapsychic cosmos, the magical passage connecting the visible world to the invisible. It carries to the invisibles the supplications and prayers of the people, and is the passage used by loas to move down into the peristyle. (In some temples a rope hanging from the roof, with a stone at its end, replaces the pole.) There is also an altar standing against one wall, on which a small red light—like the eternal light that symbolizes the divine presence in Catholic churches—burns neverendingly. On the altar one also sees various ritual objects, an amazing collection of different colorful things: candles; pious pictures and plastic statues of saints; filled and half-empty bottles of soft drinks, whiskey, rum, and other kinds of alcohol; thunderstones; Arawak pottery; ritual bottles decorated with skull and crossbones and containing sanctified rum; plastic flowers; and, sometimes, flashing Christmas lights, if electricity is available in the village.

A series of drums, much like those of Africa, line another wall. Each drum is decorated differently, has a unique shape and size, and produces a distinctive sound. Very important elements of Voodoo ceremonies, drums are not considered just musical instruments: they are the homes of the loas, who use the drummers to express themselves. The drummer becomes a medium expressing the musical language through which loas talk to worshipers.

This brings up an interesting aside. The first things destroyed by the Catholic clergy during their anti-Voodoo campaigns, were the drums, the most important ones being the *assotors,* the giant drums made of an African wood. In his book *Le vaudou haitien,* the French ethnologist and Voodoo expert Alfred Métraux wrote that there were no more assotors left in Haiti. He was wrong. I have had the privilege of seeing the only two that have survived destruction. They are still used in a small Haitian village once yearly, during the Easter Voodoo ceremonies.

The exterior sanctuaries are small rooms with shaded windows, lit only by candles on a small altar. A strange smell bathes the dark atmosphere, a mixture of the scent of burning candles and various strong perfumes that are offered to loas, particularly those who are female—like Erzulie, the energy of love and sex.

Each sanctuary has shrines over the altar, with representations of the Catholic saints who symbolize the loas to whom the sanctuary is dedicated. Like the one in the peristyle, sanctuary altars are covered with various objects, including a red light to symbolize the divine presence.

Besides being dedicated to a specific loa, each sanctuary has a further function. One may be the place where initiates come to meet with the houngan. Another is where the houngan heals and exorcizes. Some are secret places that only the houngan is permitted to enter. In the one called Bagui (the Hut of Mysteries), the houngan deals with the world of the invisibles. Initiation ceremonies are performed in the Djevo or Soba, completely dark rooms in which adepts are locked in for their entire initiation, which may last as long as a month.

CONTACT WITH THE DIVINE

Throughout history, all cultures have believed it possible to have contact with the Divine—that is, to see, hear, converse with, or have some direct relation to God or their divinities. From the first known ancient civilization up until the present, from peoples of tradition to a number of devout Catholics in our own time, there have been many instances of witnesses, prophets, and priests who claim to commune with the powers above. But who can say whether such contacts are real or imagined?

However, among peoples of tradition I have seen things that have no rational explanation other than the possibility of contact with the Divine. And while it can't be proven, those who have undergone such a mystic experience have entered a reality that is perhaps unknowable to those who haven't.

There are three ways that contact with the Divine has been realized. In the first, people see the Divine but get no messages. In the second, people see the Divine and benefit from their contact through actual messages that are heard. In the third, people converse with the Divine and can themselves become divine through trance and possession.

Seeing the Divine

In Katmandu, Nepal, I met a living goddess. Or to be exact, I met a little girl who was the Kumari, the virgin goddess, believed by the Buddhists to be the incarnation of the goddess Taleju and worshiped by the Hindus as well.

For a girl to be declared the virgin goddess she must be between three and five years of age and perfect in body and health; and she must undergo thirty-two separate trials to prove she is the incarnation of the goddess Taleju. In one such test, the little girl spends the night alone, surrounded by the heads of a hundred sacrificed buffalos, and must remain unafraid while dogs, frenzied by blood, fight over the heads; no goddess would cry.

If she passes the tests, the candidate assumes the name of Kumari and sits enthroned; kings bow before her. But the Kumari's life is a sad and lonely one. She is forbidden to speak to anyone or even to smile and nod, and since the ground is impure she must not walk, but must be carried everywhere. Her divine career ends if she loses blood from a wound, or when she reaches puberty and has her first menstrual period. Even after this time, she is not able to marry since her temporary divinity brings with it a curse: any man who dares to marry her will die within a year.

Whether or not such little girls really are the incarnation of the goddess Taleju I cannot say. However, if they are, as the Buddhist and Hindu traditions claim, it seems clear to me that the only thing their devotees gain is the belief that they have contact with the Divine. They get no messages from these girls, no body of teaching that would allow personal and spiritual growth.

Seeing and Hearing the Divine

The second kind of contact with the Divine differs from the first in that one can actually receive messages from a divine apparition.

The Bible makes many references to invisible and divine beings that suddenly appear in a visible form. God, for instance, appeared to Moses in the form of a burning bush and talked to him; the Angel Gabriel appeared to the Virgin Mary; and so on.

In the nineteenth century, the Virgin Mary appeared many times to a girl in Fatima, Portugal, and gave her revelations. In 1858, in Lourdes, France, she appeared eighteen times to a fourteen-year-old girl named Bernadette Soubirou, who also claimed that the Virgin told her what was to be done to save the world.

As I write this book, the Virgin Mary continues to appear in Fatima, Portugal, and in Yugoslavia, where she is seen even by non-Catholics. The three young men and one young woman who see her frequently and hear her messages have been examined by scientists from all over the world. Electroencephalogram tests rule out hysteria, and science can offer no further explanation.

Conversing with the Divine and Becoming Divine

The third way of having contact with the Divine is through a mystical experience that may involve possession phenomena. This happens in all cultures where religious rituals are based on the principles of trance and possession. The worshipers not only have contact with the Divine, but may converse with divine entities and, by the means of possession, become divine themselves and a channel for the sacred.

I have witnessed such phenomena throughout the world. But it was in Haiti—where I lived for five years, studying Voodoo and other Haitian religious belief systems—that I was able to observe these kinds of religious phenomena carefully. There, I have seen what the Catholic church calls *theophany*—that is, the manifestation of God or divinities in human form.

Before his initiation into Voodoo—which can take place at any age, but never before puberty, and only if he is a baptized Catholic—the novice receives a series of religious teachings from the houngan. When the master feels his student is ready, he begins the initiation itself.

Part of this process consists of getting a *loa-tête* for the novice, a loa who will be his protector for life, helping him to solve everyday material problems and protecting him from hunger, illness, and bad luck. Most important of all, this loa will be his intermediary with God, making sure his soul will find a place next to God in the afterlife.

During his first degree of initiation, which can last up to one month, the novice is kept completely cloistered in a small, dark sanctuary, where he leads an ascetic existence: loneliness and silence . . . loneliness and silence . . . broken only by the houngan's mystical teachings. And again loneliness and silence . . . loneliness and prayers. Silence broken by sacred teachings. Silence and self-confrontation. Silence and loneliness and tears. Darkness and loneliness. The silence and loneliness bring forth regrets and remorse, tears and fear. Fear of death begins and grows stronger.

At this point, the houngan brings about the ritual death of the novice, and carries out the same process of silence, loneliness, prayers, and teachings again. Fear sensitizes the body to cosmic forces; the mind calls upon the loas for help. But the passing time gives birth to a fear of the loas, who, at any time, may push the novice's spirit away, possessing his body. Tears and screams break the prayers and the silence. The neophyte becomes like a virgin excited by the male's erection, willing to be penetrated, yet fearing what will happen. The mind begins creating invocations to shut down the silence, the darkness, and the unbearable loneliness. Through teachings and prayers, discovery and acceptance of the self begin; self-love appears.

Now the houngan brings about the novice's ritual rebirth. After more silence, prayers, and teaching, the houngan returns, this time holding his *asson,* the sacred rattle that gives him the power to call loas. And for hours, his instrument produces magic rhythms—cosmic signals calling other universes. Every day the silence, the prayers, and the teaching are interrupted by the cosmic call of the rattle.

And suddenly it happens. A loa throws out the novice's mind and takes over his body. *He is possessed.* By questioning the entity through the possessed initiate, the houngan is able to recognize which loa has been incarnated in this body. And since, as time goes on, the loa comes more frequently, answering his rattle's call to possess the novice, the houngan knows that this entity has become the novice's *loa-tête*. The novice has received his first initiation into the world of Voodoo.

Through the second degree of the Voodoo initiation, he will become a Voodoo initiate. And at the end of that initiation, the houngan captures the initiate's breath by means of a magic ritual, and shuts it in a terra-cotta pot, called a *pot-de-tête*, (head pot), which will be added to all the other *pots-de-tête* for the initiated members of the houngan's community. And from then on, as long as he belongs to this community, the initiate will be magically linked to the houngan.

The release of a new initiate into the village is always cause for mystical and often frightening ceremonies, during which the power of men calls down the power of divine entities. The initiate is dressed in white, symbolizing the purity of rebirth. While he prays inside the sanctuary where he has been initiated, more and more worshipers and the other new initiates, also dressed in white, move slowly into the peristyle, talking and laughing.

The drummers start to brace their drums. Using consecrated flour and ashes, the houngan draws a large rectangle on the ground at the foot of the altar, which he fills with messages. Then he draws a series of magic designs, called *vévés,* in front of the drums and all around the *poteau-mitan.* Each of these designs represents the emblem of a specific loa who will be called by the houngan's *asson;* its function is to attract and fix this loa's energy. In addition to their masonic and alchemic symbolism, one can also recognize in these designs the influence of astrology, the Cabala, metaphysics, and theosophy.

Each design is perfectly symmetrical. One half symbolizes the loa's emblem as if reflected by the *cosmic mirror* that separates the visible world from the invisible; the other half symbolizes the emblem as if it continued across the cosmic mirror to the other side, reaching the invisible world. A small cross drawn on top marks the opening of this cosmic mirror; it is the point of connection with the source of life, the cosmic memory.

The magic power of such a vévé comes from the fact that it reflects both the visible and the invisible world, each holding forces that oppose the other. But as long as the design remains perfectly symmetrical, it cannot generate power because the two opposing forces are kept in balance. So, just before the ceremony is to begin, the houngan will add a small line on one side of the design only, in order to break its symmetry and, therefore, the balance between the two opposing forces. The effort of these two forces to re-create harmony will generate the power necessary to attract the specific loa represented by the design.

The other thing the houngan must do is put all the forces inside the peristyle out of balance. To do this, he cuts magic designs in the air with a ritual machete. This liberates the forces kept still by the harmony, and marks the opening of the ceremony.

☾

The houngan begins singing a Catholic religious chant in Latin. The new initiates enter the peristyle and move toward their families, who greet them with reverence. In the courtyard outside the peristyle, other worshipers wash animals to purify them, then cover them with colorful silk scarves in preparation for their sacrifice to the loas.

The houngan takes his *asson* and starts singing in Creole, the native Haitian language, a series of short salutations and invocations to the loas; worshipers join in on the refrains. The rattle leads the chants, marking the rhythm, and calls the loas, inviting them to join the celebration.

After an hour, the drums begin to beat; they will continue to beat until the end of the ceremony, which may last for six or seven hours, or even longer. Drums are the rhythmic foundation of a Voodoo ceremony. Each drum has a specific sound and follows its own very sophisticated rhythm. There are drumbeats to mark the beginning and end of dances, drumbeats to call for loas and drumbeats to greet them, drumbeats to chase away evil energies and undesirable entities that might cause trouble, and drumbeats to throw believers into a state of trance. And once someone is possessed, there are drumbeats to accompany each step of his possession.

Chants and wild drumbeats soon fill the peristyle with an electric energy, a feeling of the sacred, that penetrates the body through all the pores of the skin. Still shaking his rattle, the houngan moves through the crowded peristyle and stops between the *poteau-mitan* and the altar, where he turns to greet the four directions as well as the above and the below, thus marking the center of the universe. He repeats this a few times to amplify the ritual's magic.

Then he picks up a bowl of water and a bottle containing sanctified rum, and pours both water and rum on the ground to salute the souls of the deceased. He then pours water and rum on each of the different magic vévé's to greet the loas they represent, starting with the design of his *loa-tête*.

He moves to the drums and, in front of each, turns 360 degrees. He pours water at the drum's base, and takes a sip of rum, which he sprays over the drum and its drummer, thus greeting the *loa-tambour* (loa drum). He then goes to the spot where he has established the center of the universe and pours water and rum on the ground; again he takes sips of rum and sprays it in all directions, thereby greeting the below, the east, the south, the west, the north, and the above.

Moved by the incessant and hypnotic rhythms of the drums, which are reinforced by the omnipresent sound of the houngan's rattle, people begin to shake their bodies, dancing and singing chants in Creole and ancient African dialects. After an hour or two of this frenzy, the atmosphere becomes charged with powerful energies—so intense that I have to go outside and pour water over my head.

This frenzied atmosphere of music and body movements induces trance states. Already a few believers have been captured: their eyes become wild-looking or closed; their bodies, covered with sweat, begin shaking wildly and violently. In a trance state the believer is extremely receptive; he is vulnerable to possession. Unlike some other cultures of tradition, Voodoo believers do not drink alcohol or take psychedelics to create a trance state. Their trances are induced by the synergy of dancing, chants, and loud drumbeats.

Feeling the loas' presence, the houngan calls for the *manger-loa*— the feeding of the loas. As I mentioned earlier, the loas are the Voodoo initiates' invaluable helpers in the visible and invisible worlds. In exchange for this, the initiates must honor their loas with thoughts, prayers, and rituals, and must feed them during their part of the ceremony. Forgetting or refusing to do so may bring on the loas' wrath and a call for vengeance. But there are two other reasons for making the sacrifice: to give thanks to a loa for something he did, or to ask him for a favor. This latter reason follows an interesting principle, which is worth explaining since we too apply it to our behavior. In normal circumstances, there is a balanced relationship between a loa and a worshiper. The worshiper owes the loa nothing, and the loa owes the worshiper nothing. Therefore, by offering a sacrifice to the loa, the worshiper breaks the balance of their relationship, putting the loa in the position of owing him a favor. And as the saying goes, "Give something to a divinity, and the divinity will give it back to you one hundred times."

At a signal of the houngan's rattle, the drummers change their rhythms, which almost instantly calms the participants, bringing them out of their trances. The dancing and chanting continue, but at a different pace. The twenty or thirty people who will make sacrifices hug and caress their animals to show love and respect for them and to create oneness with them. Depending on the importance of the favor they want, and on their wealth, worshipers may sacrifice chickens, goats, pigeons, pigs, or even bulls.

The houngan places some grains of corn and a small bowl filled with water on each magic design. Carrying their live offerings, the worshipers, one by one, put them on the designs. If the animal eats a few grains of corn and drinks water, this shows that the specific loa accepts the offering. If nothing happens, or if the animal only eats or only drinks, it is sent back outside for another ritual bath.

With the same powder he used to create the magic designs, the houngan draws a cross on the back of the animals who have been accepted by the loas. But there is one last thing to be done before sacrificing them: the houngan must determine whether the loas are ready for the meal. He chooses one worshiper who is still in a trance, places him on the spot where he established the center of the universe, and holds a chicken in front of him. The houngan hopes the believer will be possessed by the loa protector of the houmfort, who will signify that the meal may start. If nothing happens within the next five minutes, the *manger-loa* will be delayed. But the ceremony will continue, with dancing and chanting, until the loas indicate that they are ready for the animal sacrifices.

And, indeed, it happens. The believer, at first motionless, with his eyes half-closed, suddenly seems to be hit by a powerful energy that shakes his body violently. His eyes open wide. He grabs the chicken with his teeth and beheads the animal, keeping the lifeless, bloody head in his mouth.

The houngan passes his hands over the head of the possessed man, who slowly releases the chicken's head. The loas are ready to start their feast. The animal sacrifices may begin. Drumbeats grow wilder; chants and dances express joy.

Holding a chicken in each hand, the houngan passes them over the heads of the worshipers, who, one by one, come and bow in front of him. This creates a oneness with the animals, making the believers part of the sacrifice. Then, amid a frenzy of chicken shrieks and flapping wings, of drumbeats and chants, everyone who has a chicken to sacrifice breaks its legs and wings, while continuing to dance.

This transforms the chickens: they loose their astral, etheric body, upon which the loas will feed. The tongues of the chickens are torn out—the tongue symbolizes language; therefore it can lie—and stuck on the *poteau-mitan*. The houngan places a drop of sacrificial blood on the forehead of each believer to testify to the sacrifice and to insure immortality.

Holding them by the head, the worshipers turn their chickens round and round, breaking their necks, while still chanting and dancing in a circle around the *poteau-mitan*. Afterward, they put the dead chickens, side by side, on the magic designs at the foot of the altar.

The animal sacrifices have ended. The *manger-loa* is over. The dead chickens will be cooked and eaten by the community after the ceremony in a ritual feast. The drums begin to beat wildly again. (The physical stamina of the musicians is absolutely amazing; they can play for seven or eight hours without taking a rest.) And the frenzy once again induces trances in the worshipers, conditioning them for possession.

The way in which believers experience their possession varies from one person to another. For some, it seems to be an ecstatic joy, for others, a frightful and painful emotional trial. The latter seem to be resisting the loa, who is forcing his way into their body, trying to chase their own spirit away in order to master their will and possess them entirely. Their eyes open wide, looking at the invisible presence, they scream hysterically, or cry, their faces completely distorted by pain and fear. Their fight to free themselves of the outside energy trying to break their will provokes amazing and breathtaking scenes.

Literally and visibly attacked by the loa, the body is violently shaken, and the hands are twisted in different ways. The head is brutally pulled back, as if invisible hands had grabbed the hair. (In fact, loas are called divine horsemen: they sit astride believers, who become the horses of the Divine.) Sometimes—and I have seen this more than once—the body is lifted into the air and shaken like a puppet, then thrown another direction, where it falls to the ground.

If believers don't give themselves up to the loas' will, the houngan helps them to do so by passing his hands over their heads and tying scarves around their waists; this instantly ends their struggle. And their faces become ecstatic as they finally are able to experience the divine possession calmly. Everyone who is possessed is carefully watched and handled with care, both by the houngan and by those who are not, or not yet, possessed by loas.

A possession may last for a few minutes, or for hours. A believer may be possessed many times by the same loa, or successively by different loas—even by some who do not pertain to his life. There are believers who will not be possessed at all, even if they want to be. It seems that the state of possession is not dependent upon the believer's will, but upon the loas' choice. In the same manner, loas can possess people who don't want to be chosen and those who are not in a trance, wherever they may be.

When they are possessed by loas, believers may do astounding things. I have seen people eating deadly sharp-edged glass, walking on fire, levitating, and dematerializing. Some possessed believers lie down on huge fires without their clothes catching fire. Others become channelers of the Divine, making predictions and prophecies, or delivering secret messages and giving personal advice to those who approach and question them. Many start to speak a language unknown to them, a kind of gibberish which is perfectly understood by houngans and other High Initiates only; it is the language of the Divine. This phenomenon is called glossolalia.

At last, at the houngan's sign, the drumbeats change their rhythms, sending the loas away, and bringing peace into the peristyle again. The ceremony that started ten hours ago is about to close. The houngan performs a ritual that restores the balance of energies he had broken. Harmony returns. Those who were possessed begin to recover from their mystical experience—which they never remember, for as loas leave their believers' bodies they take their memories with them. But the believers know they have been part of the sacred. And those who have not been possessed are content, for they have had a contact, and maybe have conversed, with the Divine. Everyone goes home, exhausted but happy.

Except me. For I wonder what it is that I have witnessed.

☽

I'd now like to share a few stories with you that I find interesting. The first perfectly illustrates that, indeed, loas can possess anyone at any time.

A houngan was performing an exorcism inside a small sanctuary. The sanctuary was crowded with members of the community, sitting on benches set along the walls. The only place where my former wife and I could sit was on the ground, against the knees of those sitting on the bench behind us. There was no drumming in that ceremony, just the rattle of the houngan's *asson* as he prayed and chanted invocations that the crowd repeated softly.

Sitting just behind us on the bench were two women, who were talking about clothes and prices. I whispered to my wife, "How funny it is: we do not belong to this religious culture, yet here we are, amazed and sensitized by this sacred atmosphere, while behind us, these two women seem to completely ignore where they are."

I had hardly finished talking when the woman sitting just behind me jumped over my head and, her body shaking like a puppet, floated in the air just in front of us, five feet off the ground, for a long time—much longer than the laws of gravity would allow. And then instead of falling down vertically, she was thrown to the other side of the sanctuary, where she fell down next to the houngan. It was, literally, as if the woman had been grabbed by an invisible force that shook her body before throwing her to one side. My wife and I pinched each other to be sure we were not dreaming.

☾

The second event showed me that one doesn't need to share the Voodoo faith and worldview to be possessed by a loa.

A dear friend of mine—whom I will call Jean—would offer me hospitality whenever I was in Haiti. A French scientist with several Ph.D.'s, Jean was in Haiti to restructure the university's Faculty of Science and to teach physics. He had never been interested in Voodoo, and systematically refused my many invitations to accompany me to a Voodoo ceremony. I wasn't even able to arouse his curiosity with my stories and accounts of the amazing phenomena I had witnessed. For him, Voodoo was just the naive superstitions of a bunch of hysterical people. "Religion is the last hope of weak and ignorant people!" he used to say, trying to persuade me that one day science would prove the nonexistence of God.

One day, however, he agreed to accompany me to a Voodoo ceremony that I wanted to film. He did so as a favor, because I had no one else to help me with the sound recording. "It's just to help you that I am going, Douchan," he repeated all the way to the houmfort.

The ceremony was dedicated to the Guédés, the loa guardians of the souls of the dead. They are honored during ceremonies performed day and night, starting on All Saints' Day and continuing until the end of November.

The interesting thing about these ceremonies—which do not involve animals sacrifices, and in which believers can be possessed by Guédés and souls of the deceased—is the technique the houngan uses to ascertain that worshipers really are possessed. He gives them a foot-long cigar to smoke and a special bottle to drink from. Smoking a foot-long cigar is no astounding feat, but to finish off the contents of the special bottle, which contains one liter of rum in which two pounds of hot peppers have marinated for a whole year, is something no one could do under normal circumstances.

I took a sample sip, and it immediately brought tears to my eyes; I began to sweat instantly, and for a while it stopped me from talking. And for many hours my lips, tongue, and throat burned despite all the water I drank. My skin was irritated wherever the spicy mixture had touched it. The mere opening of the bottle brought tears to the eyes of the whole Haitian crowd. Yet when possessed by a Guédé or a dead person's soul, a worshiper can drink a few bottles of this mixture without being bothered.

Jean stood next to the *poteau-mitan,* with the tape recorder hanging around his neck; he would point the two microphones toward whatever I was filming. I moved throughout the crowd with the camera to wherever something interesting was going on.

As usual, drumming, chanting, and dancing filled the air with powerful energies. Two hours later, it had become a frenzy. Some believers, in a state of trance, were shaking all over, while others, experiencing violent possessions, were drinking spiced rum and smoking cigars. (Possessions by Guédés are more violent than possessions by loas.)

As I happened to glance at Jean, I saw him jump to one side, as if hit by an electrical charge. He struggled to keep control of himself. I began filming him, and continued to do so until he fell down and disappeared into the crowd. Thinking he was perhaps having a heart attack, I rushed to where he had fallen and found him prone on the ground, motionless except for his feet, which were moving to the drums' rhythms. His usually ruddy face was pale and covered with sweat; his hands were cold. I was about to call for help when the houngan approached. "Don't worry! Your friend is just possessed by a Guédé," he said, holding Jean's head with respect and tenderness.

"It's impossible!" I answered.

"You'll see," he said, tying a purple scarf around Jean's neck. (Purple is the color of Guédés.) Jean suddenly stood up and, a wild look in his eyes, drank the entire bottle of spiced rum that the houngan held out to him and began talking to him in the language of the sacred, which there was no way he could know. Then, smoking the cigar the houngan had given him, he began dancing wildly.

I filmed and took photographs of the scene, but couldn't believe what I was seeing. Jean, who never drank alcohol or ate spicy food because it upset his stomach, emptied several bottles of spiced rum. The man who couldn't stand it when I smoked, even in a car with the windows open, smoked a series of cigars.

After an hour Jean collapsed, as if he had fainted. When he regained consciousness, he said he felt relaxed, with neither a hangover nor indigestion. But he had no memory of what had transpired. Of course, when I recounted to him what he had done during the ceremony, he didn't believe a word. "You have a wild imagination, Douchan," he said, laughing. "What are you trying to prove? Such things can't happen to a rationally minded person like me."

A week later, I showed him the photos, saying, "If these don't convince you, the next time I come I'll bring my movie." He grabbed the photos and disappeared into his room, where he remained for two days.

When Jean gave me the pictures back I knew we would never talk about his mystical adventure again. However, he made himself available to accompany me to other ceremonies—searching, I imagine, for scientific, logical explanations for what he had experienced. And he became for me a precious witness to the many scientifically unexplainable phenomena that took place in our presence.

☾

The following story illustrates how possession by a loa is not dependent on the believer's desire and will, but on the will of the loa.

If a Catholic woman decides to dedicate her life to worshiping God, she may become a nun. Among other things, she will make a vow of celibacy and wear a wedding ring, symbolizing that she belongs to God. In Voodoo, too, women—and men as well—may dedicate their whole lives to a loa and marry the divine entity. These mystic marriages, however, are rare, for being married to a loa requires draconian obligations and responsibilities that few men and women are ready to take on.

I had the privilege of seeing and filming a ceremony in which a twenty-year-old woman married Djamballah-Wedo, the loa who represents the energy of fecundity and is symbolized by a snake.

When she was nineteen, Marie, a Voodoo initiate, began seeing a snake in her dreams, and it obsessed her. The houngan she consulted told her not to worry, that the snake could only be Djamballah-Wedo visiting her in her dreams. Then, when she turned twenty, she dreamed that the snake wanted to marry her. Answering this mystical call, she decided to marry him, despite her houngan's advice that she not do so because of the responsibilities and obligations she would contract for her whole life.

As far as the possession phenomenon is concerned, her wedding ceremony was perhaps the most impressive and disturbing of all the Voodoo ceremonies I have witnessed.

The houngan—a man in his forties whom I already knew, having filmed a few ceremonies in his houmfort—allowed me to film the marriage. I was there with my friend Jean and a couple of American friends—Steven Ball and Virginia, his former wife—who had arrived the day before to witness their first Voodoo ceremony. Steven was an architect and Virginia an interior designer. Both rationally minded, they didn't believe my stories about Voodoo and had decided to come to Haiti to see for themselves.

Setting two chairs before the altar for the intended husband and wife, the *houngan* said to me, "Usually I am the one possessed by Djamballah-Wedo. So just look at me, and you'll see how Djamballah-Wedo manifests himself when possessing someone." Then, a few minutes later, as he was drawing the magic designs, he added, "I would like you to come back and show me the film you'll make tonight, because I have never seen how I look when I am possessed."

The peristyle was filled with worshipers chanting in Creole, and with the wild beating of drums. The wedding service began with a ritual opening and traditional salutations to the souls of the deceased and to various loas. Then, followed by the bride-to-be, who was wearing a colorful dress and a large straw hat, the houngan and two mambo assistants paraded around the peristyle carrying the community's sacred flags, whose many-colored weavings represented Djamballah-Wedo's emblem. This went on for about three hours, accompanied by the rattling of the houngan's *asson,* chants and invocations to the bridegroom.

Then, because Djamballah-Wedo seemed to be putting off his arrival, the houngan decided to perform another ritual to call him. Once the sacred flags were carried back to one of the sanctuaries, he appeared, shaking his rattle and leading invocations and chanting, with the two mambos at his sides, and still followed by the bride-to-be. One mambo was carrying a small bowl of milk, the other a cup of barley syrup and three chicken eggs—snakes' favorite foods. This went on for another two hours.

Then, suddenly, Djamballah-Wedo arrived, but not as the houngan had anticipated. Although the houngan was usually the one to be possessed by this loa, and although he wanted to be possessed so he could be filmed in that state, it wasn't he who was possessed, but the mambo who was holding the bowl of milk.

As if hit by lightning, the mambo jumped in the air and fell on the ground, where, her eyes closed (they stayed closed for her entire possession), she started crawling and hissing like a snake, her tongue darting out of her mouth just as a snake's does. Crawling quickly and with remarkable ease, she rapidly disappeared into the crowd, creating a real panic. The houngan and the other mambo went after her; when they caught her, they had a hard time holding on to her body, which was wriggling in all directions. Only five minutes earlier she had been an old woman barely able to carry her tired body around. Now she wasn't even a woman, but a snake moving with a woman's body.

Having finally subdued her, the houngan and the mambo set her down next to the bride-to-be. Both faced the altar, where a representative of the city government was waiting (the government recognizes such mystic marriages). The incarnation of Djamballah-Wedo suddenly calmed down, but continued hissing and moving her tongue like a snake. Holding the possessed mambo by the hand, the bride-to-be radiated joy.

The civil servant began reading the official wedding contract, which listed all the obligations, duties, and responsibilities the couple had to each other. For instance, besides promising obedience and fidelity, Marie had to agree to give herself heart and soul to her husband every Thursday for twenty-four hours, in a room in her house that would be dedicated to him. As for Djamballah-Wedo, he had to assure her protection and secure physical and financial help in her everyday life.

☾

When I was in Paris not long ago I met a Frenchman who had recently seen my movie about Voodoo. He told me the following story.

During a business trip to Haiti, he tried to convince a young maid at the hotel where he was staying to share his lonely nights. She refused, despite the money he held before her eyes. One night, however, she acquiesced. Back in France, he began having dreams in which he was attacked by a man whose head was that of a snake.

Knowing nothing about Voodoo, he never made a connection between his nightmares and the sexual adventure he had in Haiti with the maid. As his nightmares continued, he experienced a series of misfortunes: his wife left him for another man, he lost his job, and he began suffering from a nervous breakdown and other health problems.

A month later, the maid appeared in his nightmare, standing behind the man with the snake's head. And the Frenchman made the connection. He decided to go back to Haiti, find the girl, and clear up his problems. Despite his friends' warnings, he raised the money and flew to Port-au-Prince, only to find that the maid had been fired because of a health problem, and nobody knew where she was.

After a week of searching he found the girl, who told him that she was married to Djamballah-Wedo. And that in order to survive her divine husband's fury, she had undergone a series of purification rituals that put an end to the misfortune and health problems she had begun experiencing after her infidelity. She helped the Frenchman find a powerful houngan to perform an exorcism on him. And his life came back together again; he regained his wife, his job, and his health.

☾

Some scholars claim that possessions are nothing but psychopathological manifestations. Should we then consider that the 90 per-

cent of Haitians and the several hundred million other people throughout the world who practice religions based on the principles of trance
and possession are just hysterics whose faith is based on superstitious beliefs?

After years of careful observation, I still can't explain what possession phenomena are, but I know that possession is not a psychopathological manifestation, nor is it playacting. I do have some
thoughts regarding possession phenomena in relation to Voodoo,
however, for Voodoo is a religion I have observed and studied.

Voodoo rituals are based on three powerful generators of energies: music (drumbeats), chanting, and dancing. The sounds and
rhythms of drums induce trances, which put the body in a state in
which it can be possessed.

Chanting has always been an important part of all religious rituals. Perhaps as important as their meaning, the rhythm of the words,
in conjunction with the melody, liberates, or generates, energies.

Dancing is also a source of energy. Within the religious context,
dance is for the body what meditation is for the spirit. This physical
ritual can bring on an altered psychic state that puts the performer in
tune with aspects of his brain that induce higher levels of consciousness.

Now, the question is, what are the believers calling through the
synergy of music, chanting, and dancing; what is it that possesses
them? Their answer is that they call divinities, and that divinities possess them.

We can posit that divinities really do exist; or that they really exist
only for those who worship them; or that they really exist, but only
because they have actually been created by the power of man's faith; or
that there are entities that really exist among us that have been called
divinities; or that the cosmic forces and energies that rule the universe
have been perceived as divinities and labeled such.

But perhaps by dint of trying to find explanations we are com-
plicating things. For whatever divinities may be they seem to have real
powers and energies. Otherwise, why would man, over the centuries,
have had the need to perform magico-religious rituals in order to call
them?

As far as Haiti is concerned, I would say that misery opens the
door to the invisible world, because faith is needed to enter that sphere.
Perhaps Haitians more easily accept their tragic destiny because of
their faith in the sacred, imaginary, and magical. But is it only faith
that leads to the supernatural and the Divine; is it faith that guards the
world of the sacred, the imaginary, the magical; is it faith that allows
contacts with the Divine?

I don't think so. Faith is just a means by which we can get rid of the negative beliefs that inhibit us from doing whatever we would like to do and could do without limit—like moving a mountain or becoming divine. The abilities of our minds are limitless, but our belief system limits our powers and talents. The doors of truth and mysteries seem to be closed to our rational and logical minds. It is because children have a limitless imagination that they can enter the world of the imaginary. "The unitary experience of infant and mystic are alike," wrote Claire Myers Owens in *Main Currents in Modern Thought.*

MAGIC HEALING

In Haiti, I witnessed an impressive ceremony that was performed to heal a little girl suffering from an advanced state of tuberculosis. I knew this little girl very well. She lived in a small village in the back country of the Artibonite region. As a matter of fact, I had twice placed her in the hands of official medical science, The diagnosis? That she was in a terminal state of tuberculosis. And I thereafter brought her to a houngan known for his healing powers.

According to his diagnosis, the little girl was the victim of a deadly curse that had thrown her inner energies out of balance, breaking apart her protective field of energies; this allowed illness to take over her body. Consequently, he performed an exorcism to chase away the evil sent by the curse. Then, alone in a sanctuary, he did what was necessary to send the spell back to whoever had generated it.

He next proceeded to restore the balance of the little girl's energies, which automatically expelled the illness from her body. The final part of the ceremony consisted of giving her natural medication (various plants and pulverized minerals) that would repair the damage the illness had done to her body.

When I first brought the little girl to the houngan, I had to carry her, for she couldn't walk. After the ceremony she felt much better. A week later she had recovered completely and was able to play and run with her friends.

When the two doctors who had diagnosed her as terminally ill saw her and the X-rays of her healed lungs, both said that their original diagnoses had certainly been wrong.

LEVITATION

I was twenty when I witnessed levitation for the first time. The event took place in northern India, not far from Cashmere, in a Buddhist monastery where I had been given permission to stay for five days.

I had stopped in India on my way home from the Philippines to Brussels. At that time, 1967, hippies had not yet invaded India and Nepal, although the few foreign visitors who were there had followed the mystical call of Eastern philosophies, searching for a new spirituality.

The head of the monastery was a remarkable old lama who told me that he was in his fourth reincarnation. He spent quite a bit of time with me and, for hours, patiently answered my questions, sharing his knowledge and wisdom. (When I got back home, a friend asked me what language I spoke with him. I couldn't remember. Even today this remains a mystery to me.)

Among the many thoughts the monk shared with me, I remember him telling me that one doesn't get knowledge and wisdom by sitting on the bed and waiting for a master to come and teach you. It is the personal search, the quest within, that lights the way to answers. And whoever has reached that state of mind can find clues to the answers in a book, a conversation, a movie—anywhere. As he said, everything can give an answer to him who has created the need for it.

Another time I asked him why some people seemed to be more lucky than others. He answered my question with another: "How does sap move upward, reaching the last leaves at the top of a tree? Without any mechanical help, sap moves against gravity."

"I don't know," I replied. "Perhaps by capillary action."

"Because the tree creates the need for it," he replied "When, like a tree, someone creates the need for something, that something will come to him. But if someone waits passively for something, like luck, to come to him without using his imagination and intelligence to create the need for it, nothing will come to him. Needing something is a state of mind that creates energies that call and attract."

So, during the rest of my stay in the monastery, I, like a tree, created the need to get anything that would enlighten me in one way or another. And it worked: my need was answered during the religious ceremony performed on the last night of my stay.

That night, I saw the lama, who was sitting in the lotus position, praying, rise slowly upward in the air until he was about two feet above the floor, where he stayed for at least three or four minutes.

The next morning I knew I couldn't leave the monastery without asking him a few questions about what he had done. Looking for him, I stumbled upon a monk who was carrying the little bag containing my personal belongings. "Our spiritual leader has said that you must leave now," he whispered in broken English, leading me to the monastery's exit.

The second time I witnessed levitation was eight years later in a small village in Zaire, during a ceremony performed at night.

Overcome by collective frenzy, the worshipers began jumping over a large campfire, and then walking on its coals without being burned. When it came his turn to do the same, the village sorcerer dove into the fire, in the same way a diver plunges into water, but instead of falling into it, he remained three feet over the fire, parallel to it, long enough for me to ask myself what was happening. Then, as if in slow motion, his body moved until he was standing erect again, his feet touching the live coals, and he walked away.

I couldn't question him that night because he was too intoxicated to talk after the ceremony. But the next morning he said to me, calmly, as if nothing special had occurred, "That happens sometimes, when the spirits are there." I wanted to know more, but he refused to say anything further.

☾

After having seen the lama and then the African sorcerer, I was inclined to think that levitation was a real phenomenon. But the passing of time and the negative reactions of others to my accounts of these experiences slowly started to fill me with distrust, and I began to think that perhaps I had been the victim of a trick that made me think I saw what couldn't possibly have happened.

However, in later years as I traveled extensively throughout Haiti, I saw men and women levitate numerous times. And I now believe in the reality of what I saw, although I have no explanation for how it happens. And I know that it is not just a freak phenomenon but a reflection of the powers of the human mind over matter.

The first time I saw someone levitating in Haiti was in a Voodoo sanctuary. This was the incident I recounted earlier in this chapter, when a woman sitting behind me leaped into the air during an exorcism. The woman was sitting on a bench set against the wall. She suddenly jumped in the air and, passing over my head, floated from behind me to about twelve feet in front of me, where she stayed suspended in air for at least ten seconds, about five feet above the floor. From there, she moved to my left and finally hit the ground about twenty feet away. During the whole time that she was "floating" (she moved about thirty-four feet from her seat to her landing, in an L-shaped pattern), she never touched the ground.

It is interesting to note that all the innumerable levitation phenomena I observed in Haiti involved people who were experiencing a state of possession during a ceremony. They didn't always travel long distances, following a complicated or zigzag path, but they did all levitate by jumping into the air, staying above the ground for much longer than a normal jump would keep them there, and hitting the ground, not always falling straight down.

The reader may think that, since the levitations I observed often happened during nocturnal ceremonies, inside poorly-lit rooms, I could easily have been a victim of trickery contrived by a houngan to prove to me his own powers or the powers of Voodoo. In many cases I did indeed think about this possibility. Yet many of the ceremonies in which I witnessed levitations were performed inside peristyles that were usually well-lit and certainly had enough light for the ceiling to be quite visible. And some were performed during the day, with copious light in the peristyle. Consequently it would have been easy for me to see it if someone levitating was being kept in the air by some physical means such as a rope.

Moreover, since I saw this phenomenon on many occasions, I had the opportunity to study it carefully. After sufficient incidents, I went beyond the state of awe and surprise that might have clouded my first impressions, and was able to observe the situations with calm rationalism, to search carefully for possible fraud, and even to approach the subjects close enough to see the reality of what was going on.

Some of the levitations also took place during ceremonies performed outdoors, in the open air, with a canopy of bright stars above the participants. In small Haitian villages in the back country, where there is often no electricity, Voodoo communities are too poor to build large peristyles. So small huts made of dried mud mixed with straw are used as the houmfort's sanctuaries; and whenever there is to be a large crowd, the village's main square becomes the peristyle, with a pole erected in its center to serve as the *poteau-mitan.*

It was in such a place that I witnessed something quite amazing. The setting was a thirty-square-foot plaza surrounded on three sides by huts and bordered on the fourth side by a large tree, beyond which was a small dirt road. There was a large campfire on one side to light the square, projecting the shadows of the dancing believers on to the walls of the surrounding huts. The light of kerosene lamps tied to the four poles surrounding the dancers and drums lent a hallucinatory atmosphere to the occasion.

All the worshipers were dancing in a frenzy, jumping and violently shaking their bodies. Suddenly the body of one of the dancers stopped wriggling and began moving as if in slow motion. Then the man, his body completely vertical, slowly started to rise into the air as if he were weightless breaking away from the rest of people, who were still dancing frantically. Once he was above the crowd, still in a vertical position and dancing in slow motion, he slowly began to turn upside down.

Once he was upside down—with his head about six feet off the ground—he suddenly traveled through the air with amazing speed, hurtling toward the tree on one side of the plaza and landing, still upside down, on the treetrunk, halfway between the ground and the tree's lowest branches. And in this upside-down position he began climbing the tree until he reached the first branches, where he set himself upright again. To the cheers of the worshipers, he got down from the tree as if nothing had happened.

Before his levitation, the man had been dancing in a group of fifteen people, just in front of five drummers arranged side by side. With my movie camera and my portable lighting system, I was able to move easily all around the dancers, except on two sides—one of which was the one with the tree—which were too crowded with shaking and dancing villagers.

As I moved around looking for a good shot, my assistant would follow me, taking advantage of the movie light to shoot still photos with a camera loaded with normal-speed color-slide film. When I did not have the lights on he took pictures with another camera loaded with high-speed color film.

At one point I was filming no more than six feet away from the dancers, standing behind the drummers, when all of a sudden my lights went off and my movie camera stopped working. (I will consider this technical problem in a moment.) After being blinded for a few seconds, I suddenly noticed the man who was dancing slowly, because his movements contrasted with the other dancers' frenzied gyrations. When he was in the air above the dancers, starting his upside-down turn, I moved to the left side of the group, without losing sight of him, and continued to watch him. I was again about six feet from the dancers, and I stayed there until he came down from the tree.

My closeness to all this allowed me to notice that, while turning slowly upside down, the man's shirt wasn't hanging downward; that is, his shirt was also in a state of levitation.

I searched for tricks, but could find no rope tied to the man. I suppose there could have been a black rope, invisible in darkness, but it couldn't have been attached to the tree since it was too far away—at least thirty feet from the dancers—to have allowed the man to rise vertically above the other dancers, to float in the air, and to make his upside-down movement just above the dancers. Neither did I see any kind of rope stretched between the top of one of the huts and the tree to which this rope might have been tied. Besides, if a black rope had been tied around his waist, it would have contrasted with his white shirt and the white shirts of the other dancers while he was dancing, and later during the first part of his levitation. If the beginning of the rope had been painted white so as to not be seen over his and the others' white shirts, it would have contrasted with the darkness when he rose in the air. But in either case the rope couldn't have kept him vertical while he rose above the dancers, and couldn't have kept him vertical when he was upside down. And the rope would have constrained him in his upside-down movement.

But perhaps the rope was hidden beneath his shirt. That would allow him to rise vertically, but it would stop him from turning upside down and keeping that position until landing on the tree trunk.

In the end, despite careful examination of all possible explanations, I wasn't able to find any evidence of fraud. I had to face the fact that, given the way the scene was set, and the way the levitation took place, there was little or no possibility, technically speaking, for trickery to have taken place. And I have now come to the conclusion that fraud wasn't an issue in many of the other levitation phenomena I witnessed, either.

It is interesting to note that I have never successfully photographed or filmed these phenomena. Each time, something has interfered with my ability to record the incident on film.

Frequently the batteries supplying power to my movie camera died just as the levitation began. As a matter of fact, my camera batteries would not be the only ones to go; the batteries supplying the portable lighting system and those of the tape recorder, as well as my watch's battery, would all give up just at the time someone began levitating.

One set of batteries that dies suddenly can be explained as a technical failure; two separate sets dying at the same time may be considered a coincidence. But the fact that all these separate sets of batteries died at once, and repeatedly—more than twenty times, each time a levitation phenomenon occured—poses serious questions that I don't believe have a purely technical explanation.

Might it be that in order to overcome the forces of gravity and perhaps other principles of physics, someone levitating needs such an enormous amount of energy that it discharges all nearby batteries? Or should we perhaps consider that the state of levitation—that is, the manipulation of gravitational forces and perhaps forces related to other principles of physics—itself develops such a quantity of energy that it short-circuits all batteries, killing them instantly?

I must admit that each time levitation occurred, I felt the hair rise all over my body—I have a hairy body—in the same way it does when I get very close to a TV screen. Since Haitian people have very short, curly hair, I couldn't see if they experienced this. But when asked, all said they could feel a kind of shivering all along their body. This, for them, was proof of the presence of loas incarnate in believers. Also, when I was able to move close to believers in a state of levitation, I could feel heat coming from them, despite the overheated atmosphere of a peristyle. Maybe this excess heat was produced by their overexcited bodies or was due to their frenzied dancing.

There were, however, two occasions when my batteries did not die when levitation occured, perhaps because I was not close enough to the subject. Instead, something equally bizarre interfered with the smooth operation of my movie equipment or with the photographic process, influencing the quality of the picture I took. Once processed, the film showed whatever I had filmed clearly, sharply, and in vivid color—except for those portions of the film covering the levitation. During these sequences, the film was so dark and out of focus that it was absolutely impossible to see what was going on. It was as if I had filmed the whole scene through a filter that darkened and completely blurred my pictures.

As for the still photography, I was using three Nikons. Coupled with a flash, camera A was loaded with a normal-sensitivity color-slide film, camera B was loaded with a high-sensitivity color-slide film, and camera C contained black-and-white film. Thus, regardless of the kind of light, I (or my assistant, in the majority of cases) was always able to take pictures. However, here again, as levitation occurred, something interfered with the photographic process, producing equally poor or, I should say, astonishing results.

For instance, during the last ceremony I described, my assistant used camera B when my lighting system batteries died as the man began levitating. During the whole ceremony he shot five rolls of thirty-six-exposure high-speed film. They were all processed by the Kodak laboratory in Brussels, but when we examined the slides we discovered an enigma. The first twenty-one slides of roll one contained perfectly clear, sharp pictures, with vivid colors, showing various scenes shot before the man levitated. From slide 22 of the first roll of film up to slide 15 of the fifth—the 138 slides shot from the point when the man began moving in slow motion until he was about to move down from the tree—there were no pictures at all on the film; it was completely black. Then, begining with slide 16 of the fifth roll, the pictures were clear and sharp again, and showed the man as he came down from the tree, cheered by the crowd, and various scenes of the rest of the ceremony.

I met the lab supervisor and showed him the whole series of slides, including the faulty ones, emphasizing the order in which they were taken but not telling him about the content of the ceremony. I asked him what kind of technical problem might have caused so many slides to be completely black.

"The only plausible explanation is that the shutter had a momentary failure," he replied. Then, as he carefully examined the slides, he said, "The slides are not underexposed, so it would seem that the camera didn't have a shutter failure. The slides are completely black and without images because you have photographed nothing!"

If all the levitation phenomena I witnessed had been trickeries, optical illusions, special effects, the results of hypnosis, or drug-induced hallucinations, nothing whatsoever could have influenced the operation of my batteries or interfered with the camera equipment or the photographic process. Instead of showing nothing, the faulty slides would have at least captured images of the village square lit by the campfire and the bright kerosene lamps, and of the dancers moving around the drummers. Instead of being totally out of focus, the movie would have shown clearly the scenes I had shot, instead of omitting the visions we had of people levitating.

Consequently, because of the fact that, for whatever reason, something interfered with the smooth operation of the batteries and the photographic process—something that did not follow scientific logic and rules—each time we witnessed a levitation phenomenon, I have to conclude that whatever caused the interference was powerful. It leads me to believe that what we saw could have been real—unless we agree that technical equipment can react to people's hallucinations.

It is interesting to note that I witnessed these levitation phenomena when the believers were in a state other than the normal one—that is, when they were meditating, in a trance, or in a possession state. Perhaps the intoxication brought on by meditation, by the trance state, or by possession helps to shut down negative beliefs—those that keep us from levitating, for instance—and liberates the unconscious, which gives us the power to perform such feats.

8

Sorcery and Magic
Death, Zombies,
Flying Men, and
Werewolves

We all are superstitious up to a certain point, in one way or another.

Some of us would never walk under a ladder; others would consider their whole day ruined if they encountered a black cat.

At the same time, thousands of card and palm readers, psychic advisers, astrologers, and other modern-day shamans and mages in this country have opened offices to sell their services; they openly advertise their talents in all the media. And many of us will go to see them for advice.

Whether they fear a car crash, want to win a sports competition or desire a certain social position, many people try to influence the future. They might wear lucky charms or religious objects to bring them into God's good graces; they may hang a medallion of Saint Christopher in their car; or they may wear a specific dress or dress in a specific color—all to protect themselves against the evil eye or to influence destiny by some means—or, unconsciously, to protect themselves from evil energies or invisibles.

This mysterious need has survived over the centuries, despite religious teachings and man's natural incredulity, and continues to challenge our rational minds and scientific logic. Is it based on supersti-

tion, or does it result from at least some real powers? Is to be superstitious a superstition in itself? What is our attraction to the belief in
magic? Is it cultural? Instinctual? Are we that much different from the
Fourth World, which to this day believes in magic?

Tribesmen of the Fourth World, and indeed many peoples of tradition, use fetishes, gris–gris, and other jujus as a protection from the
evil eye and to neutralize evil energies. These are made of human or
animal skulls; powders; plants; dried parts of animals; animal skins,
bones, teeth, and feathers; fish bones and scales; shells; and so forth—
to which powers of protective magic have been attributed. Or they
may be figurines of wood, clay, or metal, representing tribal divinities
of protection.

But all cultures throughout history, even the most evolved ones,
have believed in magical objects. The word *amulet,* for instance, comes
from the Latin word *amuletum,* which the Roman historian Pliny used
to designate an object that preserved people from illness; illness was
seen as the consequence of an evil spell. It was made of an animal or
plant substance.

More sophisticated and powerful than amulets and fetishes are
talismans. The word itself comes from the Arabic *tilsam* or *talasim,*
which comes from the Greek *telesma,* meaning "consecrated object";
the Greek word perhaps comes from *tselem,* a Hebrew word meaning
"image." Because the influence that has been attributed to it is subject
to symbolic, analogic, and sometimes logical reasoning, a talisman is a
scientific object that can be made according to specific rules. If amulets
and fetishes protect from all evil energies, talismans, being more
evolved, each have a specific purpose. One will protect from insects,
another from sorcerers, another from evil spirits, and so on. In their
specific actions, talismans resemble *pentacles* (from the Greek *penta-
klea*).

Pentacles serve to support high–magic operations. Covered with
esoteric symbols and various religious and sacred words that can act as
catalysts of cosmic energies, pentacles not only are protective, but also
are transmitters of powerful energies. These magic objects were part of
all esoteric traditions, and all esoteric traditions have contributed to the
science of pentacles.

From India to Tibet, believers spin prayer wheels, while thanking
their divinities and asking them for favors, hoping they will influence
their destinies. For the same reasons we light candles in our churches
in front of specific saints. People drive needles into a certain stone on
the coast of Brittany as a rite of fecundity. In Katmandu, Nepal, be-

lievers drive nails into specific wooden poles and kiss the nails to expel evil spirits.

Since the rise of mankind many great civilizations, some of which ruled over large parts of the world, have studied esoteric traditions and natural and physical sciences. They have invested a great deal of time, energy, imagination, and thought in creating objects of technical sophistication and magical powers to influence their destinies, attract good luck, protect them from negative influences and malevolent spirits and entities, and prevent them from being hurt by evil spells cast by sorcerers. And they have done so because they believed in the existence of negative astral influences, of invisibles populating the invisible world, and of the power of magic, which can use and transmit cosmic forces, made good or evil only by man's will. Hence, we may speculate that there are some truths to be found in these beliefs.

SORCERY

As I have said, there is only one universal force, which is neither good nor evil. But it can be used for good or for evil, with positive or negative consequences. Therefore, it can help and heal, or hurt and kill. This principle holds true for loas as well.

Within the context of Voodoo, loas cannot hurt; they are capable only of helping by acting as intermediaries between humans and God. But outside of the context of Voodoo, bokors or sorcerers also use this force, and the loas—but for evil purposes.

There are various means a sorcerer can use—according to his degree of knowledge—to cast spells that can influence his victim's will, cause illness, or even cause death, including:

△ poisons

△ evil charms and magic dolls

△ existing negative energies or those made evil through appropriate rituals, or evil spirits and other invisibles

Poisons

We have seen that, indeed, some magicians really can heal sick people by using their pharmacopia of natural medicines. Therefore, it would seem likely that some sorcerers know of certain plants and other natural elements that can bring on mysterious illnesses or sudden death.

The traditional method for bringing on illness or death consists of mixing a poison into the victim's food or drink—thus the Asian distrust of those who have long fingernails, for they can contain poison—or of placing it directly in a victim's wound. These poisons are often made of plants that have toxic properties, like manioc root, which contains hydrocyanic acid; of certain minerals or animals, like crab spiders, tarantulas, scorpions, and so forth; or, as was the Borgias' method, of the highly toxic liquid extracted from a decomposing human cadaver.

Evil Charms and Magic Dolls

The most difficult phenomena to understand are those involving evil charms that sorcerers create during black-magic rituals and use to cast spells that can influence their victims' will and bring them illness or even death. Just as some magicians can heal the sick by restoring the balance between mind and body, so others may be able to destroy that balance and bring on illness or sudden death. An evil charm can be any substance, or object, or a combination of the two. In Haiti, *bokors* (evil sorcerers) use the bones, reduced to powder, of babies and small children who died before being baptized. Then, by the means of a magic ritual, they charge this powder with noxious or deadly properties.

Clients for such evil charms are numerous: the farmer who wants to attract his neighbor's crop into his own field; the man who wants a woman to fall in love with him; the man who wants to break apart the marriage of the woman who refused him; the man who wants his friends' wives; the woman who wants to eliminate a rival in love; someone who wants to get rid of a personal enemy.

Generally, these evil charms are spread on the path or in the yard of the victim; the half-emptied gourd that held the evil charm is left nearby, so that the power of suggestion can add to the victim's agony when he stumbles upon the charm.

In Africa and the West Indies, there is a potion that can be poured on the victim's path. When he steps in it, it gives him elephantiasis of the feet, which slowly leads to death.

Among the Gypsies, evil charms—whose main ingredient is dried toads—are left, visibly, next to the victim's house. European evil charms are usually made of the cadavers of black cats and are buried next to the victim's house.

In some cases evil charms are reduced to a powder that one throws on the victim. Love powder, for instance—powder that makes a woman fall in love with the man who throws it on her head—is made of a dried hummingbird reduced to powder, to which pollen and the sperm of the wooer are added. And there is a powder a man can throw on a rival in love that keeps the rival from sleeping for two or three months and covers his entire body with huge infected pimples.

Some sorcerers also have the power to cast evil spells without leaving evil charms on the victim's path or near his house. These are the evil charms that are kept at the sorcerer's place of ritual. They may, for instance, be hidden inside a doll made of wood, clay, beeswax, or rags that roughly resembles the victim. The sorcerer uses the charm to focus and concentrate evil energies inside the doll. Then, activated by a needle he drives into it, the doll acts as a transmitter of these energies, sending them toward the victim; this works as long as the doll is not destroyed.

Evil charms and evil dolls become more powerful when they contain something that is part of the designated victim's body, like sweat, hair, fingernails, or toenails (that is why in many Asian countries hairdressers, manicurists, and pedicurists always burn their clients' hair, fingernails and toenails in their presence); or when they contain something that, really or symbolically, belongs to the victim, like a piece of clothing, or something that has been in contact with him, like a mound of earth taken from near the hut where the victim was born.

Such evil charms are often called Voodoo dolls, yet they have nothing to do with Voodoo—first, because Voodoo doesn't deal with black magic; second, because these techniques have been used for centuries, throughout the world. From the very first sorcerers to the ancient Egyptians, the Mayas, and the Incas, evil dolls have always been powerful weapons of sorcery. And they remain so today.

In the Introduction, I described an experience from my African childhood in which our native guardian seemed to have killed someone at a distance by using an evil doll. Sorcerers of the Andes also use evil dolls in their black-magic ceremonies.

In Haiti, I witnessed many ceremonies involving evil dolls. In one ceremony a bokor used a doll to send a deadly curse to someone who was living in New York. I couldn't verify whether the curse worked, but the ceremony itself was very impressive.

According to all the sorcerers I have questioned during my travels, there is no way to break an evil spell. The victim has to quickly find a powerful sorcerer to return it to the original sender. It is not usually the sorcerer who performed the original witchcraft who will be thus hit—

sorcerers know how to protect themselves—but the client on whose behalf the ceremony was performed. That, perhaps, would explain why sorcerers insist on having their client at their side while casting an evil curse.

Outsiders rarely get the opportunity to witness black-magic ceremonies involving evil dolls, but cemeteries in Haiti abound with these figures, especially in November, which is dedicated to celebrating the souls of the deceased. Do the makers of these dolls believe that their little weapons in rags receive powerful charges from the souls of deceased? I don't know, but I have seen many of these dolls scattered on tombs, with needles stuck into them.

Existing Negative Energies

Some sorcerers have the power to subdue the negative energies of the universe and those made evil through appropriate rituals, or to use evil spirits or other invisibles (like Petro loas in Haiti).

When I asked the houngan who had healed a little girl suffering from an advanced state of tuberculosis (which I described in the previous chapter), if he had used a magic doll to send the deadly curse that had caused the girl's illness back to whoever had originated it, he said no, that there were other ways to do it.

I really don't know what kind of energies he used, but, strangely enough, a few days later a woman of the little girl's village died mysteriously. I investigated and found out that this woman had never been able to bear children; despite many attempts, her pregnancies had always ended in miscarriages. She had often been seen in the company of the little girl, and seemed to love her so much that she even asked her family to let the little girl live with her, but the little girl refused. Were these refusals so emotionally painful for her that love and desire became jealousy and hate, leading her to wishing the little girl's death? Of course, this is only a hypothesis, for no one proved the woman had seen a sorcerer to cast an evil spell on the little girl, and no one can be sure that she died from the deadly curse's return to its sender.

There is, obviously, some danger involved in attending black-magic ceremonies when one doesn't fully know what is going on, what kind of energies are involved, and how to protect oneself from evil energies.

In March 1982 I made a one-month lecture tour in the south of France. I began the tour just a week after one of my many sojourns in Haiti, where, this time, I had approached sorcerers and studied their powers and magic. Two days after I began the tour, I suddenly began experiencing weird phenomena: every electric appliance I touched blew up, due to mysterious short circuits that appeared for no apparent reason.

It first happened to my sixteen-millimeter movie projector. It happened again when I got a replacement projector. Then my sound system blew up when I touched it. And returning to my hotel after my lecture that same night, my car lights went off. I stopped at a garage, where the mechanics on duty examined my car and said that everything was working perfectly. And indeed it was—until two minutes after I left the garage, when the lights went off again. When I entered my hotel room and turned on the light switch, the electric bulbs died instantly. And the next morning I couldn't start my car, but the concierge could. In order to continue my lecture tour, I had to hire someone as my driver and technician, to run all the new equipment I had to rent.

In the beginning I thought that I was simply carrying, for mysterious reasons, too much energy. It was almost funny. Each time I started to think how ridiculous it was of me to allow my mind to accept defeat over matter, I would touch a switch . . . and watch the light bulbs die.

After a few days and further incidents, I started to seriously question myself. And I got scared, wondering what I could have done wrong in Haiti to bring on such weird things. So I went to see a French Catholic priest, known to be a powerful exorcist, and asked for help. Without mentioning my recent Haitian experiences, I told him my misfortunes.

"Are you a Catholic?" he asked.

"Yes!" I answered.

"Do you believe that it could be the work of Satan?"

"I don't think so," I said. "Maybe it's only a curse, or something like that."

To make a long story short, the priest explained that he couldn't do very much to help me as long as I didn't believe this was the devil's work. And even if I did change my mind, I would have to fill out forms and get checked by a psychiatrist, and he would need to get permission from his superiors, which could take several weeks. Understanding the urgency of my case, he sent me to a modern-day alchemist living in Nice, who also had powers of exorcism. "But please, don't tell him I sent you," the priest implored me as I left him.

I called the alchemist to ask for an appointment. He said to come right away. When I entered his office, the alchemist, a fascinating man in his fifties, immediately said, "When you called me, I knew you were in trouble. But now that I see what remains of your aura, I know you are in danger."

He asked me to sit. I had the peculiar feeling of being in a medical doctor's office. As I was about to tell him my weird experiences, he asked me to say nothing. He brought out a small bowl filled with salt and asked me to blow on it. Then he opened one side of a black box containing a Polaroid camera, pointing down. He placed the bowl beneath the camera, closed the box, and pressed a switch. "In one minute we will have the results," he said, smiling.

The picture represented the surface of the salt, covered by various shadows. He took his pencil and started to join shadows with other shadows, until the photograph was covered with his drawings. Then, while carefully studying the picture, he started to talk. And the more he talked, the more fearful I became. This, basically, is what he said:

"It is not in Africa. But I see African powers. It looks like an island. But I don't understand why this island is so far from Africa. I see a large campfire, drums, and people dancing all around. They are in a trance. You have participated in a ceremony. You and another Caucasian. A black-magic ceremony. Evil rituals. About two, three weeks ago. They have told you not to leave the magic circle, the circle of protection. Yet you have done it. You have made a big mistake. All of your life energies were sucked out of you while you were inside the magic circle. They probably were used by the sorcerer. But you would have got them back at the end of the ceremony. Instead you left the circle, and without life energies protecting you, you attracted the negative and evil powers like a magnet. I also see powerful snakes around you and your friend. And something that has to do with dogs. A sacrifice of dogs. No, I see something which is related to sacrificed dogs that tried to protect you. But that wasn't enough. It helped you until a few days ago."

"What's the verdict?" I asked in a panic when he finished the reading.

"You need one day of fasting, and I need two. Let's meet in three days, and I shall perform a ceremony that will cleanse you completely and help you to restore your life energies. Thank God you did not wait too long before seeing me."

The most amazing thing about his reading is that he told me about an event that I had indeed experienced but completely forgotten. Yes, the event he described so accurately had happened on the island of Haiti, so far from Africa, but where people still use African powers. Yes, there was a big campfire, and drums, and people in a trance, dancing and being possessed. Yes, it was a ceremony of black magic, which I was filming with my friend Jean. Yes, we did leave the magic circle, despite the sorcerer's interdiction, because I needed to get new batteries for my camera. In fact, the sorcerer was so concerned that we had left the magic circle that, after the ceremony was over, my companion and I had to undergo a horrifying cleansing ritual. The thing he mentioned that was related to sacrificed dogs was a necklace made from the teeth of such dogs, which I received from the Kirdi tribe in Cameroon. The necklace is a talisman of protection. I wear it almost always, but the alchemist couldn't have seen it because I had left it behind in Brussels.

And he was able to determine all that from a bowl of salt on which I had blown.

Three days later he performed the ceremony, a kind of exorcism. And my misfortunes disappeared all at once. He taught me how to protect myself from evil energies. And that, perhaps, was the greatest lesson I got. I always thought that nothing evil could ever happen to me, because I am a basically good person and because I attended ceremonies involving dangerous energies only out of scientific curiosity. I had no evil purpose in mind. I always thought that as long as I lived in a state of love and goodness, rejecting jealousy and hatred, I would be protected from evil and bad people. Well, I was wrong.

When I called him, Jean told me that he, too, was experiencing misfortunes. And his life became normal again after he went to see an exorcist for a cleansing.

What had happened to us in Haiti was this:

Assisted by Jean, I was filming a ceremony involving black magic. The ritual was held inside a large white circle drawn on the ground by the bokor at the beginning of the ceremony. The magic circle is supposed to protect the ritual from malevolent spirits and evil energies.

The bokor had warned us many times that, once the ceremony started, it was forbidden for any uninitiated person to step outside the circle.

"Why?" I asked.

"It's dangerous!" was all he would say.

While the ritual was taking place, the batteries of the movie camera and of the tape recorder died suddenly for unknown reasons. In our haste to solve the problem, Jean and I forgot the bokor's warning and rushed to the car to get a new set of batteries.

When we came back, the bokor's reaction was instantaneous. He called a few of his assistants, who roughly carried us into a dark room, one of the houmfort's sanctuaries. More surprised than scared at first, we rapidly became more scared than surprised, for over the noise of the drumbeats from the ceremony outside we heard the hissing of snakes coming from the corners of the room.

Partially blinded in the darkness, we moved to the middle of the sanctuary and stumbled upon a bed, onto which we quickly jumped. Getting used to the darkness, we saw a dozen human forms that, hissing, were crawling toward the bed. We were surrounded by men and women in deep trances, all possessed by Djamballah-Wedo. We were too scared to push them away from us. Still hissing, they pulled us down from the bed and crawled all over us, touching our skin with their tongues. We lay with these human snakes for more than twenty minutes until they left us alone. We then got back on the bed, where we remained, speechless, as we waited for the ceremony to end, wondering what our next ordeal would be.

After an hour, the drumbeats of the ritual stopped. Two men burst into the room and brought us back to the center of the peristyle, where we had to undress completely. The bokor gave us a ritual bath—to purify us, as he said, from the malevolent spirits and evil energies that had fallen upon us when we moved out of the magic circle.

I am not sure that this ritual fully worked.

Do talismans, amulets, pentacles, and other magic protections really work? And are there evil things that we should really try to protect ourselves from?

To the first question I would answer yes, magic protections sometimes really work, whether because of real inherent power or because by believing in them one creates and surrounds oneself with protective energies that are truly effective. The talisman may be just the focus of our positive thoughts, or it may accumulate the protective energies one generates and surrounds oneself with. Or it may work because of a combination of the power of the mind and its inherent protective qualities.

To the second question I would also answer yes. There are indeed things one should try to protect oneself from: evil energies—whether the natural ones that cross the universe, those of evil spirits and demons (if they exist), or those produced by sorcery. More than anything else, though, I fear the energies induced by evil thoughts—mainly envy and hate. People who envy and hate you are able to send you, often unconsciously, evil energies that really can hurt you. The danger is greater in big cities, where competition is everywhere. Hate and envy are in themselves powerful generators, providers, and transmitters of evil energies.

If one has no magic protection, one has to surround oneself with good thoughts. Good thoughts, like the state of love, produce positive energies: evil thoughts consume one's energies, making one vulnerable to the evil energies of others.

ZOMBIES

When we think of zombies, images from horror novels and movies dedicated to the uncanny spring to mind. Yet zombies are real, though not as depicted by the fertile imagination of so many writers and filmmakers. Zombies are not the product of black magic, nor are they the living dead; however, the reality of zombies is perhaps as scary as what fiction has made of them.

In Haiti, the term *zombie* designates someone who is *believed* to be one of the living dead, but it also refers to babies and small children who died before being baptized (and whose souls can be captured for various purposes).

Except during November, no Haitian in his right mind would ever travel near a cemetery at night for fear of stumbling upon a zombie. Haitians believe that if a zombie looks at them, they too will instantaneously become zombies, unless they throw salt into the zombie's eyes, which will render him harmless or make him disappear. So those who have to travel at night always carry salt with them.

No one knows exactly when and where zombies were first made. The fact that ancient Indian literature mentions the plant that causes people to turn into zombies leads me to think that this phenomenon may have started in India. However, when I was in Africa I heard that there, too, there are sorcerers who still create zombies, following age-old traditions.

We also don't know if there was a religious aspect to the creation of zombies, but we can speculate that zombies were commonly used as slaves. It is mainly for this purpose that bokors make zombies in Haiti today. Indeed, bokors often own large farms, and don't like to pay for the labor they need. By creating zombies, they have ready access to workers whom they need only lodge and feed. They also use zombies as drummers during their ceremonies. Overwhelmed by work, exhausted by lack of sleep, and not always well fed and taken care of, these modern-day slaves do not live very long and are easily replaced.

Most bokors shroud the zombie phenomenon in an aura of supernatural mystery. This helps them make people believe that zombies are indeed dead people they have brought back to life thanks to their powers of black magic. But the making of a zombie is really just a simple chemical process that results from a person's ingestion of a specific mixture, which Haitians call *concombre-zombi* (zombie cucumber). Much has been reported and written about *concombre-zombi;* most of it comes from the bokors themselves, who want to protect the secrecy of their mixture, and most of it is false. It took me a long time and a lot of patience to win the confidence of one of the many bokors I approached, who finally shared with me the secret of making a zombie.

Whether mixed with other plants or with a special fish that has been pulverized, the main ingredient of zombie cucumber is the flower of the datura, an intoxicating plant that grows nearly everywhere in the world and is part of many traditional pharmacopoeias because it has many different properties depending on the dosage used. It takes only a tiny dose of datura to create the amazing hallucinogenic effects used by some tribes during rituals of initiation and rites of passage. A higher dose creates zombies, and a full dose instantaneously kills anyone who has the bad luck to ingest it.

There is an interesting aside about datura. Used in a certain dosage and prepared in a slightly different way, the flower of the datura makes a powerful abortive potion. In fact, during the Hundred Years' War, the French authorities gave the order to destroy the datura and the other natural abortive plants that grew throughout the country in order to force families to have large numbers of children, thereby supplying the army with soldiers. Many plants survived, however, and even today country witch doctors in France use them to make abortive potions for farm animals, and sometimes for people.

When a bokor is in need of a zombie, he will travel to backcountry villages searching for someone who has a personal enemy he would like to get rid of. When the sorcerer finds such a person, he sells him the *concombre-zombi* powder to put in his enemy's food, convincing him that it will cause his enemy a fatal disease without leaving any proof of the crime.

If the intended victim consumes this powder, he will slowly show visible signs of a mysterious illnesss, which will appear to cause death two or three weeks later—but the victim will only *seem* dead. The illness provoked by the powder cannot be diagnosed by most doctors and modern hospitals, of which there are few anyway in all of Haiti. (Indeed, there is only one doctor for each hundred thousand inhabitants in Haiti, and there are practically none in the back country, since doctors can earn much more in the cities.)

What happens to the victim is this: zombie powder creates an imbalance in the metabolism. The victim soon loses his appetite and becomes perceptibly thinner and paler, sometimes losing his hair. And then finally one day he will seem to die, his body becoming cold and stiff. In essence, his metabolism has slowed down so completely that he gives no indication of being alive. So he will be declared dead and will be buried within twenty-four hours—to avoid the putrefaction of the body that comes rapidly in tropical climates.

Yet the victim is not really dead; he is in a deep coma, a catatonic state. His heart still beats, but only at two or three very weak beats a minute—a level that cannot be detected in his pulse. His breathing is also so slow and shallow that it can't be detected on a mirror set beneath his nose. (Because his breathing is so shallow, there is enough oxygen inside the coffin for the victim to survive for four or five days. After that, he will really die from asphyxiation.) The semblance of death is so good that, in at least one case I know of, the American hospital in Haiti issued a death certificate for a person who was subsequently buried but reappeared a while later as a zombie.

The fear that people have of zombies leads many families to bury their dead along with a bunch of sesame seeds, or a ball of thread and a needle whose eye is broken. They believe that by staying busy counting the seeds or trying to thread the needle, the deceased will not answer the sorcerer's call to be reborn. Some families will even strangle their dead, or pierce their hearts, or even mutilate their bodies by beheading them or removing their vital organs, making resurrection impossible.

The majority of zombies I have interviewed told me they heard everything that was going on around them at the time of their supposed death, and because they couldn't say anything or move any part of their body to show their family they were still alive, they themselves believed they were dead, thinking that all dead people continue to hear the voices of the living. They remembered hearing their family's cries, and the hammering on the coffin when the top was closed, and the sound of earth crashing down on the coffin.

Two or three days after the victim's supposed death, the sorcerer and a few of his zombie helpers go back to the cemetery late at night. They dig up the coffin containing the victim, close up the grave, and take the coffin back to the bokor's houmfort.

Back at his houmfort, the bokor opens the coffin inside one of the sanctuaries, which he has transformed a few days earlier into a theatrical set representing a sort of hell, with large fireplaces all along the walls. He uses a small hidden door to enter and exit the sanctuary without being seen by the victim. He then gives his victim an antidote to the zombie mixture that will slowly restore the balance of his metabolism, raise his heart rate, and increase his breathing. And he attaches long chains, tied to the walls, to the victim's ankles and wrists.

Once the victim has regained consciousness, he is nursed back to complete health, which takes about a month. All this time, though, the bokor continues the charade of making the victim think he is in hell, paying for his sins. He disguises himself as the devil and tortures his victim with physical violence.

At other times, the sorcerer appears as a kindly bokor. He brings food and water. He tells the victim that he has traveled into the hereafter in search of good people to bring back to life. The victim of course begs him for his help; he wants to go back to earth, back to his wife and family. The bokor says he will see what he can do.

The object of this entire brainwashing process is to get the victim to the point of being ready to accept any proposition the sorcerer has to offer. In return for being delivered from hell, he will readily agree to belong to the bokor forever and be his lifetime servant. He will obey him, do whatever he is asked, and never go back to his village to see his family. In addition, the bokor convinces him that he will need to drink a magic potion every day to stay alive. Without this, he will die again and return to hell to face the devil's wrath. But if he remains his master's good and obedient servant until he is old, his master will send him straight to heaven. And the victim believes the bokor has such powers.

When the bokor knows that his victim has been thus brainwashed, he orchestrates a spectacular escape from hell. But as he frees him from the chains, he says that the devil is about to come and hides his victim in a hole hidden inside a wall, telling him he will come back as soon as the devil is gone. At that point, the victim is generally so scared that he begs the bokor to take him along right away. The bokor leaves him there, though, returning to the sanctuary as the devil.

Discovering that the victim has escaped, he goes into a rage, promising himself aloud that if he catches the victim, he will throw him into the fire for all eternity. Later, the bokor joins the frightened victim still hidden inside the cavity and gives him a potion to make him fall asleep.

When the victim awakens in the bokor's houmfort, he believes the great escape from hell has succeeded, that he has become one of the living dead and must forever show his gratitude to his master. From then on he will serve the bokor, working in his fields during the day and beating drums during the night if needed.

Among the zombies I have met, the very few who could talk normally gave the same answers when I asked why they didn't escape from their master and rejoin their family. "Yes, I have a family, a wife and kids. I think about them every day, and still hear their cries when I died and was buried. Of course I would like to go back to them, but if I escape from my master to join my family, or if I even disobey him, I will not get the daily potion that keeps me alive. And you don't know what it is to be dead! You don't know what it is to have been sent into hell! The only way for me to stay alive and avoid the devil is to remain with my master, because he has the power to send me straight to heaven."

How could I have changed their minds about the reality of who they were? To get them to recognize that they were not the living dead but living human beings, I would have had to completely deprogram the weeks of brainwashing they had gone through, and find a way to convince them that there had been no hell and no devil, that there was no magic potion. I would have to fight against the memories of their own death. I would have to counter their strong belief in the living dead, which so many Haitians share.

Actually, many of them were right about one thing: escaping from a bokor can bring a sudden and real death. While some sorcerers' magic potion contains nothing special, others add a poison to it, some addictive toxic substance that the body needs to stay alive.

Very few zombies can talk normally, because there has been brain damage, as you might expect, during the zombification process. Many factors affect their ability to become normal again: the dosage of datura, the toxicity of the other ingredients sometimes added to the zombie mixture, the degree of oxygen loss when the victim is in his coffin; the chemical content and dosage of the antidote; the degree of physical and emotional suffering that is part of the brainwashing process; the poison contained in the magic potion. Each of these can in itself cause severe brain damage. Some zombies seem to be able to think, though they talk with difficulty; others can talk but have stopped thinking, their memory completely washed away. And there are zombies who have lost their powers of thought and speech, and who move like characters in horror movies, with empty, wild-looking eyes.

Those who have stopped thinking, who are no longer aware of the wrath they would incur by leaving their master, who suddenly become amnesic, are often the zombies who escape from their slavery and can be seen walking along roads or crossing cities. If they are lucky, they will be recognized by a friend or a family member. Imagine the emotions of a friend or parent upon coming across someone whom they had mourned and buried long before.

When such a thing happens, the family sometimes brings their beloved zombie to a hospital, which sends him to Port-au-Prince, to the clinic of Dr. Lamarck Douyon, a Haitian psychiatrist who for many years has dedicated his life to healing zombies, using various medicines. And he succeeds, if the brain damage is not irreversible.

When I was traveling at dusk through the Haitian back country, I often stumbled upon zombies who were going back to their houmfort from their master's fields. They were always walking in the middle of the dirt road, holding their machete on their shoulder, moving like the zombies of our scary tales. They never answered when I raised my hand high to salute them, but as we passed each other, they looked at me with their lifeless eyes. I always wished I had salt in my hand to throw into their motionless and scary faces . . . to see if they would disappear as the Haitian people believe.

FLYING MEN

Who has never flown in his dreams or dreamed of flying? I'm sure everyone has at least once. As children, our imaginations were filled with images of sultans traveling on flying carpets, witches journeying on brooms, and magicians walking through walls. To be able to fly has always been man's most powerful desire, since long before Icarus and Da Vinci. But what if man had really found a way to become a magic bird?

I have witnessed real incidents of people *flying*—that is, dematerializing, and materializing somewhere else. If someone told you that he saw a man passing through a wall, I am sure you would wonder if he was sane. But I heard just such an account from a Catholic priest who gave his word of honor it was true. What happened was this: the priest's sacristan rushed toward a wall and instead of smashing into it, disappeared in front of it as if he were moving through the wall. He then appeared on the other side, continuing his run.

The priest who told me this is a respected professor with the equivalent of an American M.A. degree in philosophy and Ph.D. in sociology. Having spent ten years as a missionary in Haiti, he became an expert in Voodoo, and wrote two books about the mysteries he witnessed firsthand. This priest is a Frenchman, and his name is Jean Kerboull.

I believed Father Kerboull's story because when I asked the lama I had seen levitating in the Buddhist monastery about the possibility of astral voyages, he answered, "Yes, it is possible to physically travel through solid objects and through space. I have done it and can whenever I need to."

"How can a human body travel through space and pass through solid objects?" I asked.

He answered with a question, as he often did.

"How could you make a piece of ice pass through a robe?"

"I don't know," I replied.

"It's easy. By changing the nature of the piece of ice. Heat it and it becomes water; heat the water and it becomes vapor. Vapor can pass through a robe. Then reverse the process. Chilled vapor becomes water, and chilled water becomes ice again."

"I understand," I said. "But how can you change the nature of the human body?"

"A human being consists of two things: a physical body, the one you see, and an invisible body, the one we call the astral or etheric body. When I want to go to a given place, which can be miles away, I only need to think of being there, since a thought can create an action; this instantly sends and places the invisible body there. Raising the wave frequency of my physical body makes it become my invisible body; then lowering the wave frequency of my invisible body makes it become my physical body. Thus I can travel through solid objects and through space, instantly."

So I believed Father Kerboull's story, but I wanted to see this phenomenon with my own eyes. Unfortunately, we were in Paris and he wasn't able to travel back to Haiti. "During your next sojourn in Haiti," he said, "try to find my sacristan; he should be working for another parish. If you don't succeed in finding him, you'll have other opportunities to see these phenomena, for there is a secret society in Haiti, called the Flying Men, that performs such things. This society has many lodges all over the island, but its members are very secretive about belonging to the sect. So be patient, and try to build confidence before asking questions."

When I returned to Haiti a few months later, I began to search for the sacristan. I visited almost all the Catholic parishes in the back country of Haiti. I never found him, but I met several old missionaries who shared with me stories of their firsthand encounters with the bizarre and the unknown. Father S., for instance, a Belgian Catholic missionary, told me the following story.

"When I came to Haiti thirty years ago, this parish covered all the villages within a radius of one hundred kilometers, with no roads at all between the villages and the church, just paths that the peasants took on foot, donkeys, mules, or horseback. When I arrived, there was only one priest in the parish to care for all these souls. Since he was getting old and tired, my function was to assist him. He was to stay here at the mission, taking care of church matters, the dispensary, the boarding school, and the college, and I was to travel around with the jeep, visiting all the villages of our parish, even the little ones that one could reach only on horseback.

"At Eastertime about twenty-five years ago, while my superior prepared for the paschal celebrations at our church, I was getting ready to leave the mission, as I always did during Holy Week, and travel to each of the main villages, where I was to perform the Easter Mass, so that our whole community would have the chance to celebrate Easter.

"At 7:00 A.M., Pierre Louis, a fourteen-year-old boarder in our college who was to accompany me on the trip as a choir boy, finished loading the jeep, and we left the mission. Around 5:00 P.M., after an exhausting ten-hour voyage covering only about seventy kilometers as the crow flies, we finally reached the first village, where I was to celebrate the Easter Mass that same evening.

"The village was crowded with worshipers who had come from all around. Pierre Louis unloaded the jeep while I decorated the altar.

"At 6:00 P.M., Pierre Louis announced to me that the large box containing the consecrated hosts was missing. I searched the entire jeep, but in vain. Since, for the people here, a Mass without communion wouldn't be a Mass, the only thing I could do was return immediately to the mission, and come back again. I turned to Pierre Louis, who I felt was to blame since he was the one who had loaded the jeep, and yelled at him to release my anger. Pierre Louis began crying and told me not to worry and wait there while he went back to the mission to retrieve the hosts. Hearing his stupid talk, I couldn't resist slapping his face. 'Yes, that's it, go to the mission alone, but never come back!' I said. And Pierre Louis left.

"Within the next few minutes, as I began reloading the jeep, Pierre Louis touched my shoulder, smiling. He was holding the box with the hosts. I slapped his face again for making such a stupid joke, and promised myself to punish him somehow for making a fool of me. But after the Mass I forgot the incident and didn't talk about it for the rest of the trip.

"A few days after we returned to the mission, my superior asked me why I had not come to him myself to ask for the box with the hosts.

" 'Because I was in the village,' I replied at first. Then, realizing that something strange was going on, I asked, 'What do you mean? Which box of hosts are you talking about?'

" 'The box of hosts you forgot to take with you and left in the garage.'

" 'Who came to pick it up?' I asked nervously.

" 'Pierre Louis,' he replied. 'Who else would have?'

" 'When?'

" 'Monday night, the day you left for your trip.'

" 'At what time?'

" 'I don't know, at six or seven in the evening.'

"Without saying anything further, I left my superior and rushed to the college, searching for Pierre Louis. When I found him, he calmly admitted that he had *flown* to the mission, seen the superior and asked for the box of hosts, picked it up, and *flown* back to the village to give it to me. He said that his father, who was the leader of a Flying Men sect, had taught him how to *fly*.

"Since that time, I took Pierre Louis along on all my trips and amused myself by giving him trials in order to test his flying abilities. I saw him many times, just as I see you, dematerializing and materializing in front of my eyes.

"I promised myself to visit his family and question his father, but since they lived far from the parish's territory I never found the time to do it. Three or four months later, Pierre Louis disappeared from the mission, leaving a note behind saying that he had to go back to his village because his father was sick. I have not heard a word from him since."

"Do you remember the name of the village, Father?" I asked excitedly.

"I don't even think that I knew it. It was one of those very tiny villages without a real name, lost somewhere in the bluffs. Pierre Louis was supposed to lead me there. But he never came back."

I was amazed by Father S.'s story, and I continued to hear similar accounts from many priests. For the next two years I tried to track down Pierre Louis, but hundreds of people of his age are called Pierre Louis. And slowly I forgot about him. Yet I continued to search for someone who could lead me to a member of the Flying Men.

When I began the fifth year of my many sojourns in Haiti, I met a Haitian named Saint-Germain, who lived in the Artibonite, a dry, harsh region. Saint-Germain, who was in his forties, was very well-educated; his family had sent him to a Catholic college. I used to bring him books from France, mainly treatises on alchemy and high magic. And he opened doors to secret sects for me because he understood my motives.

One day I heard someone calling him P'tit Louis, which is a French abbreviation for Little Louis. I asked him why he had been called so. "I prefer to be called Saint-Germain because of the man," he replied, referring to the mysterious and controversial Count Saint-

Germain. (Some say the count was a renowned seventeenth century French alchemist who mastered the alchemist's ultimate task of transmuting base matter into gold; this had in turn led him to the secret of eternal physical life.)

"So your real name is P'tit Louis?" I asked.

"No, that's the nickname my parents gave me because I was small. My real name is Pierre Louis."

Scarcely believing my luck, I asked him whether he remembered a priest called Father S. when he was in school.

For a few seconds he was reluctant to speak, but finally he said, "Yes, I remember him very well. I traveled the back country with him."

I told him what I knew about him, and that I wanted his help in investigating the Flying Men. He agreed to help me, and we arranged for me to pick him up the next day after midnight, in front of a certain houmfort.

I knew the place where I was to meet Saint-Germain very well. It was a double houmfort—one part led by a houngan and dedicated to Voodoo, the other headed by the houngan's brother, a bokor, and dealing with sorcery. I had been there several times to attend and sometimes film ceremonies.

Sounds of drumbeats led me to the little village, which I reached around midnight. The main square was filled with worshipers who, dressed in red and wearing red scarves on their heads, were dancing frantically around a huge campfire that lit their sweaty faces, and projected their shadows onto the colorful paintings covering the houmfort's walls. Since the worshipers were not dressed in white, I suspected that this wasn't a Voodoo ceremony, but one performed by a secret sect.

The place was so crowded that I couldn't see if Saint-Germain was there. Since one is never welcome at a religious ceremony without being invited, I waited in my car, parked nearby, so he could see me.

At 12:45 A.M. the ceremony was still going on, more frenzied than ever. Not wanting to miss Saint-Germain, I got out of the car and, my nerves strained, took the risk of approaching the ceremony, expecting someone to throw me out. As I reached the crowd, looking all around for my friend, I stumbled upon the bokor, who was smoking a cigarette, his eyes reddened by alcohol.

"It's Saint-Germain who told—" I started to say, mumbling, but he interrupted me.

"Ah, Douchan, we were waiting for you!" he said, exhaling cigarette smoke and the smell of run.

"I came for Saint-Germain," I said, a little nervously. "Where is he?"

"He'll show up very soon! Come with me." He grabbed my hand and led me through the crowd to a place where I could see the whole ceremony.

"What's this ceremony?" I asked the bokor.

"The one you came for. It's just the beginning."

"I came . . . for this ceremony?" I asked, surprised, but also suspicious.

"Yes. Saint-Germain told us." As he finished his sentence, the rhythm of the drumbeats changed, and Saint-Germain appeared, dressed in a magnificent white army uniform complete with military medals covering his chest and a hat. His arrival created a renewed frenzy, and the worshipers began jumping, and walking through the fire.

"Why is he dressed like that?" I asked the bokor.

"He must. He's the emperor."

I couldn't believe how lucky I was. Not only had I found Pierre Louis by chance, but he was the emperor of the Flying Men, the highest title the society can bestow. This meant he was the head of all their lodges in Haiti.

I later learned that this title is given only to the one who has the greatest ability to *fly*. Pierre Louis also told me a few things about the initiation and trials one must undergo to become a member of this society, but I had to take an oath not to repeat any of what he told me. The only thing I can say is that the rituals of the Flying Men are not performed within the context of Voodoo.

Thanks to Saint-Germain, I have witnessed many breathtaking things. During the ceremony that night, for instance, I twice saw worshipers disappear before my eyes. One was a man who was dancing with the other members of the sect, all in deep trances, when suddenly he wasn't there anymore. An hour later it was a woman's turn to disappear. When the ceremony was over, the two believers were still missing. Saint-Germain explained that only the few highly initiated believers are able to *fly* without the need of a ceremony. The others, like the two missing sect members, have to come back like normal people—on foot or by bus—from wherever their flights take them.

Saint-Germain also told me that many members of the Flying Men are able to *bilocate* themselves: that is, while the subject remains earthbound, his astral body can be seen by others wherever he sends it. (I myself have never seen this, but many reliable witnesses have corroborated Saint-Germain's declaration.)

According to Saint-Germain, in order to be able to *fly*—that is, to dematerialize in one place and rematerialize somewhere else—a believer must reach a state of trance and wait to be possessed by Erzulie-Yeux-Rouges (Erzulie-Red-Eyes), a female loa worshiped as the goddess of love and sex.

Once a year, in January, all members of Haiti's Flying Men lodges meet for one night only at a given place, to which they must travel only by *flying*. Saint-Germain invited me to such an assembly, allowing me to bring my friend Jean along. That year the meeting was to be held in the Artibonite desert. To be sure we wouldn't get lost on our way there, Saint-Germain arranged for a member of his local sect to guide us.

Around 11:00 P.M. we reached the chosen place, which looked like a movie set. By the light of twenty to thirty kerosene lamps, a dozen people were just finishing building large open shelters, using wood and palm leaves they had brought in (along with cases of beer, rum, and soft drinks) by truck. The shelters, one for each local sect, were built all around a large open space, where, according to our guide, all the Flying Men were to land sometime after midnight.

Sitting on top of the shelter for Saint-Germain's sect, Jean and I had been looking at the sky since midnight, watching for the Flying Men's arrival. We could see the bright stars between the clouds. Because of the nature of the event we were hoping to witness, and the atmosphere of secrecy and mystery surrounding it, we couldn't help thinking we were about to see something very similar to the Witches' Sabbaths of the Middle Ages—the night assemblies where witches flew on their brooms.

At 1:00 A.M. no guests had yet flown in. But then we realized that there were already about a hundred people in the large square, walking, smoking cigarettes, and chatting together. All were wearing scarves and dresses of a color that indicated to which lodge they belonged. Some were carrying heavy drums. And then, all of a sudden, hundreds of small luminescent points appeared in the sky and beneath the clouds for a second or two, their mobility contrasting with the motionless of the stars. And before we could say anything, the whole square was crowded with more than six or seven hundred believers, also dressed in the color of their lodge. And guess who was standing just beneath us? Saint-Germain, of course. He smiled at us as the drums began beating.

After a flourish of drumbeats, a life-size black coffin was brought to the center of the square, carried by men holding candles. They set it, surrounded by the candles, on a table, in front of which someone placed a large stool. Chanting, and accompanied by drumbeats, a group of people, all belonging to the same lodge, left their shelter, moved through the large circle formed by the crowd, stopped before the coffin, and began dancing. After a while they became motionless as their leader climbed onto the stool and started to address the crowd, which often posed questions or expressed itself with applause, laughter, or cries.

One purpose of this yearly gathering was to give all the Flying Men a chance to meet; but it also provided an opportunity for each lodge to report on its activities and express problems or concerns about any matters pertaining to the society.

Two hours later Jean and I were still sitting on top of the shelter in order to be able to see what was going on. Although Saint-Germain forbade me to film or photograph, I did record a speech or two. We waited eagerly for the ceremonies to end so that we could witness the Flying Men's departure. But then, due to an argument between Saint-Germain and a lodge leader who didn't want us there, we had to move to a shelter away from the square, where people went to drink when they weren't watching the ceremony.

Unfortunately, we soon were joined by a Tonton-Macoute, who asked for our papers. (Tonton-Macoutes, the Duvalier regime's special police, were free to do whatever they wanted—they even murdered people—to get information. They were feared by everyone.) Emboldened by alcohol and the .357 Magnum he had pointing at us, the agent demanded twenty dollars cash; otherwise he would arrest us. Twenty dollars is enough for a family to live on for a month in the capital, and for four months in the country. Before we could answer, he asked for one hundred dollars, and continued to increase the amount. We were able to divert his attention and run away, missing the takeoff of the Flying Men.

To be honest, I must say that often when I saw people disappearing I could have been a victim of fraud. Because it always happened at night, and because no one knows in advance who will disappear, it would have been futile, if not impossible, to focus on a single person among the believers, who were constantly dancing and moving in all directions. Except on those few occasions when I actually saw the person disappearing, the only evidence I had that a believer had dematerialized and flown away was the fact that he was missing.

During the few times that I was allowed to film, something influenced the operation of the batteries and interfered with the normal photographic process—the same things that happened when I tried to record levitation phenomenon on film. And it occurred only when someone was supposedly in the process of disappearing. This again led me to believe that something strange, mysterious, and powerful was really going on, defying all scientific logic.

☾

I often asked Saint-Germain to show me how he goes through a wall—to demonstrate the dematerialization and rematerialization process. He always refused, saying that doing this outside the context of a religious ritual was against the rules of the Flying Men. One night, however, we were drinking rum (or rather he was; I was just pretending to drink in hopes of getting him to perform in front of me) and talking in my hotel room in Gonaive, a small seaside town bordering the Artibonite region. Intoxicated with rum and exasperated by my never-ending questions and requests, he asked me why I was always pushing him to prove his abilities. "Don't you trust me?" he screamed at one point. "You think we are tricking you?"

"No, no, no, my friend," I replied gently, trying to calm him. "I just want to see you do it for me, as a favor!" Silently he continued to drink for another hour.

"Okay!" he said all of a sudden, getting up, his face covered with sweat. "Okay, what do you want to see?"

I asked to see him go through the wall of my hotel room and then to perform an astral voyage, such as flying to the room I had in my friend Jean's house in Port-au-Prince, about a hundred miles away. He said nothing, but when I asked if I could film the scene, he replied, "What for? It will not show up in your movie, just like all the other times!" And he laughed.

I set up the camera anyway, and said I was ready. He was looking at me with his sweaty face—I wasn't sure it was due to a state of trance or to alcohol and heat—and turned toward the wall and walked right to it. As he was about to smash himself against the wall, with my very own eyes I saw Saint-Germain walk through the wall of my hotel room. Or to be exact, he literally disappeared—he dematerialized himself—before smashing himself against the wall. As this happened, my body was covered with chills and I felt my hair being pulled up. I also felt a kind of heat coming from where Saint-Germain had disappeared.

I rushed from the room and found him waiting in front of the wall he had gone through.

When we came back into the room, I discovered that the batteries for my movie equipment were dead, including extras I had in my room. When I asked Saint-Germain if he knew anything about this, he offered no explanation. "It happens even to the batteries of our flashlights when we keep them too close to us," he said.

I may have been hallucinating, but something did discharge my camera's batteries and all the other batteries I had in the room. The only thing the camera recorded was Saint-Germain as he was looking at me before starting to walk toward the wall. Then nothing.

Afterward I asked Saint-Germain to go and pick up something, anything he could find, from my room at Jean's house in Port-au-Prince and, before coming back, to enter Jean's room and say hello to him.

"Why?" he asked, surprised. "I don't understand you. If I can walk through a wall, I can go to Port-au-Prince without problems. It's the same principle whether I decide to go through the wall or I decide to go to Port-au-Prince or elsewhere."

He was right. Walking through walls and astral voyages should be based on the same principle: sending the astral body to the final destination. As the astral body materializes itself and becomes the visible body, the visible body dematerializes itself and becomes the astral body, which can be called back to the visible body, and vice-versa if the astral voyager wants to come back to where he started.

"I agree with you, my friend, but . . . as a favor . . . please!"

Saint-Germain emptied another glass of rum and asked me to explain carefully where the house was, and where Jean's room and mine were.

"Can't you find it by yourself? I mean if you can fly you could—" Saint-Germain interrupted me nervously. "What you just told me isn't very smart!"

"I'm sorry, I . . . I was just thinking aloud. I didn't mean to . . ." I didn't know what to say to calm him.

"Flying is one thing, but if I don't know where I must go, how do you want me to reach the destination?"

He was right. So I told him in detail how to find the house and the rooms.

And he disappeared suddenly in front of my eyes, dematerializing completely. It was not a slow process during which some parts of his body disappeared before others; no, he disappeared all at once, in the blinking of an eye. Moving my hands in front of me, I walked to the place where he had been standing, and then throughout the whole room, but Saint-Germain wasn't there. He had really disappeared.

During the time Saint-Germain was away, I was hoping that Jean would be home to testify that he had seen Saint-Germain during the night, and I regretted that I had not thought to provide a note for the astral voyager to give to Jean or to leave in his room in case Jean wasn't there.

I stood next to the door to have the whole room in my sight so that I could see him when he reappeared. Exactly thirty-two minutes after he had disappeared, Saint-Germain reappeared. He materialized next to the bed, holding a small notebook in which I used to write notes about my sound tapes after listening to them—a notebook that I never took along when I left Port-au-Prince, because I was scared of losing it.

When Saint-Germain disappeared, and again when he reappeared I experienced chills and felt the hair on my body rising. And I felt heat coming from where he disappeared, and again from where he reappeared after his astral voyage.

I was speechless. I was excited and on the verge of fainting. I couldn't control my heartbeat, and my legs began shaking. What I had experienced was far more amazing to me than having seen levitation or Saint-German walking through the wall. I had to force myself to realize that what I was now holding in my hands was my own notebook, which indeed had experienced an astral voyage; my notebook, which, for a while, had dematerialized.

"Where did you find it?" I asked.

"Where you left it, on the table with your tapes!" he said.

"Did you see my friend Jean?"

"He wasn't there."

❦

I am sure that you have many doubts about the reality of levitation and astral voyages, and I don't blame you. I would never have believed in any of these phenomena if I had not seen them myself. And while it is my intention to convince you that some people are able to manipulate gravitational forces and defy the laws of physics, I do hope that some of you will reconsider the possibility that such phenomena exist. After all, hagiography—the history of the lives of saints—is filled with stories of levitation, astral projection, and astral voyages that have been experienced by members of the Catholic clergy.

And psychic research also strengthens my accounts. According to parapsychologists, man indeed could have both a nonmaterial body—an astral body—and a physical body. Under certain circumstances the two bodies could separate, with consciousness accompanying the astral body. Furthermore, there are many parapsychological reports concerning astral projections, called out-of-body experiences, in which the subject remains earthbound. Though the astral body often remains invisible, there are cases where it has been seen by other people. (Please see books treating this subject, such as *Journeys Out of the Body* by Robert A. Monroe or *The Enigma of Out-of-Body Travel* by Susy Smith.)

In describing the mysterious disappearances I have witnessed, I left out one interesting and important detail. During those few times that I was sure that I saw someone disappear during a ceremony—because I was close enough to the subject—and again when Saint-Germain disappeared as he passed through the wall of my hotel room, I noticed that my eyes picked up a distinct image. This image was always the same: the person who had just disappeared, seen from the back, appeared to be followed by something that looked like a bunch of feathers. In pondering this, my first thought was that it looked like someone riding a broom, an image similar to representations of witches traveling to their Sabbaths.

Long before I traveled to Haiti, I read a book called *Vingt et un ans chez les Papous* (Twenty-one years among the Papuans), written by Father André Dupeyrat, a French Catholic missionary who lived with Papuans in New Guinea. In this book he described his contact with the Cassowary Men, a sect of sorcerers who make astral voyages. Father Dupeyrat recounted amazing stories about a sorcerer friend of his who was able to disappear instantly in front of him and, traveling long distances over mountains and valley, instantly reappear in a given village. Father Dupeyrat was of course incredulous until he went to the village and investigated. Indeed, the sorcerer had arrived in the village just as he disappeared from Father Dupeyrat's sight.

He wrote that these sorcerers are called Cassowary Men because anyone who witnesses their disappearance reports having the impression that the men flew away riding a cassowary, a native ostrichlike bird with very large tail feathers.

When I decided to go to New Guinea, I contacted Father Dupeyrat and, thanks to him, eventually met one of the sorcerers he mentioned in his book. And the sorcerer did what I asked him to do. At night—they only *fly* at night—he disappeared in front of my eyes, accompanied by a strange noise that sounded like the wings of a large bird flapping in the air, and I, too, thought I saw him riding a cassowary.

However, it was in Haiti—when I first noticed that my eyes picked up the same image each time someone dematerialized in front of me—that I made the connection with the Cassowary Men. When I saw something like feathers following the Papuan sorcerer as he disappeared, I concluded it was the tail feathers of a cassowary because that was what I was expecting to see; that is what people told me would happen. If nobody had told me this I would have picked up only the image of the sorcerer seen from the back, followed by something that looked like a bunch of feathers; and I would have concluded that he was riding a broom because that is my cultural reference. If this same image is picked up by the Papuans when a sorcerer dematerializes, they, having no cultural references to brooms, would naturally conclude that the sorcerer left riding a cassowary.

According to accounts of Europe during the Middle Ages, people used to see witches flying away riding brooms. If cassowaries existed in Europe perhaps these people would have seen the witches riding cassowaries instead of brooms.

In Arabia, when people saw a magician dematerializing—I have met some Arabs who claim that such magicians still exist nowadays—they also picked up the image I have described. Since their cultural references included neither cassowaries nor brooms, Arab witnesses perceived the image as being the tasseled end of a carpet. This gave rise to tales of people traveling on flying carpets. In each of these cultures, people ascribed the image their eyes picked up whenever an astral voyager began his trip to whatever it was that they already knew—a broom, a cassowary, a carpet. The few Haitian priests I spoke with who had seen some of their parishioners vanish said that they suddenly shone brightly and disappeared at once, leaving behind a luminous wake. All this, of course, doesn't prove that *flying* actually occurs. What does happen is that whenever people see, or believe they see, someone dematerialize, they experience the same visual image.

Even if you don't want to believe in astral voyages, this phenomenon at least gives evidence that something powerful goes on at that specific moment; otherwise, why would people of different cultures, living in different times, experience the same image?

Is it possible that all myths and legends are really born from realities, that a myth is not really a myth but a true story based on one of man's ancient powers? Now, more than ever, I believe this to be true. And that perhaps is the most fascinating idea of all, at least for me, for it means that everything is possible.

WEREWOLVES

Late one afternoon, while I was driving in the Haitian back country, I saw two men running in the distance. They were dressed in black, and were moving zigzag fashion through a field, each carrying one end of a stretcher on which was set a long, black box that looked like a coffin. Surprised by the scene, I stopped my car and looked through my binoculars. The black box was indeed a coffin, and the two men were wearing frock coats and top hats. As you might expect, this aroused my curiosity, so I sped up and passed them, got out of my car, and ran back toward the bizarre procession.

Exhausted, their black faces glittering with sweat, the two men were visibly afraid and didn't stop when I reached them. I had to run alongside them to be able to ask questions.

"Hi! How are you?" I asked. They didn't answer.

"Why are you running like this?"

"To lose the devil!" said one of them, out of breath.

"How long have you been running?"

"Since this morning," said the other man.

"When will you stop?"

"When we're sure we have lost the devil," said the first man.

"Then what will you do?"

"Find a cemetery and bury him!"

"Bury who?"

"The one who's inside the coffin."

"Who's inside the coffin?"

"A werewolf!" both answered at the same time. I couldn't believe what I had heard.

"My friends," I said, starting to run out of breath myself, more out of excitement than exhaustion, "I think you deserve a cigarette! I have American cigarettes in my car. One pack for each of you. Okay?" They didn't answer.

"What about a small gift to reward you for your efforts?" I said, showing them a ten-dollar bill. No answer. "One for each of you, of course!" I continued, holding the bill in front of the first man.

"Okay," he said. "Let's go to your car!" And, still running, but in a straight line, we reached the car.

"What about taking a short break?" I said while opening the car's door and grabbing two packs of cigarettes. "Just put the coffin here on the ground."

"We can't. It's dangerous," replied the first man.

"I'll give you twenty dollars each if you do that and let me photograph what's inside the coffin."

"We can't. It's too dangerous for all of us," repeated the other man. I searched my pockets trying to find more twenty-dollar bills, but could find only fifty-dollar bills.

"Fifty dollars for each of you, or you can go without any gift!" I said, thinking that one hundred dollars was a fortune for them and a lot of money even for me. But I wanted to see a werewolf.

"Give us the money," said the first man, while they put down the stretcher. "And the cigarettes! Call us when you finish closing the coffin, and we'll come to pick it up." And they ran away like two crazies.

While I started to open the coffin with a tire iron, I saw that the two men were waiting about a hundred yards away, smoking the cigarettes.

When the coffin's cover was ajar, I saw the two men running even further away as fast as they could, and I began feeling some uneasiness growing in my body. Not that I believed I would really find a werewolf inside the coffin, but the two men running away and me opening a coffin, alone in the back country, imparted a strange atmosphere to the whole scene. Holding my camera in one hand, I opened the coffin with the other, ready to shoot if something was to suddenly jump out of the coffin.

Nothing jumped out of the coffin. And even if the man lying inside had wanted to jump out, he couldn't have because his hands and feet were nailed to the bottom of the coffin. The man was in his fifties and was wearing a shirt and pajama bottoms, both covered with blood. Besides the strong nails through each hand and foot, there was a long crucifix piercing his heart and another one driven into his forehead. I quickly closed the coffin and called the two men.

"Who's this guy?" I asked when they joined me, obviously surprised that nothing had happened to me when I opened the coffin. I could see them relaxing because it meant there was no longer any danger for them.

"The werewolf," they answered in concert.

"When did you catch him?"

"Around three or four this morning," said one of the men.

"How do you know he is a werewolf?"

"He was a werewolf when we caught him, but as soon as we killed him by piercing his heart with the crucifix he became a man again."

"You saw it, both of you?"

"I didn't see it. I wasn't there when they caught him, but he was there. He saw him becoming a man again," said the first man, pointing at the other.

"Yes, I saw everything, everything . . . like I see you. I helped to catch him and kill him. I saw how he became a man again!" he said, starting to stammer with emotion as he remembered what he had seen. And the two men told me their story.

During the past week, the people in their village had found four mutilated bodies—one man, two women, and a child—in the fields. The wounds indicated that the four victims had been attacked and killed by an animal that had sharp, pointed claws and powerful jaws with long teeth. Moreover, and this is why the villagers knew it wasn't the work of dogs, the animal had used the power of his hands to dismember his victims, open their chests, and tear out their hearts.

Then, two nights ago, three different villagers saw a strange creature the size of a man and walking upright on his hind feet. He was covered with long, black hair and had a long tail. Above his head, which was that of a huge dog, there was a weak but glowing light. And his eyes were red.

"We must go now!" the first man said suddenly.

"Hey, wait! I want to know the whole story. I want to know how you caught this guy!" I begged.

"Not now. We have to bury the werewolf, and I want to be back tonight in my village. I want to be part of the party that will hunt and try to catch the other werewolf."

"What do you mean? Is there another werewolf? How do you know?" I asked, my heart racing.

"Just after we had caught this one, a woman saw another one. That means there are two werewolves."

I asked where their village was and sped off in that direction, ready to confront the supposed werewolf. As I headed there, I remembered a story from my childhood.

In the jungles of Zaire, where I spent my early life, I often heard my parents talking about a secret sect, called the Leopard Men. They told me that these men were ravaging the whole region where we lived, hunting people like prey and killing them, as part of their nocturnal rituals, which were held once a month. The natives believed that during their ceremonies, members of this sect were transformed into real leopards. Indeed, their victims were found mutilated as if they had been attacked by leopards; the deep wounds were inflicted by long, powerful, sharp claws.

When traveling at night through the country, my father and, another time, a Catholic missionary who was a friend of the family each saw in their headlights a small band of men running across the dirt road, covered with leopard skins. They were armed with long claws made of iron, and it would have been easy for them to hunt their prey and kill them in the same way leopards would. These sightings seemed to put an end to the legend of men transforming themselves into leopards—unless the leopard men seen by my father and the missionary were just neophytes.

In any case, as I reached the Haitian village where I hoped to meet a werewolf, I wondered if the werewolves of Haiti were not similar to the alleged leopard men of Africa.

I met the villagers who had seen and examined the mutilated bodies; they confirmed that the wounds couldn't have been made by dogs, for dogs can't use their paws to dismember their victims, open their chests, and tear out their hearts.

I talked to the four people who claimed they had seen a werewolf; they all gave similar descriptions of the beast.

And I interviewed seven of the eight men—the coffin carrier wasn't back yet—who had caught and killed the werewolf. The shoulder of one had been wounded by the werewolf during the fight. I saw it: the deep wound had been made by a strong blow with a claw.

The members of the werewolf-hunting party, among whom were the mayor and the two policemen of the village, told me their story.

Coming back home, one of them had stumbled upon the werewolf crossing the village's main street, walking upright on his hind feet, like a man. He rushed to alert a policeman who lived in a nearby house. The policeman's wife answered the door and said he was playing dominoes at the other policeman's house. The villager rushed to the other house and found both policemen. It was about 11:00 P.M. They grabbed their handguns and flashlights and rushed out with the villager, looking for the werewolf.

On their way they called the mayor, who joined the party, also with a powerful flashlight. Searching the village, they were joined by the coffin carrier and a friend of his, who grabbed a long crucifix and held it in front of him during the whole hunt, believing that it would scare werewolves and vampires.

Around 1:00 A.M., the group encountered a villager completely maddened and frightened because he had just seen the werewolf: his wife had been one of its victims. He led the party to where he had seen the beast. After a short search they spotted the creature, and chased it but lost it. They met another villager (the hunting party's eighth man) who had just seen the werewolf first running on all fours like a dog, then standing up on his back feet to open the door and enter the house of a man named Sophocle, a widower.

The party rushed to Sophocle's house and searched each room, creating a panic among the three servants. When they reached Sophocle's bedroom on the second floor, the door was locked from inside. They broke the door down and found the werewolf lying on Sophocle's bed, but Sophocle wasn't there. Then the fight began, during which one villager was attacked by the werewolf's claws. Knocked out, the beast stopped resisting.

Helped by one of the policemen and the coffin carrier, one man drove the crucifix into the werewolf's heart, using a handgun as a hammer, while the others held the beast tight in case he awoke. The werewolf screamed and his whole body started trembling as he began to die. As the party searched for another crucifix to drive into the forehead, the werewolf turned into Sophocle before their eyes.

So it was Sophocle's body I had seen in the coffin that afternoon. It was hard for me to believe this story, despite the fact that some of the witnesses were people of education and credentials—the mayor, for instance, who repeated, "I always had a hard time myself believing these tales, but when I saw the werewolf metamorphose into Sophocle. . . . I have been emotionally shaken, and still am."

I asked him if he had been drinking that night. He said no, that he was sober when he went to sleep at around 9:00 P.M.

For two nights I accompanied the werewolf-hunting party, which soon numbered fifteen. Unfortunately, we had no success. Perhaps the werewolf moved into another village, or perhaps someone in this village realized it wasn't the right time to play werewolf.

☾

I will probably never see a werewolf myself, but I have heard so many eyewitness accounts that I wonder what is behind this phenomenon. Here is one of the many corroborating accounts.

About a week after the werewolf hunt I was in a café in Saint-Marc, a small seaside town not very far from Gonaives, drinking and chatting with a group of Haitians. Three of the more interesting people there were the mayor, the army commander, and the chief of police. The mayor, who had been educated in Paris, was well versed in French literature (as are the majority of educated Haitians). He was constantly quoting the great French poets and dramatists and would encourage me to give him a quote, upon which he would respond with the author's name. So, calling on my own classical education, I ended up reciting Verlaine, Rimbaud and other great French poets, and talking about the works of Baudelaire and Saint-Exupery.

The army commander and the chief of police were both raised in the United States, where their families had taken political asylum. One studied in New York and the other took various degrees in Miami. Both came back to their homeland when Baby Doc, who succeeded his father as president reopened the doors of the country to the political adversaries of his father's regime. They decided to settle down in Saint-Marc since they were both from there and still had family there. (I mention the social position and functions of these men only to indicate the good authority of their testimonies.)

After a few hours of literary games, I told them the story of the werewolf-hunting party, concluding with a remark to the effect that I was amazed at what people living in the back country could believe in. The mayor looked at the men sitting at our table and then at me and said, very seriously, "You shouldn't laugh about that. Werewolves really do exist!"

And for the rest of that evening and over the next couple of days these three men and, later, the deputy director of the region told me incredible stories, all firsthand accounts, about werewolves (and about vampires, which I will discuss later).

Following is one of their stories. I believe it is true, having known the people who told it to me.

One night, the army commander was driving through town, with the chief of police and the mayor beside him in the front seat. They were searching for one of the many street vendors to buy a snack. As they passed a small cross street, someone in the car caught sight of a food peddler walking down it. The army commander stopped the car, backed up to the intersection and saw that, indeed, there was someone walking there who appeared to be a food peddler: there was a light above his head that looked like the glow of the hot coals of the charcoal pan that food merchants carry on their heads.

As the car turned into the dark street, the army commander and his two friends saw in the headlights that what they thought was a food peddler was in fact something else. While the commander sped up to try reach the creature, which was running away like a man, the police chief grabbed his handgun and shot at the beast. It stopped, turned to face the car for a few seconds, and then crossed the street, running on all fours, and vanished between two houses. Despite their search, they could not find the beast again.

The three men knew that the strange creature they had seen was a werewolf. They had seen it long enough to know that it was neither a dog nor a man. It fit every description they had heard from others who had seen werewolves: it was completely covered with long, black hair and had a long, hairy tail. Its head was the head of a huge dog, with red, luminescent eyes, and a glow emanating from it. When they saw the creature face-to-face, the mayor and the army commander had time to catch sight of its penis, which was pink and therefore well visible on the black fur. When it was crossing the street on all fours, it ran with long, high strides unlike a dog's.

These men had been called into small villages many times to examine bodies that had been mutilated by werewolves. Even before their own encounter that night, their previous investigations had led them to the conclusion that the werewolf phenomenon wasn't a product of people's imagination and that it could be linked to secret sects.

Following their advice, I began reading the local newspapers more carefully and found that, indeed, more often than I would have thought, there were many official reports of people who had seen werewolves, as well as reports of murders supposedly committed by werewolves.

According to the many tales concerning werewolves that were so popular during the European Middle Ages and are still told in some parts of Africa and Europe, a werewolf can change his victims into werewolves and subdue them. My investigations in Haiti revealed that this could be possible there thanks to the cooperation of a certain Petro loa. (As I mentioned in chapter 7, Petro loas are easily charged with evil energies and are used in black-magic ceremonies; whereas Voodoo ceremonies call only upon Rada loas, which are of a neutral energy or are charged with good energies.) This loa had the ability to manifest itself in animal form and to give this power to any of its initiates who, in turn, could transform themselves or their victims into werewolves.

In the same manner, initiates of other secret sects can use the powers of other Petro loas that exist in the Haitian pantheon of black magic to transform themselves or their victims into other animals—pigs, roosters, dogs, cats, donkeys, bats, and screech owls.

Since I had already witnessed an amazing ceremony during which a Javanese shaman had psychologically transformed his neophytes into wild animals (I described this in chapter 7), I didn't see why a man couldn't, indeed, be turned into a werewolf (or into a screech owl, a vampire, and so forth)—not merely acting like such a creature, but thinking, feeling, and being a werewolf. It was all due to the power of the mind: a bokor could make a man, or himself, believe he was a werewolf; or he could disconnect a man's human consciousness, or his own, as some shamans do, and replace it with the conscious state of a werewolf; but in this case the subject would keep his human form.

What bothers me is that in all the corroborating descriptions witnesses have given of werewolves, in no case was anything sighted that looked like a human being. Is the power of the mind such that it can create a complete physical metamorphosis of a man into an animal? This of course is possible if we allow the possibility that a spirit possessing a man could cause such a physical transformation.

SCREECH OWLS

It was in a houmfort known for sorcery that I first heard stories about a certain secret sect of sorceresses who could incarnate their souls in screech owls, fly over houses, and kill young children by magically taking away their life force.

I knew the master of this houmfort, a bokor known for his power to cast spells. He had let me attend several black-magic ceremonies that took place inside various sanctuaries, each dedicated to a powerful and bloodthirsty Petro loa. I had thus seen most of his houmfort's sanctuaries. There was one, however, that he forbade me to enter.

One day, after I had been visiting him for months, he decided, for no apparent reason, to show me this sanctuary. Poorly lit by some candles burning on a small altar, the mysterious place was decorated with mystic paintings and was guarded from inside by a motionless zombie sitting next to the central pole, who was armed with a razor-sharp machete attached to a rope tied around his waist. He was holding a conch shell and looked at me with wild-looking, lifeless eyes. At his feet and all around the pole, the ground was covered with gourds decorated with black crosses, pre-Columbian stone and terra-cotta figurines and artifacts, and dozens of terra-cotta pots completely sealed—*pot-de-tête* vases, each containing the breath of an initiate.

Large dead screech owls were hanging head down and wings opened wide, their feet tied to a rope stretched between two of the sanctuary's walls. "What are these?" I asked the bokor, who had been silent the whole time, smoking cigarette after cigarette.

"Owls," he replied, exhaling smoke.

"I thought so . . . but since it's the first time I've seen something like this in a sanctuary, I was wondering why you have them hanging here?"

"How many are there?" he asked me.

"Eight," I answered after counting them.

"Look at them closely and tell me what you think!"

I looked at them carefully. "They are well preserved. What have you done to keep them like this?"

"Nothing!"

"How long ago did they die?" I asked, wondering what the bokor wanted me to say.

"Some recently, some a long time ago . . . a very long time."

"How come they have not rotted? With this humidity, they should have decomposed."

"That's the point! They are like dead toads; they never rot!"

"Yes, that I know." And indeed I knew that dead toads always dry up instead of rotting. "But generally birds don't dry up. So, what happened to these?"

"These owls are the incarnations of women. Unfortunately, they have been killed."

"Who, the women?"

"No, the screech owls!"

"By whom?"

"By villagers! Villagers know that witches can metamorphose into screech owls, so they fear them, and kill them whenever they can."

"What happened to the witches?"

"They died, too!"

"But if these birds are metamorphosed witches, once the bird dies it should become the witch again."

"Not really, because in fact the witch keeps her physical body, it's only her soul that she incarnates in a screech owl. But when the owl dies, by transfer the witch dies, too. But the owl will never rot!"

"How do you know all of that?" I asked, though I knew what the answer would be.

"I am the leader of the local screech owl sect. That's why these birds are here in my houmfort. Whenever a screech owl in which one of my sect has incarnated her soul has been attacked and wounded, it can return here, guided by the call of the conch," the bokor said, pointing to the zombie.

Among the many stories I have heard of women whose souls metamorphosed into owls, I have chosen the following one because it had already been investigated carefully by Father Jean Kerboull before he recounted it in his book *Voodoo: magie ou religion.*

In a small town now known as Duvalierville there lived a happy family with many children. Suddenly several of them died without apparent reason. The father went to the police and vowed to shoot and kill anyone who approached his house too closely.

One evening, the man's mother told him that she was going to the nearby city for business and would be back the next day. She then left the house. That night, the family heard the noise of a huge screech owl landing on the roof, followed by shrieking. As this happened, one of the children began to faint. The father rushed out of the house with his shotgun and, seeing the screech owl, shot at it twice. Wounded in the legs, the bird took off with difficulty, and the child recovered consciousness.

The next morning, the family was surprised to discover the

grandmother lying in her bed instead of being in the city. When asked, she claimed that she hadn't been able to travel that night, having come down with a high fever. Wanting to keep her warm, her son moved the covers and discovered blood all over the bed: both her legs had been wounded by dozens of small pellets of buckshot. Questioned by her son, she finally admitted she was a witch and was responsible for the deaths of the children, but said that she had been coerced to do this by an inexplicable force.

VAMPIRES AND CANNIBALISM

Related to the psychological transformation, or metamorphosis, of men into animals is vampirism. Vampires were known to ancient civilizations: stories about them can be found in Oceania, China, Japan, Africa, the Antilles, Europe, and South America. (I have heard descriptions of vampires in the Andes.) But the most noted vampire is of course, Dracula.

According to historians this man really existed. Born in Transylvania and raised in Turkey, Dracula (the name means "son of the dragon" or "son of the devil") returned to his country to become prince of Walachia. He was most well known for his cruelty: he tortured and killed over forty thousand innocent people. In 1476 the Turks put an end to his bloodthirsty life by beheading him. Since then, his name has become synonymous with vampirism and his reputation has spread throughout Europe and the rest of the world.

In Haiti, I learned that there are sects of vampires that continue to hunt human prey. Although it is believed that some women are born vampires—a mother transmitting her bloodthirsty condition to her daughter—anyone can become a vampire just by joining one of the many secret sects that practice vampirism, such as those involving transformation into werewolves and other animals, and communication with Satan.

According to my investigations, many of these secret sects in Haiti—and elsewhere—hunt human prey. But all don't do the same thing with their victims. Some just draw their soul and vital force away, while others use their blood for rituals. Some kill their victims to drink their blood; others kill them as a human sacrifice. And there are sects that practice ritual cannibalism, calling their victims goats or pigs.

These criminal sects, which in Haiti are very small in number, have nothing to do with traditional Voodoo and must be seen as isolated phenomena. The tenets of vampirism, as well as of secret sects dealing with werewolves and so forth, are those related to the magic produced by the rituals of human sacrifice and cannibalism. Marcel Mauss, a French anthropologist, wrote about this in his book *Sociologie et anthropologie*:

> The topic of sacrifice and, particularly, the sacrifice of children, is common to what we know of ancient magic and that of the Middle Ages; one can find examples of it nearly everywhere; however, they come to us more from myth than magic practice.

Sacrifice as part of a rite of passage or fertility, or as an offering to the deceased or the divinities, has been practiced by all cultures at one point or another in history, and in some places it still occurs today. In the Asian jungles, a headhunter must behead his victim in order to show his courage and to be fully accepted into manhood. In many African countries, the dead bodies of tribal chiefs must be buried over the heads of children; the more heads, the more energies the deceased's soul has to reach existence in the hereafter.

The Old Testament itself indicates how extensive human sacrifice was. There is also evidence that, in addition to human sacrifice, ritual cannibalism was practiced at that time in that part of the world.

Wherever cannibalism was or is practiced, human meat always has been referred to by the name used to designate the meat of a pig because it looks, smells, and tastes like pork. In a major modern city of central Africa, I carried out the following experiment. I went to the native open market and asked for pig meat. The vendor said he couldn't get any. I then sent a native to buy some and he came back with some meat, which cost a fortune, wrapped in newspaper. The analysis performed by a friend of mine who was an M.D. showed it to be human meat.

From alimentary cannibalism to sacred ritual cannibalism, anthropophagy was developed and spread all over the world. Like human sacrifice, it has been practiced by all cultures throughout history, and in some places it is still practiced.

One of the major reasons people eat human flesh is that it was, and still is, believed that this will increase one's mental and physical powers: one assimilates the qualities and virtues of the victim by eating his flesh—and assimilates youth if the victim is a child.

The ancient Greeks proclaimed that blood was the carrier of qualities, virtues, and memories. Therefore, eating an animal together with its blood meant assimilating its bestial qualities, virtues, and memories. So people began to eat the meat of only those animals that had been killed, bled, and blessed by their religious leaders. However, in India the Hindus, realizing that no matter what one does to meat it still contains blood, declared that eating meat was forbidden.

I totally agree with the anthropologists Carl Vogt and and Girard de Raille that the most primitive nations are not systematically cannibalistic and that cannibalism is also present in modern nations. And as the American writer Herman Melville wrote in *Typee,* "As reprehensible as this custom [cannibalism] is, I affirm nevertheless that those who follow it are . . . honest and human."

❦

I have met sorcerers in Africa who could see at night as sharply as during the day. They claimed it was one of their powers. However, after investigating this supposedly supernatural power, I discovered that it is just an ability that they keep secret, passing it from initiate to initiate.

The technique is simple. In fact, they discovered it by observing cats, who can see perfectly at night. A cat's eyes are closed at birth and remain so until the animal's ocular system has developed fully. So when among these people a pregnant woman is about to deliver, she is put into a dark place; on Easter Island, they used deep natural caves for this purpose. When the child is born, no light whatsoever is allowed to come into contact with the child. Not until the eye and ocular system are completely formed and have grown in strength and resistance to light, which takes a few weeks, is light allowed in. As a result, the child can see in the dark as clearly as in daylight. This would explain how paintings could have been made inside pyramids and other sacred places where there is no trace of smoke or soot to show that a light had been used.

Although one can find rational explanations for some phenomena, there are others that remain a mystery—like the rainmakers with whom I lived in the African Sahel, a large and harsh extent of savannah that borders the southern part of the Sahara and stretches south to the tropics. I have witnessed their mysterious powers to call the rain.

On small islands in the Indian Ocean, in Africa, in Sri Lanka and in other Asian countries, I carefully observed firewalkers and people who lie down on live coals without suffering burns and without their clothes catching fire, and was convinced that there were no tricks involved. Elsewhere I have seen men eating razor-sharp glass without being hurt.

I was drawn to a small village in Zaire, by stories about a powerful sorcerer living there who could dip his hands into boiling oil without suffering from burns. When I met him, he agreed to perform that feat for me, and under my total supervision.

When the palm oil began boiling inside the large iron pot set over the campfire, I asked the sorcerer to allow me to inspect his hands. I wet my finger and passed it all over both his hands, then licked it to see if I could taste anything strange with which the sorcerer might have covered his skin—some mysterious unguent, perhaps. But I found nothing. Still, I asked him to wash his hands in front of me, using the soap I was carrying in my backpack.

After he did so, he sat in front of the pot of boiling oil and said, "Sit next to me." Then he asked for some money. Thinking that I would again be the victim of a charlatan, I took out some nearly worthless paper currency. He looked surprised and said, "This will burn inside the oil. Give me some coins instead!"

I was the one who threw two coins into the boiling oil. The sorcerer began whispering some chants, and soon started to sweat under the influence of a trance. Then he suddenly plunged his right hand into the boiling oil up to his wrist, moving it about in the boiling oil as he searched for the coins. After leaving his hand in the oil long enough to cause third-degree burns, he took it out, holding the two coins in his fingers. Smiling, he stretched his hand toward me. Dumbfounded, I opened my palm without thinking. He dropped one coin into my palm. I screamed with pain. It was excruciating. The sorcerer was laughing. I still wear the scar left by that burn.

Indeed, I have witnessed innumerable phenomena that have no scientific explanation. Yet they exist; they are real. Perhaps because the people involved in these phenomena have a different worldview, what for us is impossible becomes for them a reality. The respected ethnologist Alfred Métraux noted: "From an early age, the Haitian has heard of werewolves, people who cast spells, and malevolent spirits. . . . Without completely accepting [these amazing stories], one asks oneself if, behind those devilries, there are not ancient 'African secrets' that would allow houngans . . . to defy our wretched science."

We people of the modern world are not trained to use the trance phenomenon—induced by chanting, dancing, meditation, and prayers, or by alcohol or drugs—that would enable us to reach that altered state that removes rationality and shuts off the negative beliefs that prevent us from using our mind powers. Peoples of tradition are more inclined to believe they can do anything, since they have been brought up in a culture that has not polluted their reasoning with our kind of logic and rationalism. It is our *reasoning based on scientific logic:* "understand first and you will believe" versus their *understanding based on faith:* "believe first and you will understand." It is the power of belief creating miracles versus miracles created by science. Our intelligence allows us to build spaceships to reach the heavens; their intelligence is more like an ongoing meditation that enables meetings with the Divine—a deep awareness of our connection with the universe's eternal forces.

9

The Afterlife

There are a great number of books and essays about life after death, some by physicians and other scientists, and some by people who have had an after-death experience. Many of these publications purport to give evidence that life after death is possible, that the soul continues to exist and, perhaps, is reincarnated in a new body, to start a fresh round of life on earth.

I don't claim to know the truth about the afterlife, since I have not yet died and come back to earth—or at least I don't remember doing so. Nor have I ever known anyone who called me after his death to tell me how life is lived there—although I have experienced something very strange in connection with my deceased father. However, I have some opinions on this topic, based on what I have learned in my sojourns around the world.

In this chapter I would like to share with you how the people of the Fourth World, and the peoples of tradition living in the Third World, view the afterlife, and how they react to death.

THE EXISTENCE OF SOULS

As I mentioned in the Introduction, when I was a child growing up in Zaire, our family servant Joseph appeared to my mother as he was dying in a faraway hospital. And my father concluded that it was Joseph's soul that, after Joseph's death, had appeared to my mother. At the time, this gave me evidence that a soul can survive death.

And my belief became even stronger when my own father passed away several years later. Upon his death, he became even closer to me than he had been in his lifetime. I felt his presence around me and within me. I missed his voice, his hugs, his kisses, and his physical presence, which had been so reassuring. But I never felt abandoned by him. On the contrary, he became an everyday companion with whom I could chat. I could hear him talking to me within me. And many times I even wondered if I had not become an explorer because of him. My life became what he had dreamed of for himself in his lifetime—the realization of his own desires for adventure. And if today I am still alive, I owe it to him. I am convinced that he was the one who confronted me with deadly dangers, and who helped me to survive the worst of them. But after many years of his companionship, one day I felt lonely and realized he was gone; he had moved away, slowly and gently, to continue his own voyage.

Today, I am not so sure that it was Joseph's soul that appeared before my mother. Perhaps it was, but perhaps it was Joseph himself who came to our house via astral projection, or by an out-of-body experience, or by an astral voyage.

But I still believe in the survival of the soul after death. And my belief has grown stronger in my travels all over the world, because wherever I go, I encounter cultures that believe in the existence of a soul and in its survival after death. It is a belief that belongs to all peoples of tradition—in itself a curious testimony to the possible truth that may lie behind it. Furthermore, so many peoples of tradition have strikingly similar customs surrounding the death experience that one has to ask whether there isn't some lost universal consciousness that our modern-day Western civilization has repressed.

Among peoples of tradition, it is believed that the soul is located in the head. Some peoples of tradition therefore have a taboo related to touching the head of a child. In the back country of Thailand, for instance, I inadvertently made the mistake of putting my hand over a little boy's head, as if to say "nice boy," and thus brought the wrath of his father down upon me. Fearing that I had cast an evil spell on his son or had tried to take his soul away, he became so angry that I, unable to explain my actions to him, had to run away to save my life. Since then, I never touch the head of a child when I am with a people of tradition.

Headhunter tribes behead their enemies when the enemies are still alive because they believe that, thanks to a magic ritual, the soul will remain inside the skull and that, by offering food to the captive souls, they can use its power. For the same reason, the Asmats of New Guinea hang their fathers' skulls around their necks and use them as pillows when they sleep.

Funeral Rituals

When someone dies in our society, we get through the proper rituals as quickly as we can: we shed a tear, say a prayer, put flowers on the grave, and try to forget. But peoples of tradition do exactly the opposite, drawing out their farewell to the departed.

For cultures of tradition, death is not an end; rather, it is just another state of being. In death, there is a separation of the soul from the body; the body is dead forever, but the soul goes back to the primordial world—the Garden of Eden, the world of the invisibles—where the divinities, ancestors, and souls of the dead continue to live for eternity. In that invisible world, life goes on in the same way as it does on earth, except that, since it is an eternal paradise, there is no struggle for survival.

Nearly every culture of tradition considers death as the last and most important rite of passage an individual experiences during his life on earth. As a result, they engage in elaborate and often extended funeral celebrations. Performed by the religious leaders of the community and the family of the deceased, the funeral ceremony frequently consists of a series of rituals that are intended to perform five main functions:

△ To chase away malevolent spirits, which can harm the soul of the deceased and capture it for evil purposes.

△ To ease the separation of the soul from the body. The soul hesitates to leave this world despite the eternal paradise it will find, because it still has the desire to experience human passions—love and physical pleasures, such as eating and sex.

△ To *fuel* the soul on its voyage to the primordial world where its ancestors live. (This voyage is perilous because of the malevolent spirits and other evil entities and energies that the soul encounters on its way to the invisible world.)

△ To help the soul be accepted among its ancestors. Once this has occurred, the deceased's family and clan have the opportunity to be helped materially and spiritually by the deceased's soul.

△ To keep the soul alive. The energies sent by the memories of those who have survived the deceased fuel the soul's existence. Without these energies the soul would cease to exist.

These funeral rituals comprise magical incantations and prayers; music, dancing, and chanting; animal, and sometimes human, sacrifices; and offerings of food and clothes. The acts of sacrificing and offering have the same purpose: to transport what is sacrificed or offered from the visible to the invisible world so that the spirits, ancestors, and other souls of the dead can enjoy it. Sacrificing or offering liberates the quintessence or astral body (which animates the physical body of an object or an animal; without this quintessence, the object or an animal stops existing). It is believed that if the quintessence of food is sent, the divinities, ancestors, and souls of the dead will actually feed on it. Similarly, a sacrificed animal will serve as an animal. A dress will actually be used as a dress.

Without appropriate, perfectly executed funeral rituals, the soul of the decreased will remain on earth, or will not make the journey to its ancestors safely, or, if it does, will not be accepted by them. In any case, the soul of the dead person will cause various misfortunes for his family and his clan—disaster or illness. In this manner the soul will express its displeasure, and will let the family know, through a shaman or other spiritual leader, what further rituals are required to enable it to join its ancestors. The Tao recognizes that souls who do not receive appropriate rituals, as well as those of people who have committed suicide, may become angry ghosts who spend their time annoying the living.

According to Voodoo, besides the physical body that dies and returns to dust, a human being is composed of the *small angel* and the *great angel*. The former is the spirit that keeps the body alive. For nine days after someone dies, his spirit wanders around the corpse, and then merges into the cosmic force of Life.

The latter is the spiritual double of the individual—his soul. After the individual's death, the soul cannot bring itself to abandon the world of the living, because it still wants to live, love, and enjoy earthly delights. So it remains near the dead body for one hundred to two hundred days, perhaps in the hope that the body will somehow revive. (It is interesting, and yet disturbing, to note that many cultures of tradition—in fact, a great majority of them—believe not only that the soul remains around the dead body but also that it does so for the same period of time and for the same reasons; and they perform funeral rituals that attempt to force a speedy separation of the soul from the body.)

When a Voodoo believer dies and is buried (generally within twenty-four hours after death, because the warm Haitian climate speeds up decomposition of the body), the houngan opens the *pot-de-tête* containing the dead person's breath—which had been captured the day the believer became a Voodoo initiate—and releases it. Then he performs a series of rituals to help the soul separate from the body and leave the world of the living. These ceremonies may last a few weeks or longer, depending on the strength of the soul's desire to remain with the living.

Once the houngan has decided that the soul has departed, another ceremony begins. In this ritual, the soul is sent into purifying waters called *purgatories*—a reminder of Catholicism—where it must remain for 101 days, washing its sins away. If after this period of time the soul has not been asked for (in a later ceremony and with the help of the dead person's loas), it is lost and will remain in oblivion forever—the Voodoo idea of hell. If the soul is asked for, it leaves the purifying waters and begins the long and dangerous journey to the invisible world—a journey that it can make safely with the help of the dead person's loas. There it reaches God and divine eternity, and may become in its turn a loa that the family of the deceased can invoke for assistance. In this way the family can incorporate the intelligence, knowledge, wisdom, and powers of the deceased.

During one ceremony of sending the soul into purifying waters— which is always performed in a cemetery, using the dead man's tomb as an altar—I saw the dead man's widow using her hands to dig a narrow hole one foot deep next to the grave, on a line with where the head of her husband would be. When she finished digging, she placed a love letter in the bottom of the hole, a letter she had written that very morning to her beloved. Then she put in a half-dozen cigarettes, and a small bottle of rum. She did this because she believed that the quintessence of the gifts she had placed in the hole would reach the world of the invisibles, where her husband's soul would use them.

When someone dies among the Apayaos of the Philippines, his family sacrifices several animals, which later are fed to those who come to mourn—often the whole village and members of the dead person's clan. The funeral lasts a minimum of three days, but may go on for as long as the family of the deceased can continue to feed the participants.

After being washed and dressed in ceremonial clothes, the deceased is the first person to feast. While a member of his family keeps his mouth wide open, pushing his tongue aside, rice and meat are pushed deep inside his throat. To end his final meal, some rice wine is poured into his mouth. After this, his mouth is closed and tied shut.

Before rigor mortis sets in, the deceased is placed on a funerary chair and tied upright to it. And throughout the entire funeral—one that I know of lasted five days—his family distributes tobacco, betel, and rice wine to all participants, who, singing, crying, laughing, drinking, smoking, and eating, visit the deceased, dance in front of his body, and honor his life with endless chants.

When there is no more food, the relatives carry away the deceased, still sitting on the chair of death, accompanied by a chant: "We are leaving you forever. By performing all these rituals and sacrificing the animals, we have given you the prescribed funeral. . . . Now you must go. And do not curse us, but beseech your ancestors to give us happiness and prosperity."

Next there is a procession in which the deceased is carried through the village. During this parade, the people chant, "You have all you need: rice, chicken, and pigs to feed you, and the clothes to wear during your stay in the dwelling place of your ancestors. You leave your earthly goods with your children and relatives, so that they can enjoy life in the same way you enjoyed it while you were living."

As the procession winds its way to the burial place, the crowd sings, "Beseech your ancestors to give us happiness and prosperity, and protection against our enemies; make abundant game for our hunt. . . . Take away rats, insects, and other predators that destroy the rice plants. . . . Prevent disease from killing our poultry and our animals. Send them fertility so that we will be able to make more sacrifices for you. Give us good health so that we will live as long as possible, continuing our traditions and offering sacrifices."

Then, before the deceased is put into the burial place and left there in the fetal position—symbolizing his birth into another world—along with food, drink, and sometimes his weapons or jewelry, the crowd chants, "We are saying farewell forever. . . . This is the last place we can go for guiding you to the dwelling place of your ancestors. . . . Go and live with your ancestors forever."

The burial itself puts an end to the collective funeral ceremony, but additional rituals performed only by the family will continue for some time so as to help the soul along on its perilous voyage.

In Mustang, a Himalayan kingdom bordering southern Tibet, I witnessed the funeral ceremony of a worker killed by a rock slide. The ritual followed the customs of Buddhism and Bon-Po, an ancient indigenous Tibetan religion that survived Buddhism and, in many places, has mixed with it. According to Bon-Po, the dead man's body must be returned to one of the four natural elements: water, earth, fire, or air. It was the holy astrologer of Mustang who, studying the worker's horoscope, decided that his remains should go back to the air.

Three stones, piled one upon another, were put in front of the entrance to the dead man's house to drive evil spirits away. Inside, while some members of the family prepared food to sustain the soul on its voyage to Nirvana, others placed the body in the fetal position, and wrapped it like a mummy. Then, carrying the corpse on a stretcher, a procession of family, relatives, and villagers left the dead man's house and set out for the nearby river.

The long parade was headed by Buddhist monks playing traditional Tibetan religious music, using drums, trumpets, and horns. A long white cloth was tied to the dead man and to a lama walking ahead of him, leading him on the *way of clear light.* The Bon-Po shaman read from the Tibetan Book of the Dead. "O noble son, the time has come to lead you to the path of paradise; the guide is showing you the way."

Then, on the riverbank, the dead man's body was solemnly dismembered for the *servants of the air:* the vultures. The plaintive sound of a conch summoned the birds who would carry the corpse away. And again the crowd performed ceremonies that were to guide the dead man's soul to Nirvana.

🕮

No culture can top the Toradjas, who live in the mountains of Celebes, Indonesia, for the amount of time they devote to dying and funeral rites. Here, a funeral, which they call the Festival of Tears, can last up to twenty years, and is divided into several stages.

First, when a man's heart stops, he is declared to be sick, not dead. His body is kept at home from nine months to ten years, until his first funeral can be arranged. Then a water buffalo is killed, and he is declared officially dead; his soul can now start on the long and dangerous journey to the afterlife. However, his body will be buried only when a second funeral can be arranged, and that may take equally long. This second ritual will help his soul enter the Toradjas' heaven and be accepted by his ancestors.

There is a practical reason for the delay between the time a man is clinically dead and each of his funerals. The Toradjas believe that the more animals they sacrifice, the better are the soul's chances of traveling safely to the hereafter and reaching its ancestors; and since a large number of animals costs a fortune, it takes a long time for the family to raise the necessary money.

These Toradja funerals also create new life. Young men and women come from miles and miles away to attend. Dressed in their finest, the men dance and the women cry. Everyone is emotional, and falling in love is easy. Two months after a funeral there are always many marriages; nine months after a big funeral many babies are born.

I witnessed a second Festival of Tears for a man whose heart had stopped twenty years earlier. The departed was a prince, so it took time to build the magnificent guest houses for the relatives and friends who were to attend. People from ninety villages had been invited—in all, about twenty thousand guests—to a funeral that would last several weeks.

For this important event, the family and guests supplied a great number of pigs and buffalo for sacrifice, whose souls would accompany the dead man on his long journey to heaven, and whose meat would be used to feed the crowd. (Because the deceased was a prince and therefore huge numbers of animals were needed, some guests contracted a lifetime of debt in order to contribute their share—another reason this funeral was not arranged in a hurry.) Each animal is given a ritual name before it is killed; the time, the place, and the method of each sacrifice is set by tradition.

Guests from nearby villages arrived first, carrying gifts. In turn, they received betel, tobacco, and rice wine from the dead man's family. With their arrival the Ma-Badong began a eulogy for the dead—a mixture of poetry, song, and dance that lasts through the entire Festival of Tears. It is led by the *tominas* ("the one who knows"), who chants, "All of us who came here at dawn to witness, all who came in the evening, all who came in the dark of night, we will not talk, we will say prayers and sing songs of praise. So it will be for everyone: not talking, but singing; no words, but poetry for you who have died."

The members of the dead man's family sat in silence. When he first died his body was kept at home on the ground, with its feet toward the west, and the family continued to offer it food. When the prince was declared officially dead, his body was moved to the attic, and everyone continued to visit and talk with it, keeping his soul alive in their memories.

As the Ma-Badong continued, the *tominas* recited verses that told of the prince's life, and the crowd answered in chorus. For the Ma-Badong everything—good and bad—that people can remember about the dead man's life is presented in song and dance. "You did not cry when you were circumcised," the *tominas* sang. "You were brave when your front teeth were shortened. You did not cry when it came time for the burn marks on your arms and thighs, the marks of fire that give men protection from devils."

The *tominas* sang of the prince's adolescence, his first love, his wife, and his joy in having children. He praised the women of the village—creators of life, responsible for the harvest and for the family's wealth. The Ma-Badong was not always solemn and sad, however. Although I saw people break into tears, at other times their faces lit up with smiles and people laughed, remembering something funny the dead man had said or a clever thing he had done.

At a signal from the *tominas,* the mourners gathered to hear him talk about the critical point each soul must face on its journey to the heavens: "At the western horizon, there is a doorway guarded by a crippled blacksmith named Lankuda. He lets children pass by. But Lankuda asks all men, 'How many heads have you taken?' And he asks women, 'How many lovers have you had?' If the answer does not satisfy him he smashes the soul, but if the deceased has had a full life, Lankuda opens the doorway to elsewhere."

Day after day, week after week, people arrived with gifts and food. And, providing a rhythmic background for the animal sacrifices and rituals, the Ma-Badong continued. The *tominas* sang, "Your head burned with fever and your hair fell out; the will of your ancestors calling you to join them was strong. So we asked the priest of death what rite we should follow for you, which animals should be sacrificed and where."

The mourners continued, "Father, now I repay you for all the love and care you gave me. Reach down and kiss me one last time. Let me glorify you. You will become as glorious jewelry and as pure as gold."

I sat with the family inside the dead man's house. His body (or what was left of it) had been at home for twenty years. People broke down and cried to think that this was to be his last night here. The body had been oiled and was lying in the next room, with its feet toward the east and its head toward the west. (Among the Toradjas, as among the ancient Egyptians, rituals of life and fertility are always directed to the rising smoke—that is, the sunrise, the east. Rituals of death are directed to the falling smoke, the west, where the sun goes to join the gods.)

Near the village, there was a large field covered with standing stones that symbolized all the dead of the village. The stones representing the closest dead relatives of the prince had been decorated. Some of the stones were twenty feet high and weighed tons. (They reminded me of menhirs, the standing stones of the Celts. Such stones, typical of many ancient religions, symbolically connect the earth and sky, providing a passageway for the blessings of the divinities and the souls of ancestors.) A group of men carried a small effigy of the prince through the field of standing stones and formally introduced it to each of his ancestors. Some people put offerings to the gods on top of high bamboo poles planted in the field (which also bridged the gap between this world and the sky).

The prince's heart had been still for twenty years, but the final journey of his body was to take place today. Long reduced to bones, the body was wrapped in many layers of clothes to form a cylinder, called a *banka* (which means "boat"). Thousands of years ago the Toradjas were sailors, and they still use a ritual boat to carry their dead from the village to the burial cliffs.

While the *banka* was being moved out of the house, the Ma-Badong continued: "O gods of falling fire, this is the ritual for the dead so he will protect us and bless us. O gods of the west, gods who guard the sunset, you who give plants, you who guard the world, a man is returning to his ancestors."

With the *banka* rocking on human waves, the procession formed, moved once around the dead man's house, crossed the village, and headed out through the rice fields. During the procession the closest relatives and loved ones hid their tears with their long white clothes. While they carried him, they sang a chant about how he would soon leave all this.

Celebrating the departure of a soul is important, not only for the dead, but also for the living. By transporting the body all around his domain, the family harvest would be blessed in future years. The *tominas* often stopped the procession to choose the proper animal for the next sacrifice, and the people waited in silence.

After crossing fields of rice and groves of bamboo, the *banka* docked at its final port—a cliff twenty feet high, where decorated wooden doors opened onto tombs cut into the solid rock, one tomb per family. Once inside, the body was removed from its wrapping and arranged next to the other bones, the head of one skeleton touching the feet of another. Offerings were left and the Ma-Badong echoed against the rock wall: "The rain falls on all of us, doesn't it? The shower drenches everyone, doesn't it? The rain drenches free people and slaves; it falls on old people and on babies. When the rain falls, it falls on one and all; nobody can avoid it, no hiding place is sufficient. It chooses each of us in turn, it soaks us when and where it chooses. And I am not sad in my heart because it is written that the rain will fall."

A menhir had been erected for the prince who had died, and during the night a life-size statue was carved in wood, representing the dead prince. The *tominas* prayed: "The statue looks like a man, but does not breathe; the statue becomes the man, but does not talk." The statue was dressed in the man's clothes and then put on one of the many balconies dug out of the cliff for that purpose, where there were other statues of ancestors, all looking down toward the village to remind the villagers of their dead. As long as the statues could be seen, they believed, the souls of their dead would be immortal.

The Festival of Tears ended with the Ma-Badong's last chant: "Once the loved one enters the heaven beyond the clouds, he will be wrapped in fog. There, there is no fire, but he is happy because there he no longer wanders, there he is with all his ancestors. The moon will be his house, the stars his fire. He will become a god; he will become a brilliant yellow star; he will become the constellation of the Pleiades. We will never forget him. When he looks down and sees us he will start to cry, and his tears will be the morning rain."

The Existence of Hell

For the majority of peoples of tradition, there is no hell. A man is punished for the mistakes he commits in his lifetime by his clan, and he fully atones for them while he is alive. They do not mark his soul with sins, nor do they interfere with his life after death. Or perhaps it is hell to die without funeral rituals.

(It is interesting to notice that many peoples of tradition do not have a word to designate *hell,* just as they don't have words to designate *guilt* or *sin,* among other things. If a language has no word for guilt, maybe guilt doesn't exist; we can use the same reasoning for hell and other words missing in their vocabulary. On the other hand, if a language has a word for the concepts of guilt, sin, and pardon, it allows an individual to commit a sin, experience guilt, and be pardoned.)

Entertaining the Souls of the Dead

In many cultures it is believed that the dead—or rather their souls—like to be entertained and taken care of by the living. For example, in our culture, on All Saints' Day we have the habit of paying a short visit to cemeteries to say a prayer, bring flowers, and think of our beloved departed. Similarly, in some countries like the Philippines, whole families gather around the tombs of their ancestors, where they picnic and chat for a whole day.

In Haiti, people believe that the souls of their loved ones who died during the year are bored, waiting endlessly for their corpse to return to life. So, beginning on All Saints' Day and continuing through the first week of November, the cemeteries in Haiti are transformed into comedy theaters. People stand on tombs where, in front of a live audience (and the dead one of the invisibles), they jump with joy, dance, play music, sing, and tell obscene stories—as if talking about genitals and sex could exorcize death and make the dead laugh.

COMMUNICATING WITH SOULS

All around the world, many people believe that one can contact the souls of the dead and communicate with them. There are many shamans, magicians, sorcerers, witch doctors, medicine men, and other religious leaders of peoples of tradition who claim they are guided by spirits and have mediumistic talents that give them the power to converse with the dead. Some even maintain they have the power to make dead souls materialize; they perform their rituals in cemeteries and places of worship.

Those who claim to be mediums for conversations with the dead are often chosen by a master at a young age because of their mediumistic talents. The master then trains and develops their abilities during an apprenticeship.

In Taipei, the capital of Taiwan, there is a temple, called the Temple of Evil, where women who are professional mediums practice their abilities to communicate with divinities and souls of the dead. Anyone wanting to converse with a dead person may hire their services. The medium enters a state of trance and begins calling the wanted soul until the soul takes over her body. Then she talks in the same manner as the dead person did, answering questions posed by the client. Sometimes she writes messages, in a writing style that resembles that of the deceased.

We in the United States have been invaded by spiritualism, which maintains that human beings have souls, that souls survive death—that there is a life after death—and that communication with the souls of those who have crossed over can be achieved by mediums. Whether practiced in the religious context of spiritualism or independently, there are several different techniques for achieving communication with the dead.

The communication usually takes place during séances. The dead soul expresses itself either by banging on the table or moving a drinking glass over the letters of the alphabet on a Ouija board; at other times the medium gets a message from a soul and passes it on to the person who wanted to communicate with it. Or the medium may experience a state of trance and be taken over by the soul, which then communicates verbally or through automatic writing.

I cannot confirm the validity of these techniques, as I have always refused to participate in séances, being aware of the real dangers of such rituals, which can, often accidentally, involve evil spirits.

Bokors and houngans of the Voodoo religion also claim they can communicate with souls by various means, many of them similar to those described above. However, their task is made easier since it seems that sometimes, even without being called upon by its relatives, the soul of a deceased person can incarnate itself in someone whose state of trance has conditioned him to be possessed. I witnessed one such phenomenon while attending a Voodoo ceremony in Haiti, and found it very disturbing.

At the exact moment when the houngan opened a dead woman's *pot-de-tête,* releasing her breath, many members of the community who were attending the ceremony fell down, suddenly possessed. One of them began speaking like the dead woman, thanking the rest for having been present at her funeral and giving personal messages to a few of them.

The most disconcerting instance I have seen of the souls of the dead becoming incarnate happened during the Gúedés ceremonies, which are always performed in November. During these ceremonies, the believers are put into a trance state by drums, chanting, dancing, and an overall frenzied atmosphere. In this state they are conditioned to be possessed by an entity, be it a loa or a dead person's soul. But when a believer becomes the incarnation of a dead person's soul, and is recognized as such, his face is covered with powder to differentiate him from those who, in the same ceremony, are possessed by Guédé loas or other entities. And when they become possessed by souls of the dead, believers react in the same way they would if they were possesed by loas; they fight off the assault, jumping high in the air and, sometimes, even levitating or lying on live coals.

One might think that the soul of a dead woman would possess only a woman, and that a dead man's soul would be incarnated only in a man. Well, this turns out not to be true, and I found that disturbing. Many times I observed women being possessed by the souls of dead men, and men being possessed by the souls of dead women.

When a woman becomes the incarnation of a dead man's soul, her dancing movements become wilder, and her voice changes into a male voice as she communicates with people in the crowd. A man's voice becomes soft and feminine when he is the incarnation of a dead woman's soul, and he attaches a scarf around his chest as if he needed a bra.

Many times someone in the crowd recognizes in the possessed person the manners, the voice, the intonation of a family member who died a few months earlier. I remember one man who was possessed by the soul of another who had been recently killed in a car crash, and through the voice of this possessed man the one who had died told his son, who was attending the ceremony, where he had hidden some money. I drove the young man to the house, where he searched through the attic, as his father, speaking through the possessed man, had told him to do. And there was the money, hidden in an old can.

Some psychiatrists and psychoanalysts are beginning to reconsider certain mental illnesses, such as schizophrenia, as being possession by one or more than one entity—without exactly calling that entity the soul of a dead person. In Los Angeles, I have been privileged to attend a monthly meeting of some of the world's most renowned psychiatrists and psychoanalysts. One of the featured guests was a woman who had real and recognized mediumistic talents. As the attendees concentrated their thoughts on one of their patients, the medium entered a state of trance. Then she began talking like one of the doctors' patients, with the voice, words, attitude, and mannerisms of that patient in a state of crisis. The concerned doctor questioned the entity that was talking through the medium about its identity and its reasons for possessing his patient. Usually, the entity said it was a lost soul that wanted to continue to be part of the world of the living in order to fulfill its desires. To do so, it had simply possessed someone who was experiencing a nervous disorder and who would therefore present no major resistance.

Afterward, instead of treating their patients, these doctors dealt with the entities possessing their patients, trying to make them leave the patients. (When the entities do leave they find someone else to possess, I guess.)

In modern societies there are also many reported cases of souls of the deceased having materialized in one way or another—in the form of a ghost for instance. And there are hundreds of reports describing haunted houses. One explanation is that the walls of such a house may have been impregnated by, and become a repository of, something awful that happened to someone living there. Or it may be that a suffering soul has taken refuge in the walls until appropriate death rituals can be performed.

Using Dead Souls for Evil Purposes

The fact that, according to many cultures, the souls of the dead have a hard time leaving the world of the living and, therefore, remain around the body for a certain period of time provides sorcerers with ideal places for practicing their sorcery—cemeteries. There they can use the energies of the souls of the dead. They will go to cemeteries, for instance, when they want to transfer someone's illness to a healthy person, or charge charms with evil energies so they can use them to cast spells.

In Haiti, one of the most sought-after ingredients, because of its energies, is any part of the corpse of a child who died before having been baptized. Sorcerers search children's graves to appropriate their finger bones. Sometimes they even snatch the whole corpse, to perform rituals to capture the soul.

However, the most powerful sorcerers deal directly with the souls of the dead, hiring them to take some action, often malevolent. I once witnessed such a search for a soul—a dreadful experience. The ceremony took place at night in a cemetery in the back country of the Artibonite region of Haiti.

The meeting place was the bokor's houmfort. The members of his community were all gathered together—about twenty people whom I knew well, all dressed in white. The women and some of the men wore white scarves on their heads. The bokor let me know I couldn't use a flashlight or any other source of light in the cemetery as the brightness would frighten away the souls and perhaps anger them. Since I was short on high-sensitivity film, which would allow me to film by the light of the moon and the torches and candles that the people were carrying, I left my movie equipment inside the houmfort and brought along only my tape recorder, two sets of batteries, and two microphones.

Although I was supposed to spend the night in the houmfort (the place was far from any hotel), the bokor advised me to drive to the cemetery, which was quite far away. Since he didn't feel like walking that night, he would ride with me. So, with the bokor and four drums aboard, I drove directly to the cemetery, where the community members joined us about an hour and half later.

First a ceremony was held around the drums, with dancing and chanting to induce a state of trance, preparing the believers to be possessed by the souls of those who died recently. Then, carrying candles and torches, the whole group began walking between the graves. The people dressed in white, the flickering lights, the full moon, and the bright stars lent a hallucinatory atmosphere to the setting.

Leading the procession was the bokor, who was chanting incantations that the crowd repeated in chorus. He addressed the souls, calling on them to manifest themselves in the believers, who were ready to be possessed.

All of a sudden, one of the men started shaking and jumping. The bokor approached and asked him questions to determine which entity was possessing him. From his answers, the bokor could tell it wasn't a loa but the soul of a dead man. The bokor calmed the frenzied believer by putting his hands on his head. Using his own scarf, he gently wiped the sweat off the believer's face and tied it around his waist. Then he asked the soul if it would agree to do whatever he wanted it to do for three months. Speaking through the possessed man, the soul asked to first make love before giving an answer. The bokor accepted. For a few seconds, the possessed believer remained calm, looking all around him. Then he began walking slowly through the crowd and, in a sudden frenzy, fell on a woman and kissed her. Then he started making love to her, screaming and crying.

When their sex act was over, the possessed man approached the bokor and burst out laughing. Then, suddenly, he fell down on the ground, unconscious. A few people gathered around, trying to revive him. The bokor knew that the soul had left, making a fool of him. As the believer regained consciousness, the group began walking again among the graves, chanting and continuing their search for a soul that would make a deal with the bokor.

According to what the bokor told me, when the soul of a deceased person accepts his deal, it will do whatever he wants it to do for the whole time of the agreement—from helping him with ceremonies of black magic to increasing the powers of the bokor's protective talismans; from annoying someone to bringing a person illness or death. In exchange, the bokor will provide the soul with people who are ready to be possessed by it so that it can fulfill its earthly passions.

A sorcerer dealing with souls of the dead has the power to force the soul to stick with the deal; only when the time of the agreement is over will he release the soul and perform the necessary rituals to speed it on its journey into the hereafter.

Many souls of the dead answered the bokor's calls that night and manifested themselves in believers, only to drink rum, smoke cigarettes, and have sex. Twice, souls began fighting with believers.

At one point, I was standing next to the bokor, recording his conversation with a soul that had been incarnated in a woman. As they were about to agree on a deal, a woman standing opposite me became possessed in her turn and, in a frenzy, pushed away the people around her and fell upon me. Since I was using one of my hands to carry the microphone boom, I had only one hand free to protect my tape recorder, which was hanging on my chest, and push her away.

I began moving backward, hoping that someone would stop her; by this time, she was spitting on me, her wild-eyed face covered with sweat and distorted by hatred and anger. Then she began insulting me, not in the soft voice of a woman, but in the deep voice of a man. A few people tried to grab her, but her strength was too great. In backing away, I stumbled and fell back. She tried to get on top of me; I let go of the boom and, with my two hands, grabbed her throat and squeezed it, while keeping my arms stretched out to keep her from hitting my face.

Some of the believers finally managed to grab her firmly and began moving her away from me. I released her throat, and she burst out laughing. I froze because her laughter had such a strong, masculine tone to it. And in a deep man's voice she began insulting me again and telling me things I couldn't understand. While the houngan calmed her, some of the crowd helped me stand up.

I had fought pirates, escaped from wild animals, survived fierce tribesmen, and faced the worst dangers imaginable, but I had never been attacked by the soul of a dead person. My legs were like cotton and I was shaking all over. I needed a cigarette.

Realizing that I had lost my pack of cigarettes in the confrontation, I went to my car to get a new one. After the nicotine had relaxed me, I looked over at the cemetery and saw the white bodies of believers running all around. I heard their chants and screams as one of them became possessed again, and I knew I wasn't ready to face another soul of the dead, not that night, not ever again. I started the engine and drove straight to Port-au-Prince, 250 miles away, where I spent the rest of the night in a bar, drinking beer and watching pretty girls that sell love for a few bucks—my way to exorcize my experience with the unknown.

Sleep washed the nightmare away. I decided to listen to my tape, but the recorder refused to work. Thinking the batteries were dead, I connected the tape recorder to the electric power-supply pack, but still nothing. Yet it couldn't have been my fall that had broken my tape recorder—a Nagra, the Rolls Royce of tape recorders. As I was trying to figure out what had happened, my friend Jean arrived to pay a visit. I told him the story while he examined the Nagra. (At that time he had not yet experienced the possession I described in chapter 7.)

"It won't work because the fuses are burned out!" Jean said. Indeed, the two fuses, each 250 volts and 5.5 amperes, were burned out. That didn't make sense, since I used a set of twelve batteries of 1.5 volts each, and 18 volts couldn't burn out two 250-volt fuses.

"Maybe you burned them out this morning by plugging it into

the electric outlet," said Jean, looking for a logical explanation. But that couldn't have been the cause, because in Haiti the electricity is 110 volts. Besides, I checked the electric power-supply pack and found it perfectly set to 110 volts.

We repaired the fuses, but the Nagra remained lifeless.

To make a long story short, on my way home to Europe one month later, I left the tape recorder at a place in New York that repaired Nagras; they promised that it would be ready when I returned a month later.

Curious to know what had happened to my tape recorder, I called the repair shop a week later. The technician told me that my sound engineer must have plugged the Nagra into a high voltage, higher than 500 volts (some condensers that were supposed to withstand 500 volts had burned out), destroying the Nagra's whole electrical system. I explained to him that I had been the one using it when it burned out, and at that time it was supplied by the 18 volts of the twelve 1.5-volt batteries. Following his silent reply, I asked him to start the repairs.

On my way back to Haiti, I stopped in New York and picked up my Nagra. "Something very peculiar must have happened to your Nagra," said the technician, explaining that a high voltage had entered the microphones' inputs and had spread out through the tape recorder and moved through the electric power-supply pack's input, burning out the two fuses; some of this voltage had also destroyed a few of the batteries that were still in the Nagra.

"The only two rational explanations for this business," he concluded, "are that someone mistakenly connected an electrical source to the microphones' inputs, or that lightning hit the microphones themselves. In that case, your microphones would be burned out, too." We tested the microphones and found that they were indeed burned out.

I didn't bother telling him that that night the sky was filled with stars, and that if lightning had hit the microphones I would have known it since I was the one who was carrying the microphone boom. No, that night there wasn't any lightning—just a woman possessed by the soul of a dead man who attacked me, and laughed and screamed into my microphones. But why and how the dead man's soul destroyed my tape recorder I will never know. And if it wasn't the soul that did it, then who or what was it?

When, two days after the cemetery incident, I returned to the houmfort to pick up the movie equipment I had left there, the bokor asked me why I had left so hurriedly after the possessed woman attacked me. I lied and said I remembered I had something to do in Port-au-Prince that night. Then I asked him if I could see that woman again. He called someone to fetch her.

When she joined us, she looked quite fragile for someone who had been able to overcome the strength of many men in the cemetery. And as she gently shook my hand, she begged for forgiveness in a soft, feminine voice. "The others told me what I did to you. I am very sorry. But it wasn't me who did it. I have no reasons to have done it. I have never fought with anyone in my life, not even with a woman." Suddenly becoming emotional, she added, "It was the man's soul that possessed me who did it."

"Why?" I asked her. "Do you remember why the soul did it?"

"No, sorry!" she answered. "I never remember a thing after I have been possessed. Nobody does."

"The dead man probably had his reasons, but I had no time to ask him," added the bokor.

"How do you know that I was attacked by the soul of the dead man? Couldn't it be that the woman had been possessed by a Petro loa?" I asked the bokor when she had left us.

"No. Loas only speak in *language*." He was referring to the language that is understood only by the highly initiated. "The dead man's soul was speaking in Creole."

On our way to the sanctuary where he had locked my equipment for safekeeping, the bokor stopped in front of the door to another sanctuary, where he used to practice black magic, and opened it. In the room, whose walls were covered with magical drawings and colored paintings representing various Petro loas, there was a black coffin.

"So, you have succeeded in making a deal with a soul," I said. He nodded. "And I guess the owner of the soul is there," I added, pointing at the coffin.

"Yes, it's a man, and it's his own coffin. It wasn't easy to get it out of the grave and carry it here without your car!"

"Aren't you afraid of the soul?" I asked.

"No, I have a deal with it," he said. "And as long as I keep my promises, the soul can't hurt me. And if the soul refuses to cooperate, I can force it to since I have the dead man's body here."

"What about the other dead's souls? Can't they hurt you?"

"I have my talismans."

"What if a soul incarnates in one of your community members to try to hurt you?"

"Impossible! Besides, I know how to calm down someone who's possessed by touching his head. Anyway, none of my people could hurt me, even the possessed ones. I control them because I have their breath."

"Can't the souls possess you and hurt you?"

"I condition myself to be possessed only when I am in my houm-fort, and certainly never in a cemetery!"

As I was about to leave, the bokor invited me to stay. "I am doing my first ceremony with this soul. Stay and watch."

"Thanks, I would love to, but I must go back to Port-au-Prince. Another time, I hope," I said. But I was thinking, "No more of that, thank you very much!"

REINCARNATION

Of all the world's hundreds of religions, only a very few share a doctrine of reincarnation—the idea that the soul of a dead person is reincarnated in another human body, to start a new life as another person. And very few believe in the resurrection of the original body, as Catholicism does. This is interesting, for if the tenets of a religion were simply the product of man's hopes and ultimate dreams of becoming eternal, then all religions would believe in physical reincarnation in one way or another—unless some cultures see life as such a harsh and difficult adventure that they prefer to believe that once they die they will not be forced to live on earth again.

Few religions maintain that the soul is permanently reincarnated in matter. For the Indians of the Andes, for instance, matter is eternal since it transforms itself continually. A human being draws his origin from the earth and goes back to it after his death. Earth is therefore the Indian's Nirvana; an Indian will be reincarnated in a mountain, hill, or lake if he had a good life; if he had a bad one, he will remain a wandering spirit forever, reincarnation in matter being refused to him. This explains the Indians' respect for nature: it holds reincarnated human souls.

☾

The fact that there are common threads linking all cultures of tradition makes me believe that there are truths to be found in them; why else would people throughout the world believe the same thing? Let's examine the common beliefs concerning the afterlife.

△ Besides a physical body, a human being has a soul that is invisible and survives the death of the body.

△ After the death of the body, the soul has a hard time leaving the living and, therefore, remains near the corpse for a certain period of time. (If this is true, cremation poses a serious problem concerning the survival of the soul, for burning a body would also destroy the soul. That is what was done to witches and anyone society wanted to get rid of completely: they were burned alive to make sure that their souls were destroyed and couldn't survive to haunt the living.)

△ Living people can call on and communicate with the soul of a dead person.

△ The soul of a dead person can manifest itself and communicate with the living by possessing someone who has been conditioned for that or who has a natural predisposition to being possessed. But letting souls of the dead possess living persons is not without certain dangers; that is why, among peoples of tradition, this is done by, or under the supervision of, religious leaders, who by their knowledge can protect believers from being possessed by malevolent souls, evil spirits, or other dangerous entities.

△ There is an invisible world where all souls gather together. It might be the primordial world of eternity—the primal Garden of Eden—where the Divine lives, or the Cosmic Intelligence that a soul reaches and feeds as part of its self-transformation.

△ The soul of a deceased person needs funeral rituals. These protect the soul from evil energies, help the soul free itself from the corpse and from its desire for human passions, fuel and protect the soul on its long and perilous jouney to the hereafter, and help the soul be accepted by its ancestors or the Divine—whatever that may be.

△ The souls of dead can help the living on a material and spiritual level.

△ The souls of dead people who didn't get appropriate rituals, or of those who have experienced a tragic death—like suicide—may continue their invisible existence among the living and annoy them in one way or another.

△ Rituals and live people's memories help keep the souls of the dead alive.

After more than twenty years of journeying around the world and living with people of different traditions, I wonder if the fundamental function of the cult of the dead—funeral rituals, responses to the need the souls of the dead have to be entertained and taken care of by the living—is nothing more than to produce continuous love and remembrance of the deceased, which generates the energies that keep his soul alive. Indeed, love being the greatest and most powerful act of creation and magic, the energy of love together with the power of memory could truly be capable of safeguarding the eternity, the immortality of a soul. Perhaps someone really dies only when there is no one who thinks about him anymore; as long as a dead person is alive in the hearts and memories of the living, his soul is kept alive in eternity.

The Ifugaos of the Philippines, the Maoris of New Zealand, the Dayaks of Borneo, and many other tribes can recite the names of their ancestors going back twenty generations at least. Immortality, for them, is to be remembered by the living. Therefore, if you live a bad life on earth you are perhaps running the risk of dying without leaving behind enough mourners to provide your soul with the energies it needs to stay alive, make its voyage of transformation, and be assured of immortality. And if hell exists, then true hell is perhaps to see yourself dying due to lack of energies sent by the living. And if paradise exists, it is made of love and memories.

According to many peoples of tradition, this is true also for gods, since we have been created in their image (and thus we close the circle: from the Divine to humans, we go back to the Divine). They believe that the gods themselves vanish when humans no longer honor them; when the people don't need them anymore and they disappear from their memory, the gods will lose their immortality.

A headhunter of Borneo once told me, "The gods need us as much as we need them. They are our hope for a better life, and we are their immortality. They have created us so they will be fed by our offerings and will exist on the energies of our faith; in exchange, they have created nature to feed us, and paradise where we will live like gods.

☾

If there is something to be learned from peoples of tradition, I would say it is the value they give to death, because that gives a greater value to life. Eliphas Levi once wrote, "To love life much more than one fears the threats of death is to deserve life."

We don't witness death anymore in our modern societies; we even avoid the word. Instead of saying "He died," we say "He departed," "He left us," "I lost him," and so forth. We use the term *life insurance* for something that in fact should be called *death insurance,* since that is its purpose. We see our dead in mortuaries, bathed in soft waves of classical music, made up to give back the color of life, and perfumed to hide the smell of death. Death has become a hidden phenomenon, and we believe we are immortal.

Everything in our society reinforces this belief. The credit-card system assures us that we will be alive in a month; otherwise why should the banker give us plastic? Buying a car in installments over three years, or a house over thirty, gives us a three- or thirty-year credit for living; otherwise why should the banker give us the loan? We subscribe to pension plans because we are told we will get the money back when we're sixty-five. And we believe that one day we will reach that childhood and never had the time to realize—so busy were we with living for tomorrow, for the next weekend, the next holiday, the next salary raise, the next house, the next car. And when we die, it is with a silent scream that life is too short.

In smelling the odor of death and seeing their dead decomposing, peoples of tradition realize how great life is. In other words, we can appreciate day if we acknowledge that night exists and are ready to experience it. Experiencing the deaths of their loved ones gives the peoples of tradition the need to live life deeply and fully, as if tomorrow will never exist.

As long as we are alive, we may never know the truth about what awaits us after we die; we can only speculate. Therefore, I choose to focus more on living my life in such a way that, if there is something after death, my soul will be part of the self-transformation state, whatever that may be. That is, I choose to fully live life with love and passion, since that is my duty as a person who is alive; to remember that since I am a man with the ability to effect change, it would be a crime not to try; to consider that I am my own god and that my religion is love—love that includes respect, compassion, and understanding—love for my mate, my children, my family, and the people around me; and to accept that my freedom ends where others' begins.

I deeply believe that when I die, the only question God will ask me—God, or the Cosmic Intelligence, or She—will be: "I have given you life. What have you done with it?"